THE FAMILY Handyman

100 THINGS EVERY HOMEOWNER MUST KNOW

How to Save Money, Solve Problems, and Improve Your Home

Reader's digest

The Reader's Digest Association, Inc.
New York, NY/Montreal

EDITOR: Gary Wentz

CONTRIBUTING EDITORS: Elisa Bernick, Spike Carlsen, David Radtke

CONTRIBUTING EXPERTS: Jeff Gorton, Travis Larson, Rick Muscoplat, Mark Petersen

ART DIRECTION: Vern Johnson

PAGE LAYOUT AND PROJECT MANAGEMENT: Teresa Marrone

CONTRIBUTING DESIGNER: Mary Schwender

COVER DESIGNER: George Mckeon

COPY EDITORS: Donna Bierbach, Judy Arginteanu

INDEXING: Stephanie Reymann

EDITOR IN CHIEF: Ken Collier

PRESIDENT AND PUBLISHER, BOOKS: Harold Clarke

Warning: All do-it-yourself activities involve a degree of risk. Although the editors have made every effort to ensure accuracy, the reader remains responsible for the selection and use of tools, materials and methods. Always obey local laws and codes, follow manufacturer's instructions and observe safety precautions.

Table of contents

Table of contents

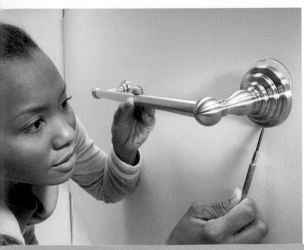

The first thing every homeowner must know

When you have questions, The Family Handyman has answers

Since 1951, *The Family Handyman* has been dishing out the best do-it-yourself home advice available. Our recipe is simple: Go straight to the pros for real-world, field-tested expertise. And then explain the projects so that anyone can be successful. Our team of more than 1,000 Field Editors includes home experts of every kind, from contractors and real estate agents to architects and engineers. And our readers—more than 4 million across North America—are constantly sharing their tips and experiences with fellow homeowners. This book contains some of that expertise. But there's a whole lot more...

Our first issue sold for 35¢ back in 1951

Homeowners in Australia & New Zealand like us too!

The Family Handyman Magazine

Get North America's top home improvement magazine at The Home Depot, Lowe's and other retailers. Or subscribe and save at FamilyHandyman.com.

Our North American Edition reaches more than 4 million readers

FamilyHandyman.com

Get instant access to thousands of home improvement projects, step-by-step repairs, storage solutions and more!

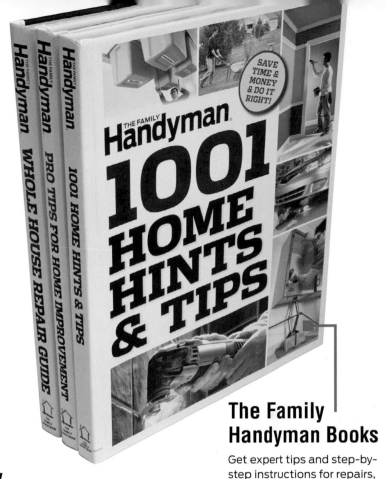

The Family Handyman Books

Get expert tips and step-by-step instructions for repairs, improvement projects, organizing and more. Shop at FamilyHandyman.com.

The Family Handyman for iPad®

Get every issue of *The Family Handyman* as it's published, plus extra tips, articles and videos. Find it at the App Store.

The Family Handyman Newsletters

Get ideas, tips, projects and repairs delivered to your in-box every week—FREE! Sign up at FamilyHandyman.com.

Tip Genius App

More than 300 FREE tips for storage and organizing, simple repairs, easy improvements and more! Download it at FamilyHandyman.com/diy-tip-genius.

Understand your plumbing system

Basic knowledge for better decisions

When it comes to home repairs and improvements, you're in charge. But when the plumber seems to be speaking a foreign language, it's tough to make a smart call. So take five minutes to get acquainted with your system. The basics are simpler than you might think.

The DWV system

The drain, waste and vent system carries waste out of your house and into the city sewer lines. Sounds simple enough. But for plumbers, it's trickier than the supply system. There are more code requirements to follow, and more know-how is needed to make it work well.

The most important DWV rule is this: Every drain must have a trap, and every trap must have a vent. Traps, those U-shaped pipes you see under sinks, hold wastewater, which prevents nasty sewer gas from flowing up into your home. Vents are simply pipes that lead outside through the roof. Without a vent, water flowing through a trap creates a vacuum and siphons the trap dry. By allowing air into the system, vents act as a vacuum breaker.

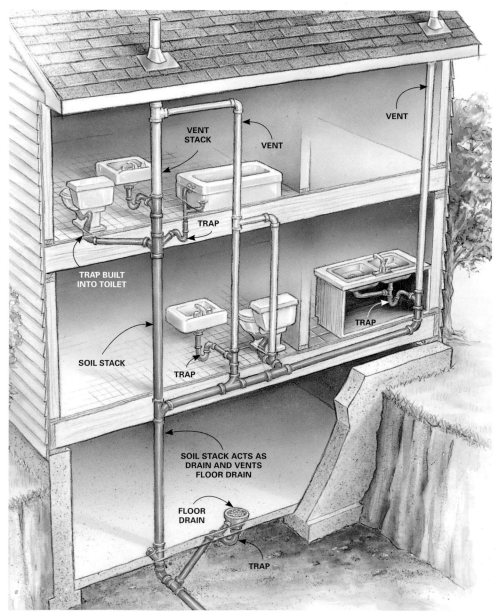

VENT STACK

VENT

VENT

TRAP

TRAP BUILT INTO TOILET

TRAP

SOIL STACK

TRAP

SOIL STACK ACTS AS DRAIN AND VENTS FLOOR DRAIN

FLOOR DRAIN

TRAP

Drain, waste and vent system

Drain and waste lines (shown in blue) must include traps, which keep sewer gas from entering your home. Vents (shown in yellow) break the siphon effect of flowing waste to keep water in the traps.

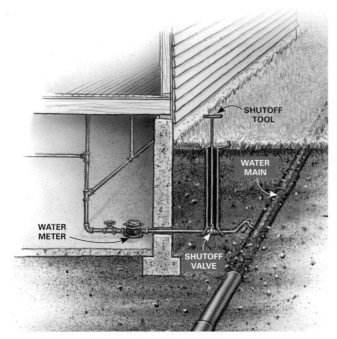

SHUTOFF
TOOL

WATER
MAIN

WATER
METER

SHUTOFF
VALVE

AAV

The water supply system

Your water supply system taps into the city water main, runs through a meter that measures your water usage and then branches throughout your home. The branch lines in your home may be any of the types shown below. Older homes are sometimes museums of pipe history, including several types of pipe.

Air admittance valves

An AAV lets air into the DWV system, but not out, so it can take the place of a vent pipe running up through the roof. On remodeling projects, that can save the plumber a lot of work—and you a lot of money—if it's allowed by your local code. AAVs aren't allowed in all situations.

Pipe types for water supply

MINERAL
BUILDUP

Galvanized steel

Unlike other types of pipe, galvanized steel almost always has threaded, screw-together connections. Its life expectancy is about 70 years, but some century-old galvanized pipes are still in service. If you have galvanized pipe and low flow at faucets, chances are the pipe is to blame. Galvanized pipe is prone to mineral buildup that eventually chokes off the water flow. Complete replacement is the best cure, but you can often improve flow just by replacing any exposed horizontal pipes.

Copper pipe

Copper was the standard water supply pipe for decades until less costly materials became available. It can be connected in several ways, but most joints are sealed by melting metal solder into the joint. The lifespan of copper depends on the local water. In some areas, it lasts as little as 25 years. In others, it lasts two or three times that long.

SOLDER

PEX

PEX is flexible, so it's much easier to install than other types of pipe. That, plus low cost and immunity to aggressive water, make it the most common choice for new water lines. PEX is a latecomer to North America, but has been used for decades in Europe. PEX comes in a range of colors.

CPVC

Unlike metals, this plastic pipe doesn't corrode, so it's been common in regions with "aggressive" water for the past 40 years. CPVC connections are usually made with a glue-like cement, but compression fittings (shown here) and other methods can also be used.

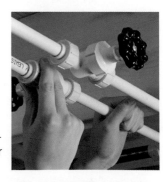

Understand your heating system

Basic knowledge for smarter decisions

When an HVAC (heating, ventilating, air conditioning) system breaks down, most homeowners are at the mercy of the repair technician because they know nothing about the system. And that's a shame, because the basics are easy to understand.

Most homes have "forced-air" systems; air is heated and distributed throughout the house. The main advantage of this approach is that the air can also be cooled or humidified. Hydronic systems (which heat water rather than air) can't do that.

How it heats

The heart of any furnace is the heat exchanger, the steel box where gas or oil burns. Outside the box, air from the return ducts is heated and flows throughout the house. When heat exchangers wear out, they crack, and dangerous fumes from the burning fuel seep into the air. (That's one reason you must have a carbon monoxide detector in your home.) Heat exchangers are expensive. Replacing the whole furnace usually makes more sense than replacing the exchanger only.

How it cools

In summer, the heat exchanger is idle and air flows past it and up through the "coil" or cooling unit. The cold fins of the coil remove heat from the air. That heat is carried outdoors through tubing that contains refrigerant. The outdoor unit then removes heat from the refrigerant, which flows back to the indoor coil.

The duct system

The duct system has two parts that work together: supply ducts, which distribute heated or cooled air to rooms, and return ducts, which carry air back to the furnace. A blower fan keeps air flowing through the system.

The vent system

With traditional vent systems, exhaust gases are carried outside by gravity—warm gases rise

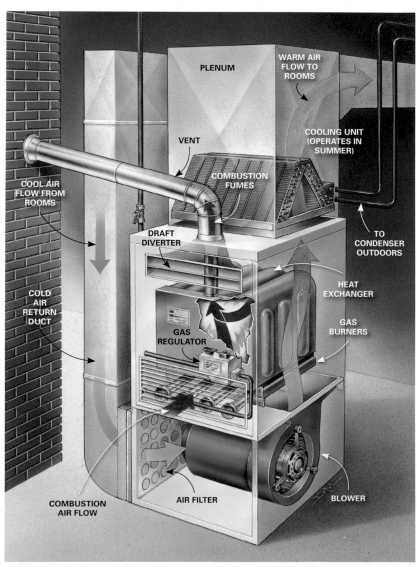

up the chimney (as shown). But newer, higher-efficiency furnaces squeeze so much heat out of the burning fuels that the exhaust gases aren't warm enough to rise. So those furnaces include a small fan to blow gases outside, often through a plastic pipe that exits through a wall. A second pipe carries outdoor air inside to supply combustion air.

Need a new furnace? Buying advice from an HVAC pro

■ **DON'T GO WITH THE LOWEST BID**
If you get a bid that's much lower than the others, be suspicious. The contractor may be using low-cost (and low-knowledge) labor. Most breakdowns are caused by poor installation rather than defective equipment.

■ **HAVE A PRO INSTALL A NEW THERMOSTAT**
Furnaces and thermostats have become computerized. Making them work together takes some serious know-how.

■ **TOP EFFICIENCY PROBABLY WON'T PAY OFF**
Furnaces with the highest efficiency ratings cost more up front and much more to repair. So a furnace rated in the low or mid 90s is likely a better deal than one in the high 90s.

■ **GET IT ALL IN WRITING**
Go with a contractor who provides a detailed, written proposal covering everything that will and won't be done. It should list the model numbers of the equipment and the costs of any plumbing, venting or electrical work.

Dave Jones, PE, HVAC engineer and
***The Family Handyman* Field Editor**

Is your ductwork robbing you?

Leaky ductwork can waste 40 percent of your heating and cooling dollars. Ductwork without insulation can waste 30 percent. The solutions are to seal duct connections with aluminum tape and silicone caulk, and to insulate ducts in attics and crawl spaces. The work is simple and you can save money by doing it yourself. But working in attics and crawl spaces is just plain miserable. So before you go through that ordeal, hire an HVAC pro to inspect and test your ducts. If your home was built within the last 15 years, your ducts are probably well insulated and sealed.

ALUMINUM FOIL
TAPE

Understand your water heater

Basic knowledge protects your home and your wallet

It's one of the best things about living in modern times: hot water whenever you want it. But it comes with risks. Ignored or mistreated, a water heater can harm you and your home.

EXHAUST VENT

WATER SHUTOFF

HOT WATER

COLD WATER

RELIEF VALVE

GAS SHUTOFF

GAS LINE

TEMPERATURE CONTROL

DRAIN VALVE

Water heater anatomy

A water heater is basically a big holding tank. Beneath a gas water heater (shown here), a burner—similar to the one on a gas range—heats the tank. On an electric water heater, two heating elements inside the tank heat the water.

Never, ever block the relief valve

As water heats up, it expands with tremendous force—enough to fracture the tank and launch the water heater through the roof (seriously, that does occasionally happen). The temperature and pressure relief valve prevents this by opening if the tank pressure becomes too high. But when a relief valve lets off a little pressure (or just leaks), some homeowners "fix" it by plugging the valve or the pipe connected to it. A very, very bad idea.

Turn down the heat

Water heaters set too hot send thousands (mostly kids) to emergency rooms each year. Most safety experts recommend a setting of 120 degrees F. But since most temperature controls don't have any numbers on them, setting them isn't so simple. Here what to do: Run hot water at the tap closest to the water heater for at least three minutes. Then fill a glass and drop in a cooking thermometer. If the reading is more than 120 degrees, turn down the dial, wait about three hours and test again.

Fix or replace?

To make that decision, keep two things in mind:
■ A water heater's life expectancy is 10 to 15 years.
■ Even the smallest repair done by a plumber will cost you at least 10 percent of the cost of replacement; 20 to 30 percent is more likely.
So if your unit is 10 years old, replacement is usually smarter than professional repairs. Even if it's just 8 years old, consider replacement rather than large repairs.

The two most common breakdowns

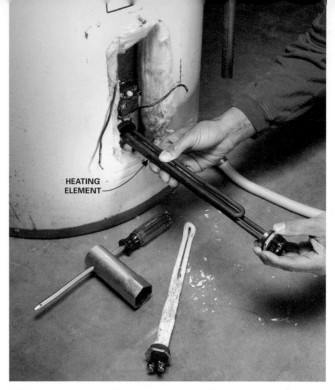

Gas water heater failure

A bad thermocouple shuts off the gas and you get no hot water. Replacing the thermocouple is a simple fix.

Electric water heater slowdown

One of the two heating elements burns out, which leaves you with insufficient hot water, lukewarm water or just cold water. Replacing the elements is the solution.

Got a puddle? Look out!

Water heaters sometimes leak from the drain valve or relief valve. Those valves are easy to replace. But if a leak is coming from the tank, you've got serious trouble. The tank is lined with a thin coat of glass. Over years, that glass begins to crack, the steel begins to rust away and a puddle appears. Left alone, the tank will eventually rupture, causing an instant flood. It may take months for a leak to become a flood, or it may take days. But it will happen. Don't gamble. Replace that time bomb now.

Will a tankless water heater save money?

A tank-style water heater wastes a lot of energy, just by keeping water hot until you need it. A tankless heater, on the other hand, heats water only when you need it. And that makes it 30 to 50 percent more efficient than tank-style heaters. But tankless heaters are expensive; installation, plus the cost of the unit itself, often add up to a price tag two or three times the cost of a tank-style heater. Here's how to weigh the costs and savings: Start with a couple bids from professional installers. Make sure it's a total bid that covers everything involved. Then search online for "tankless water heater savings calculator." Supplied with details (your energy costs, water use, etc.), an online calculator can estimate your savings and payback period.

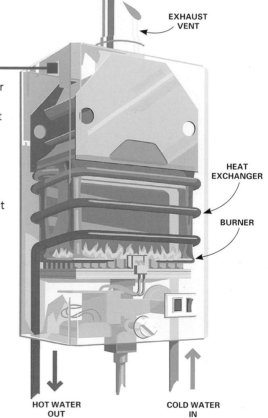

Push a button, save $100

Don't call for a repair until you check for power

Repair technicians report that a huge percentage (up to 30 percent!) of their service calls require only the push of a button or the flip of a switch to restore the electrical power. That costs the homeowner a minimum service charge (typically $50 to $100), plus embarrassment. Here's how to make sure that doesn't happen to you.

Press the reset button on GFCIs

Sometimes all the bathroom outlets or several exterior lights are powered through a single GFCI located in one bathroom or elsewhere, such as in a basement. Simply push the reset button on the GFCI and you could be back in business.

Voice of experience

It's happened a million times: The only 'repair' I make is to plug in the unplugged appliance. But I still have to charge for the service call.

Costas Stavrou,
appliance repairman
and *The Family Handyman*
Field Editor

Check the breaker

When a light goes out or a switch doesn't work, you should first check the main electrical panel for a tripped circuit breaker. Look for a breaker switch that's not in line with the others. That means it's tripped. Switch it to the off position and then back on.

Reset the disposer

All disposers have an overload feature that automatically shuts off the power when the motor becomes overloaded and gets too hot. Once the motor cools, simply push the reset button on the side of or under the unit.

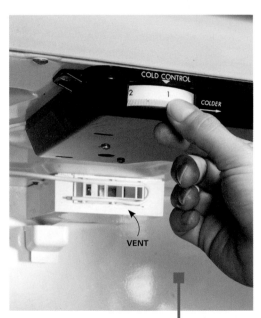

Check the outlet

If any electronic item suddenly won't turn on, don't immediately assume it's broken. Plug in a radio or a lamp to make sure the outlet is working.

Check the temperature dial

Make sure the temperature control dial in your fridge or freezer hasn't been turned way down. Curious kids may have messed with it, someone may have bumped the knob or it's just set too low. Also make sure the vents in the fridge and freezer compartment aren't blocked by food containers—these vents supply the flow of frigid air.

Make appliances last

Bad habits cost you—good habits save thousands

Appliance repair technicians and salespeople often say the same thing: "If people treated their appliances right, I'd have to find a new line of work." So you if you want to keep them employed (at your expense) ignore these pages. Otherwise, read on and save big.

Don't overload your washer or dryer

You may think you're saving time, water or energy by cramming more clothes into your washer and dryer. But overloading any washer or dryer causes damage to motors, belts and other moving parts. Some of the repairs are so expensive that you're better off buying a new machine.

Clean fridge gaskets

If you keep your refrigerator door gaskets clean, they'll seal properly and last the life of the fridge or freezer. But if you let sticky foods like syrup and jam build up on the door gasket, they'll glue the gasket to the frame. Pulling harder on a stuck door eventually tears the gasket, and that'll cost you $100 or more. Plus, if the door doesn't seal properly, the fridge has to run longer, and that'll boost your electric bill. Clean the door gasket with warm water and a sponge. Don't use detergents; they can damage the gasket.

Don't block air vents

Freezers and refrigerators require proper airflow inside the compartments to keep foods at the right temperature. Blocking the vents (often at the back of the compartment) can cause cooling problems and force the compressor and fans to run overtime. At best, that wastes energy. At worst, you'll have to replace the appliance. So think twice before you jam warehouse-size packs of frozen food into the freezer.

Don't drag clothes out of the washer

Dragging a heavy bundle of clothes in or out of a front-loading washing machine may save your back, but zippers and buttons gradually tear up the door gasket. It's just a piece of rubber, but it costs $100 or more. So lift out the wet clothes.

Don't slam appliance doors

If you continually drop or slam the lid to your washer or dryer (top or front load), you're going to break the lid/door switch. That'll cost you at least $100. Avoid this repair by lowering the lid and gently closing the door.

Clean the lint filter

A clogged lint filter means clothes dry slower while the machine works harder and wastes energy. If it gets bad enough, this will lead to repairs or even complete replacement of the dryer. Avoid all of this simply by cleaning the lint filter after each load.

Clean the refrigerator coils

Dust buildup on the coils underneath or on the back of your fridge reduces airflow and wastes energy. Worse, it leads to repairs that may cost more than a new fridge. That's quite an incentive to vacuum the coils every six months.

Don't spray switches

Most people clean knobs and touch-control panels with spray cleaners. But those liquids can easily work their way into the sensitive parts behind the controls and short them out. So instead, spray just a little liquid cleaner onto a rag or sponge and wipe controls clean.

Clean your dishwasher screen

If your dishwasher has a filtering screen under the bottom spray arm, clean it regularly. If you don't, the stuck food particles degrade into slime that blocks water flow and reduces cleaning performance.

Keep your water softener healthy

Easy care prevents expensive breakdowns

A water softener removes minerals from water; that means cleaner laundry, a longer life for water-using appliances, less mineral buildup on plumbing fixtures and lots of other benefits. And with some basic care, it can provide these benefits for 20 years or more, trouble-free.

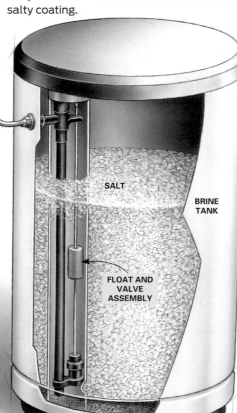

HARD WATER SUPPLY

SOFT WATER TO HOUSE

CONTROL PANEL

SMTWTFS

SOFTEN CYCLE

RESIN TANK

RESINS

DRAIN

SCREEN

GRAVEL

SALT

BRINE TANK

FLOAT AND VALVE ASSEMBLY

How a water softener works

Water flows down through the resin tank, which is filled with salt-coated polystyrene beads. Minerals in the water stick to the beads and softened water flows out of the tank. At scheduled times, the minerals are rinsed off of the beads and flushed down the drain while salty water from the brine tank renews their salty coating.

Break up salt bridges

A "bridge" of salt can form in the brine tank—essentially a fixed crust on top of the salt. Beneath that bridge, the salt gets used up, but the tank still looks full. So if your softener isn't consuming salt like it used to, ram a broom handle down into the tank. You might find that there's a hollow cavern under the upper crust. Break up that crust and the problem is solved.

How to add salt

Refill the brine tank only when it's nearly empty and then fill it no more than two-thirds full. Filling it too often or too full leads to salt bridges.

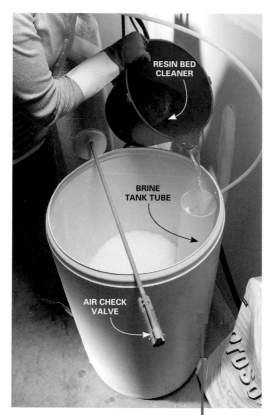

Clean the resin bed

If your water contains iron, pour resin bed cleaner into the brine tank tube once or twice per year. Without cleaning, your softener will eventually lose its ability to remove iron. Just pick up some resin bed cleaner at a water softener dealer and follow the simple directions.

Adjust the softness

Most softeners allow you to remove more minerals or fewer just by turning a dial or pushing a button (check the manual). The mineral content of your water supply can change over time, so you may have to make adjustments to maintain the same level of softness.

Reset after power outages

Your softener is probably set to clean and recharge the resin bed at night while you're sleeping. But after a long power outage, it might recharge as usual, not recharge at all or do it in the morning, delaying your morning shower and making you late for work. To reset the timer, check the owner's manual.

DIRTY ROCK SALT

Cheap salt is expensive

When I was a young, dumb cheapskate, I saved a few bucks by using rock salt in my softener. It worked fine for a few years, but eventually the impurities in that dirty salt plugged up parts, wrecked valves and cost me $600 for a complete replacement. As an older, wiser cheapskate, I'm now happy to pay a couple bucks more for salt.

Gary Wentz, *The Family Handyman* Senior Editor

Clean out the brine tank

Wait until the salt level is low and scoop out the salty gunk at the bottom of the brine tank. This mush consists of impurities in the salt, which don't dissolve well and reduce the performance of the softener. So clean it out once a year.

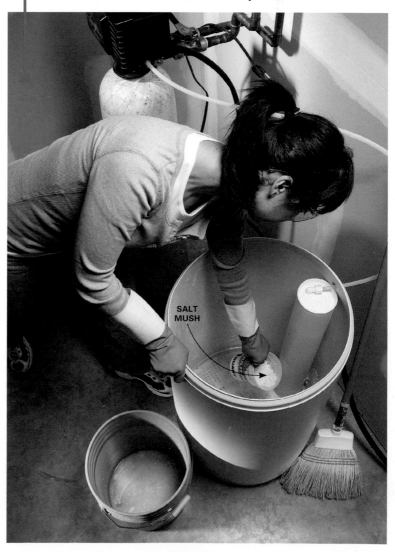

Save water

And buckets of money

Shrinking supply and growing demand are driving water bills up. Add the cost of heating water and rising sewer fees and you can see how thousands of wasted gallons turn into hundreds of wasted dollars. You can save water by fixing drips and leaks. But in most homes, replacing water-wasting fixtures results in the biggest savings. Those savings depend on your local water costs; the estimates given here are based on average costs.

Efficient (but effective) toilets

A toilet manufactured before 1994 wastes almost $100 per year, compared to a modern, efficient model. A toilet made before 1980 wastes almost twice as much. The cost of a new toilet, plus installation, is typically $200 to $400—so your return is 25 to 100 percent per year, guaranteed. (Try to match that on Wall Street!) Unlike earlier models, which often required double-flushing, most of today's water-saving toilets do their job in one flush.

Where's the water going?

Bathrooms use more water than any other room. More than a quarter of household water is literally flushed down the toilet.

Clothes Washer 22%
Shower 17%
Faucet 16%
Leaks 14%
Toilet 27%
Other 5%

Source: American Water Works Association Research Foundation, "Residential End Uses of Water," 1999

Low-flow showerheads

Showerheads are not only the second-heaviest water user but also major energy eaters. That's because 70 percent of the water flowing through the head comes from your water heater. By reducing both water consumption and water heating, a low-flow showerhead can pay for itself in just one month! And an efficient showerhead no longer means settling for a drizzle instead of a downpour. Many water-efficient showerheads change the shape and velocity of the water stream—even the size of the drops—to provide the high-flow feel.

Delta Faucet

Water-saving bath faucets

Like showerheads, efficient faucets save both water and energy. So—for a family of four—an efficient faucet will tyically pay for itself in just a year or two and continue to save money for many more years. Most water-saving faucets use special aerators that increase airflow to compensate for decreased water flow, giving you the same feel as other faucets.

If your home was built before 1994 and still has the original plumbing fixtures, you're using 30 to 40 percent more water than a comparable new home.

The badge of efficiency

Just look for the WaterSense logo. To earn this label, products must use at least 20 percent less water and still perform as well as or better than other products in that category. Go to epa.gov/watersense for more info. Some utilities are even offering rebates to sweeten the deal. Visit http://epa.gov/watersense/rebate_finder_saving_money_water.html to find rebates in your area.

What about kitchen faucets?

Efficiency in kitchen faucets is a matter of debate. Some say more efficient is always better. Others say that in the case of kitchens, low-flow is bad; it just takes longer to fill the sink or a pitcher. For now, the naysayers have the upper hand. WaterSense doesn't rate kitchen faucets and few low-flow models are available.

Prevent burst pipes

A frozen water line can wreck your home

A little ice can tear open a water supply line. That's bad enough, but the real disaster often occurs as the ice thaws and water flows freely into your home. In just a few minutes, that flow can do thousands of dollars in damage.

Why pipes burst

When water freezes, it expands in volume by about 9 percent. And it expands with tremendous force: The pressure inside pipes may go from 40 pounds per square inch to 40,000 psi! No pipe can hold that much pressure, so it breaks open. The break may occur where the ice forms, but more often, it occurs where water pressure finds a weak spot in the pipe. That may be inches or even feet from the frozen area.

Let the water run

A tiny trickle from faucets protects pipes in two ways. First, it prevents pressure from building up inside pipes. Second, it creates a constant flow of water through pipes and that makes freezing much less likely.

Temporary steps

The first sign of ice forming in pipes is reduced flow at faucets. So if the flow slows to trickle during a cold snap, or if you suspect your pipes are vulnerable, take action. Here are a few things you can do:

- Turn up the heat.
- Set up fans to blow heat into cold rooms.
- Open vanity or cabinet doors so warm air can reach the pipes under sinks.
- If you have exposed pipes inside closets or pantries, leave doors open.
- Disconnect garden hoses from outdoor faucets. Even "frost-proof" faucets can burst if a hose is connected.
- Keep the garage door closed.
- If you have reduced water flow, heat the most vulnerable pipes (usually in basements and crawl spaces or near exterior walls) with a hair dryer. Leave the faucet on while you apply heat. As you melt ice, the flow will increase.

Permanent protection

Long-term freeze prevention is usually a major project, like insulating a crawl space, replacing standard outdoor faucets with frost-proof models or even rerouting pipes away from cold spots inside the home. Start by calling in a professional plumber to assess your situation and make recommendations.

Heat the pipe

Electric heat cable is good protection during cold spells. A thermostat switches on the heat only when the temperature drops, so heat cable won't waste electricity when it isn't needed. But if you need to protect lots of pipes for long periods, heat cable is an expensive solution.

HEAT CABLE

Dry up a wet basement

Chances are, you can do it without paying a contractor

Solving basement water problems isn't exactly easy. Diagnosis can be tricky, there are often multiple causes and most solutions aren't guaranteed. On the other hand, some of the most effective cures are also the simplest. So before you call in a contractor, do your own detective work and try some easy fixes.

Multiple moisture sources

Before you can tackle water problems, you have to know where the water is coming from.

■ Rain and snow

If water shows up after a heavy rainfall or snow melt, your first strategy is to channel water away from the foundation by sloping the soil and extending downspouts.

■ Groundwater

Rainfall and snow melt may completely saturate the soil around your basement or raise the water table above your basement floor. Sealing leaks in walls and floors and coating them with waterproofing may solve the problem. Or you may need drain tile and a sump pump.

■ High humidity

Moisture carried by humid air condenses on anything cold, forming droplets and drips. Most condensation occurs on walls and floors, but it can also form on pipes and ductwork. To lower the humidity, run a dehumidifier and use the exhaust fan in a basement bathroom. Insulating cool walls and pipes also cuts condensation.

■ Leaky plumbing

Plumbing leaks can imitate seepage through walls and floors. After evaporating, water from leaks can contribute to condensation. The solution is simple: Fix the leaks.

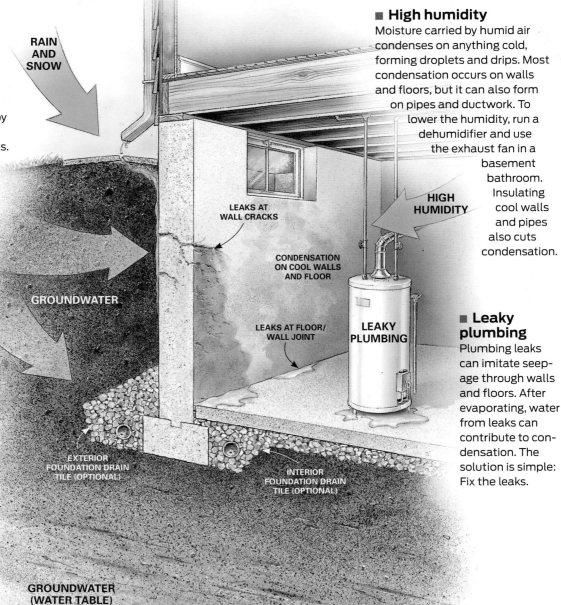

RAIN AND SNOW

LEAKS AT WALL CRACKS

HIGH HUMIDITY

CONDENSATION ON COOL WALLS AND FLOOR

GROUNDWATER

LEAKS AT FLOOR/WALL JOINT

LEAKY PLUMBING

EXTERIOR FOUNDATION DRAIN TILE (OPTIONAL)

INTERIOR FOUNDATION DRAIN TILE (OPTIONAL)

GROUNDWATER (WATER TABLE)

MOISTURE

ALUMINUM FOIL

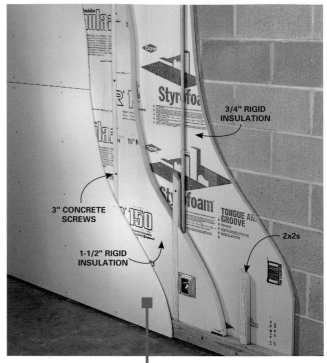

3/4" RIGID
INSULATION

3" CONCRETE
SCREWS

TONGUE AND
GROOVE
EXTRUDED FOAM
INSULATION

2x2s

1-1/2" RIGID
INSULATION

Don't get fooled by condensation

Condensation on walls and floors makes them wet and
might make you think water is seeping in from outside. So
here's a simple test: Tape aluminum foil to your basement
wall and inspect it a few days later. Moisture on the outside
of the foil is condensation. Moisture behind the foil is
coming through from outside.

Insulate walls

Aside from saving energy, properly insulated walls
drastically reduce condensation. There are several good
ways to insulate walls, including the method shown here.
But don't take this step until after you've stopped outside
water from entering—moisture trapped behind insulation
feeds mold.

FOAM
INSULATION

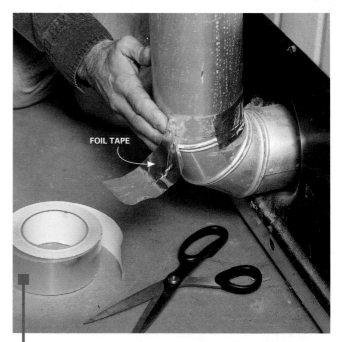

FOIL TAPE

Insulate pipes

Cover cold water pipes with insulation to prevent condensation. Foam pipe insulation is inexpensive and easy to install.
Insulating the hot water pipes won't help to dry up your
basement, though it may save energy.

Seal the dryer vent

A leaky dryer vent allows water vapor from your laundry to
become condensation on your walls. Seal the joints with foil
tape. Don't just use duct tape; it'll eventually fall off.

Extend downspouts

Make sure your downspouts dump water at least 6 ft. from the foundation. If you don't have gutters, consider adding them. The rainwater load from your roof is enormous, and channeling that water away from your basement is an effective way to reduce or eliminate incoming water.

Waterproof the walls

Basement waterproofing goes on like paint and is an easy DIY project. In order to bond well, it must be applied to bare masonry, not over existing paint. And don't skimp on the coating; applying it too thin is a common mistake.

Slope away from the foundation

Soil or pavement should slope away from the foundation for at least 6 ft. In many cases, this is the most practical way to stop snow melt and rainwater. A slope covered with plastic sheeting and decorative rock is even better. If you add landscape edging, make sure it doesn't trap water.

Patch the walls

Holes and cracks let water seep in. Plugging them probably won't solve basement-leaking problems, but it'll help. Hydraulic cement (a powder that you mix with water) is the perfect filler for this job. Chisel out any loose material before you fill cracks or holes.

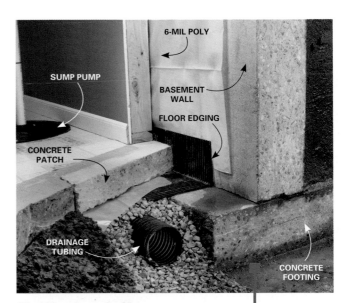

If all else fails...
install a drainage system

Adding drain tile and a sump pump is a major project that costs thousands of dollars, so it's smart to try other approaches first. But when other cures for incoming water fail, a drainage system is the way to go. If properly installed, it's a sure solution. Most systems are installed inside the foundation walls, though pros occasionally install them from outside by trenching around the house.

Save on home insurance

Surefire ways to slash your insurance bill

You might think your homeowner's insurance is like your property taxes—a fixed expense that you just have to pay. But you can actually trim hundreds off your insurance bill, cutting your costs by 10 to 45 percent. Here's how:

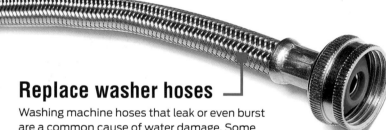

Replace washer hoses

Washing machine hoses that leak or even burst are a common cause of water damage. Some insurance companies offer a discount of up to 10 percent on your premiums if you replace the rubber hoses on your washing machine with no-burst stainless steel hoses. In 10 minutes, you could save five times the cost of the hoses on your next bill, but this is a smart move even if your insurer doesn't offer a discount.

Increase your deductible

This is the easiest way to cut your insurance costs. Bumping your deductible from $500 to $1,000 can save you up to 25 percent on your premium.

Think twice before filing a claim

Paying for a smaller loss yourself will almost always cost less than the premium increase you'll face later. Don't file a claim if it's worth less than $1,000 over your deductible.

Get a list of discounts

You may be missing out on discounts for features your home already has. Ask your agent if the company offers discounts for safety features and home improvements such as sprinklers, dead bolts, smoke detectors, updated plumbing and electrical service.

Certain Teed Corp.

Choose a tough roof

Insurance companies offer big discounts (up to 45 percent) for tough roofing materials. Talk to your agent to learn about the exact discounts for materials other than standard asphalt. In most cases, metal roofing gives you the largest discount, but it also costs two to four times as much as standard asphalt shingles.

Rate raisers

Insurance companies have a long list of things that raise the likelihood of claims for them—and raise rates for you. Here are a few:

- Swimming pool, especially with a diving board
- Hot tub
- Trampoline
- Certain dog breeds, such as pit bulls and Rottweilers
- Dangerous cracks or depressions in steps and walks

Install trouble detectors

Some companies discount your premium 2 to 5 percent for warning devices. These include battery-operated or plug-in temperature sensors ($20 to $60 depending on the type), which detect furnace breakdowns, and leak detectors ($15 to $200 depending on the model). For purchase info, search online for "leak detectors" and "temperature sensors."

Zircon

Choose fire-resistant siding

If you're installing new siding, install Class A rated fire-resistant materials such as metal, fiber cement shingles and clapboards, and masonry. Using these materials can reduce your premium by up to 20 percent, especially in dry areas of the country that are more susceptible to fire damage.

Certain Teed Corp.

Install storm shutters

In hurricane-prone areas, installing wind-resistant shutters can cut your bill by almost 20 percent. So in many cases, these shutters will pay for themselves in three to five years.

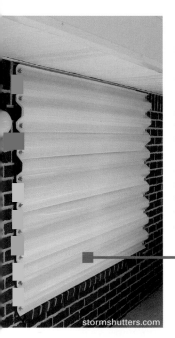

stormshutters.com

Monitor your credit score

A poor credit score can increase your premium by 35 to 40 percent so keep an eye on yours (get a free credit report at annualcreditreport.com). If your credit score has improved since your policy was issued, have your agent recalculate your premium.

Drop additional structures coverage

Many insurers just assume that your house isn't the only building on your property. If you don't have a stand-alone garage or shed, drop this coverage and save 5 percent.

Make automatic payments

Many insurance companies will discount your premium by 2 percent if you pay by automatic withdrawal from your bank account.

Shop around every five years

You may get better coverage or a reduced rate with a different insurer, so it pays to check periodically.

Avoid a water damage claim

Think twice before filing a claim based on water damage, and consider paying for repairs yourself. Water damage is a red flag to insurance companies since it hints at mold elimination costs or chronic plumbing problems in the future. That can mean increased premiums.

Make your carpet last

Keep it clean, double its life span and save thousands

Dirty carpet doesn't just look bad. Dirt is abrasive, so when you walk across a dirty carpet, dirt grinds away at the fibers. The result is carpet that looks dull, stains easier and soon becomes matted down. That's why cleaning is the best way to maximize the life of your carpet and delay the heavy cost of replacement.

Vacuum smarts

■ Vacuum often. Vacuum entrance areas and high-traffic areas twice a week and the rest of the carpeting at least weekly.

■ Set the height right. Raise it to its highest setting, turn it on and lower it until you can feel the vacuum trying to tug itself forward.

■ Slow down. It's OK to make one quick pass over low-traffic areas, but make two slow passes over high-traffic areas.

■ Start with a clean filter. A dirty bag or filter reduces your vacuum's cleaning power. Replace filters on bagless vacuums every three months. Replace vacuum bags when they're three-quarters full.

Use doormats, in and out

A pair of mats at each door keeps carpets much cleaner. Drop a coarse-textured mat outside your door to remove soil. Use a water-absorbent mat inside to prevent wet shoes on the carpeting.

Hire a quality cleaning pro

Most carpet manufacturers recommend professional hot-water extraction as the primary cleaning method for synthetic carpets. The best strategy is to hire a professional every year or two and clean the carpet yourself between pro cleanings. Here are some hiring tips:

■ Hire a pro who uses truck-mounted equipment rather than portable steam cleaning equipment. Truck-mounted equipment exhausts the dirty air and humidity outside. Its stronger suction leaves carpets drier, too.

■ Ask for a high-pressure rinse. This agitates the pile and neutralizes the carpet's pH.

■ Ask the pro to set furniture on blocks or pads after cleaning. This prevents stains from transferring from furniture legs to the damp carpet.

■ Make the estimate include everything—such as furniture moving, vacuuming (some charge extra for this, so check), routine spot removal, preconditioning and deodorizing as part of a standard cleaning package.

Clean carpet yourself (sometimes)

DIY carpet cleaning saves the cost of a pro, but it's not a substitute for pro cleaning. Rented equipment just can't do what pro gear and know-how can do. So a good strategy is to alternate between pro cleaning and DIY cleaning. Here are some ways to get the most from rental equipment:

■ Clean the carpet before it becomes really dirty. If you wait until the carpet is filthy, cleaning it will be much more difficult, take much longer and cost more.

■ Vacuum well before and after cleaning. Vacuum beforehand to remove large particles of soil. Vacuum again after you clean and the carpet is completely dry to pick up soil that wicks to the surface during drying.

■ Pretreat stains and high-traffic areas. Mix a drop of detergent with hot water in a spray bottle and lightly mist the dirtiest areas. Let sit 10 minutes before the general cleaning.

■ Use less soap than directed. The soap used in DIY machines foams a lot and leaves behind a lot of residue, which acts as a dirt magnet. Use a tablespoon or less of soap to 1 gallon of hot water to prevent soap residue.

■ Use a mild acid rinse. DIY machines are often sold with a neutralizing rinse, or you can make your own using 1 cup of white vinegar to 1 gallon of hot water. Rinse after you make one pass with the detergent solution.

■ Don't overwet the carpet. DIY machines put a lot of moisture into the carpet, and most don't have enough suction to extract it thoroughly. Make only one pass with the soap-and-water solution. Make one pass with the neutralizing rinse. Then make three drying passes with the water switched off.

■ Let it dry thoroughly. After you clean your carpets, open the windows, use fans and a dehumidifier, or put the AC on a

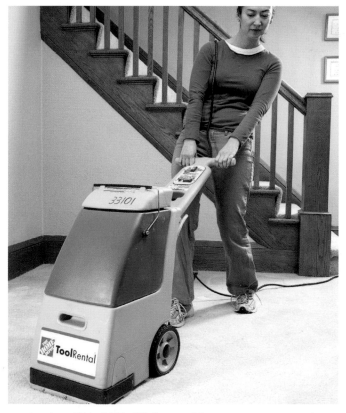

moderate setting (72 to 78 degrees) to remove excess moisture from the air. Don't replace the furniture or walk on the carpet until it's completely dry. This can take up to 12 hours, though six to eight hours is typical.

Improve your insulation

Is it a good investment? Here's how to find out

Better insulation can be a great investment with a quick payoff. Or it can be an expensive mistake. Done badly, it can even cause serious trouble. Here's how to determine whether you need more insulation and an overview of your options.

R-11 LOW DENSITY

R-13 MEDIUM DENSITY

R-15 HIGH DENSITY

Is your insulation adequate?

That depends on a complex combination of factors. Luckily, there's a simple way to answer that question. Contact your utility company about an energy audit. It can recommend an auditor and may even pay part of the cost. The auditor will visit your home, perform some tests and make recommendations on energy savings, including insulation if needed.

What's R-value?

R-value is the resistance to heat flow, a way of indicating insulation's power to stop heat from moving though it. The higher the number, the better. Insulation is labeled by total R-value. There are two things that determine that number: The thickness of the insulation and the insulating power of the material. The fiberglass batts shown here, for example, are all the same thickness, but differ in R-value due to different density.

The best insulation

Closed-cell foam insulation seals air leaks and delivers about twice the R-value per inch of other common choices. And since it's sprayed on, it's perfect for situations where installing batts would be difficult. The catch, of course, is the price. It typically costs at least twice as much as other options. Another version, open-cell spray foam, costs less but doesn't provide the same R-value, sealing power or resistance to moisture. Foam insulation is also sold in 4 x 8-ft. sheets at home centers.

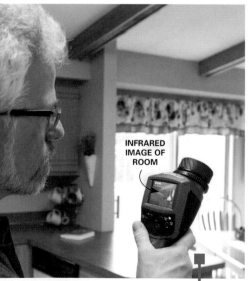

INFRARED IMAGE OF ROOM

Insulation checkup

An infrared camera shows how well-insulated walls and ceilings are. An energy auditor will also test the air-tightness of your home, the efficiency of your furnace and more.

Walls aren't so easy

In old homes that were built without insulation, adding insulation is straightforward. Contractors can drill holes into each stud cavity (from inside or out), blow insulation into the empty walls and patch the holes. If your walls are already insulated, improvements are tough: You can either tear into walls or add a layer of foam insulation, inside or out. Those methods rarely pay off in savings. In many cases, you're better off leaving poorly insulated walls alone.

Add attic insulation

Unlike walls, improving insulation in attics is usually practical and economical. There are two standard approaches: adding fiberglass batts or blowing in loose-fill insulation. Contractors usually recommend the blow-in method. It provides a more consistent, gap-free blanket than batts (plus, it's easier for them). DIYers can choose blown-in by renting a blower from a home center.

BATT INSULATION

Roll batts across the attic

Covering existing insulation with a layer of fiberglass batts is simple. But that doesn't mean it's easy. Crawling through a dark, hot, cramped attic—without stepping through the ceiling below—is a tough job.

Blow in insulation

A long hose connected to a blower outside blasts loose-fill insulation (fiberglass or cellulose) into the attic. This is dusty work, but easier and faster than rolling out batts.

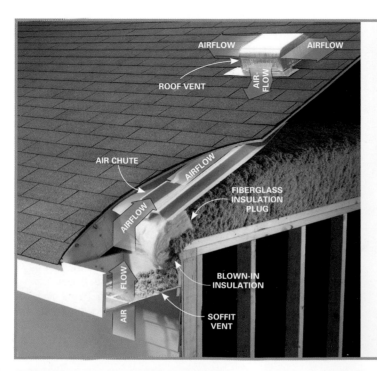

AIRFLOW   AIRFLOW

ROOF VENT   AIR-FLOW

AIR CHUTE

AIRFLOW

FIBERGLASS INSULATION PLUG

AIRFLOW

AIR FLOW

BLOWN-IN INSULATION

SOFFIT VENT

Don't block ventilation

Good attic ventilation is critical. In summer, it extends shingle life and allows you to cool your house with less energy. In winter, it prevents ice dams on the roof and condensation in the attic. But adding insulation can block off soffit vents and stop the airflow. Make sure your insulation contractor plans to add or extend air chutes and to plug the edges of the attic.

Cut heating costs

Little air leaks can lead to big heating bills

Major upgrades like more insulation or a new furnace can pay off in energy savings. But in most homes, especially older ones, sealing air leaks is the easiest, most efficient place to start. Plus, sealing leaks makes your home more comfortable and cuts cooling bills.

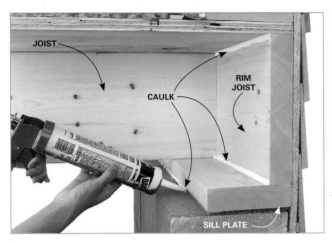

JOIST

RIM JOIST

CAULK

SILL PLATE

Seal basement air leaks

Sill plates and rim joists are usually poorly insulated (if at all) and very leaky. So if you have an unfinished basement, grab some silicone or acrylic latex caulk to seal the sill plate. If you simply have fiberglass insulation stuffed against the rim joist, pull it out. Run a bead of caulk between the edge of the sill plate and the top of the foundation wall. Use expanding foam for gaps larger than 1/4 in.

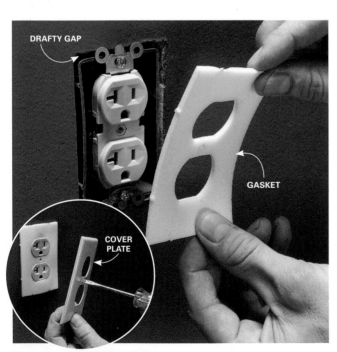

DRAFTY GAP

GASKET

COVER PLATE

Seal electrical boxes

Electrical boxes that hold switches or outlets are major sources of heat loss. Foam gaskets may not completely seal the boxes, but they'll help. They're quick to install—just take off the cover plate, stick the gasket over the box, then put the plate back on.

Get an energy audit

An energy audit includes a series of tests, including a blower door test that measures the overall leakiness of your house. On the basis of the test results, the auditor will recommend improvements and estimate the costs and savings. Audits take two to three hours and cost $250 to $400. If you set one up through your utility company, you might get one at a lower cost or a rebate.

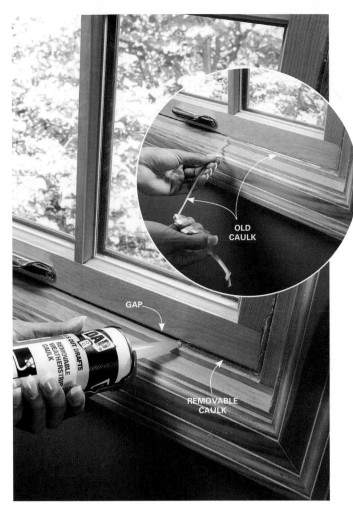

Fill gaps under sinks

Pull back the escutcheons where pipes enter exterior walls and you'll probably see generous gaps around the pipes. Use expanding foam to seal those gaps. Shake the can vigorously, then squirt the foam around the pipes inside the wall. Don't completely fill the gap—the foam will expand.

Stop fireplace heat loss

Wood-burning fireplaces can warm up a room, but more often, they rob a house of heat by letting it escape up the chimney. If you have a modern fireplace with a cold air intake from outside, make sure you equip it with an airtight door. If you have an older fireplace that uses room air for combustion, equip it with a door that has operable vents. And only keep those vents open when you have a fire in the fireplace. Otherwise, heat will constantly be sucked out of the house.

Seal windows with removable caulk

Leaky windows lead to major energy loss in a typical home. A quick, low-cost solution is to seal the gaps with removable caulk. Just apply the caulk over gaps and pull it off in the spring. Clean off any residue with mineral spirits.

Consider new storm windows

Storm windows aren't new, but they've definitely improved over the years: New ones open and close and can be left on year-round. Some offer low-emissivity coatings to further cut heat loss. You'll see the biggest payback when they're used over single-pane windows. But don't use storm windows over aluminum windows—heat buildup between the two windows can damage the aluminum, and drilling holes for installation can cause leaks.

Stop leaks under doors

If you can feel the breeze or see daylight under your entry door, that's bad news. The good news is that most thresholds adjust up or down just by turning a few screws. Turn all of the screws equally until the door opens and closes without much drag and any draft is eliminated.

Will new windows pay off?

Replacing your old leakers with new windows *will* lower your heating bills. But in most homes, the energy savings alone won't justify the high up-front costs. Other factors, like appearance, draft-stopping and easy operation, are usually better reasons to replace windows.

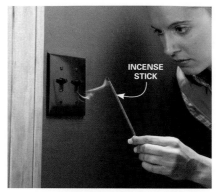

Low-tech leak detection

Locating air leaks can be tricky, but here's a clever way to find them. Close all the windows in the house, turn off fans and the furnace. Light some incense and walk slowly around the outer walls of the house. The smoke will tell where air is leaking in or out.

INCENSE STICK

DOUBLE-SIDED TAPE

Cover windows with plastic film

Plastic window film seals air leaks, reduces window condensation and can be used with curtains or blinds. Exterior or interior window film kits are available at home centers.

Check the dryer vent

If cold air comes in through your dryer vent, check outside where the vent goes through the wall. The vent should have a flap (or flaps) at the end to stop air infiltration. Make sure the flap closes and isn't stuck open. If the flap doesn't close on its own, replace it. If the flap works well, check the caulking. If it's cracking and peeling away, it's probably allowing air to leak in. Cut away the old caulking and apply new caulk.

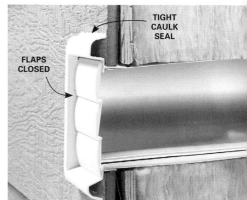

TIGHT CAULK SEAL

FLAPS CLOSED

The ultimate air-sealing job: attic leaks

Crawling around your attic and wallowing in insulation is a big, ugly job. But in many homes, airflow through ceilings into the attic is the biggest source of heat loss. So if you're really determined to tighten your home, get up there and seal those leaks! Most leaks occur where the chimneys and electrical and plumbing lines pass through the ceiling. Although the attic is a nasty place to work, plugging these leaks is simple—mostly caulking and foaming gaps.

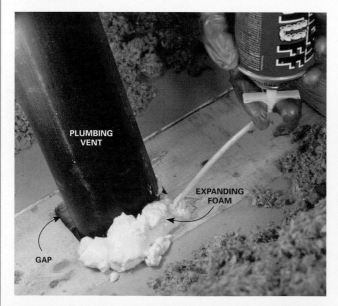

PLUMBING VENT

EXPANDING FOAM

GAP

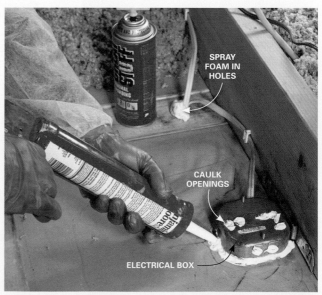

SPRAY FOAM IN HOLES

CAULK OPENINGS

ELECTRICAL BOX

Clean your air conditioner

DISCONNECT BOX

Restore efficiency and cut energy bills—in 10 minutes!

The outside unit of your central air conditioning system is basically a fan surrounded by a wall of tubing and tiny fins. If those fins are plugged with dirt and debris, airflow through them is reduced. In the short term, that means lower efficiency and expensive energy wasted. In the long term, it leads to repairs or replacement. But keeping those fins open to airflow is faster and easier than washing your car.

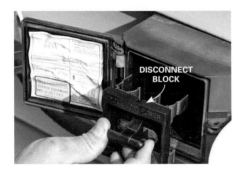

DISCONNECT BLOCK

Turn off the power

Open the disconnect box and pull out the disconnect block. Set the block aside and close the box. Don't forget to push the block back into place when you're done cleaning.

Clean the unit

Washing air-blocking debris off of the fins is as easy as using a garden hose. Here are a few tips for best results:

■ If the fins are caked with fuzz from dandelions or cottonwood trees, vacuum before you rinse with water.

■ Rinse with moderate pressure. The fins are made from flimsy metal, which will bend under strong pressure.

■ As you spray, peer down into the unit from above. You should see water streaming through the fins. If not, the fins are blocked and need more rinsing.

■ Rinse off all the fins, but pay special attention to the fins just under the lid of the unit. Aim the water upward to drive out debris buildup there.

Straighten crushed fins

A bump from your knee or a stray soccer ball is enough to crush the fins, leaving them closed and blocking airflow. If you have a few crushed fins, you can straighten them with a butter knife. If you have large crushed areas, do the job faster with a fin comb (available at appliance parts stores and online). Get a kit that has different combs to suit different fin spacing.

Cut cooling costs

And still keep cool

Staying cool is expensive. Even in moderate climates, it costs a few hundred bucks per year. In hot climates, that cost might reach four figures. So reducing cooling bills is worth some effort. And as a bonus, many of the steps that cut cooling costs also save on heating.

Keep cool with shade

Shade from trees, trellises and vines blocks direct sunlight through the roof and windows, which is responsible for about half of the heat gain in your home. Carefully positioned trees and horizontal trellises on the east and west sides can save up to 30 percent of a household's energy consumption for heating and cooling.

Clean or change filters monthly

Dirty air filters are the No. 1 cause of air conditioning breakdowns and they cost about 7 percent more in energy costs in hot climates. Change central AC furnace filters monthly during the summer. Most window units have a removable filter behind the air inlet grille that you can take out and rinse monthly.

Feel cooler at higher temperatures

Ceiling fans save money by keeping you comfortable at higher thermostat settings. Each degree higher than 78 degrees will save you 5 to 10 percent on air conditioning costs. The moving air from a ceiling fan increases evaporation from your skin and helps cool you off.

Hampton Bay

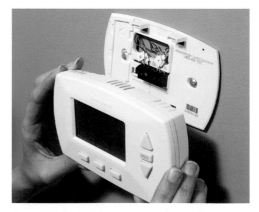

Install a programmable thermostat

This easy upgrade pays back quickly. Setting your cooling system four to six degrees warmer when you're away at work or on vacation and automatically lowering it to 78 degrees when you're home can cut 5 to 20 percent off your energy bill.

Maintenance pays

A neglected air conditioner uses 10 to 30 percent more energy, so professional service every two to three years cuts cooling bills. Regular service also adds years to the life of the system and reduces breakdowns.

Replace an old air conditioner

Replacing a 15-year-old window or central AC unit with a new, efficient unit can save you enough over the new unit's lifetime to offset its purchase price. This is especially true if you live in a hot, humid climate. Use the savings calculator at energystar.gov to figure out whether it makes financial sense to replace your AC, and get a list of the most energy-efficient units.

Voice of experience

My new, more efficient, AC unit not only cut my electric bills in half, but is much quieter. My neighbors are happy and so am I.

Gene Hamolka,
The Family Handyman
Field Editor

Block out the sun

Roughly 30 percent of heat comes in through your windows. Shades, curtains or tinted window film on south- and west-facing windows can save you up to 7 percent annually. Insulating curtains will save even more on both heating and cooling costs.

Protect your electronics

Power surges can cost you thousands

Sensitive electronics are showing up everywhere. Aside from places you'd expect them—like TVs and computers—they're also in many appliances, even in newer furnaces and water heaters. All of that high-tech circuitry is vulnerable to power surges. The destruction can be gradual or sudden, but it's always expensive; repairs often cost more than completely replacing the victim. But you can protect your electronics (and your wallet).

COAXIAL CABLE

SURGE SUPPRESSOR

COAXIAL CABLE

Two sources of surges

The most dangerous surges come from outside your home. These "external" surges are caused by lightning or an unstable power grid. Any device connected to coaxial cable (cable TV or a computer, for example) is also prone to lightning. Smaller "internal" surges are generated within your home by heavy power users like your fridge or furnace. These two types of surges require different solutions—and it's smart to employ both.

Point-of-use surge suppressors

Small surge suppressors that protect one or several devices offer only fair protection against external surges. But they're good for internal surges and many include protection for coaxial cable. Some suppressors are much better than others, so check the technical specifications (usually on the packaging). You don't have to understand the details—just look for three things:

■ Clamping voltage: You want 330 volts or less.
■ Clamping speed: 5 nanoseconds or less.
■ Energy dissipation: 500 joules or more.

The standard version

Most surge suppressors are similar to this one. You just plug the cord into a wall outlet and plug devices into the suppressor. Many include coaxial cable protection.

Built-in protection

Some outlets contain surge suppressors—much neater and more convenient than a bulky separate device. They lack coaxial cable protection, though.

For tight spaces

Low-profile surge suppressors are thin enough to fit behind most wall-mounted TVs. This model includes coaxial cable protection.

Whole-house surge suppressors

A whole-house suppressor protects every device in your home against external surges, and does that far better than a point-of-use suppressor. But a whole-house suppressor won't stop internal surges. There are two types, and both require an electrician for installation. Expect a total cost of $400 to $600.

METER SOCKET

METER SOCKET SURGE SUPPRESSOR

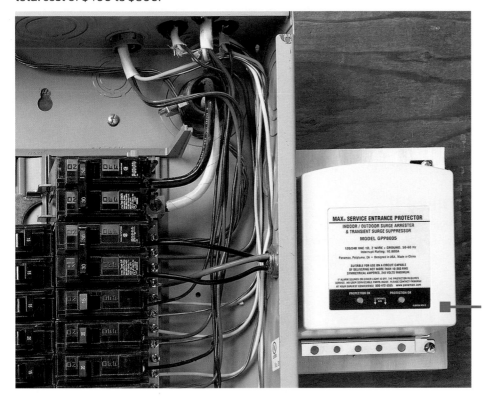

MAX. SERVICE ENTRANCE PROTECTOR
INDOOR / OUTDOOR SURGE ARRESTER & TRANSIENT SURGE SUPPRESSOR
MODEL GPP8005

At the meter
Some whole-house suppressors connect to the electrical meter, which is typically outside the house.

At the main panel
Most whole-house suppressors are mounted near the main electrical panel and require a connection within the panel.

Does it need protection?

You can't always tell if a unit has sensitive electronics inside just by looking at it. But here's one clue: If it has a digital display, it definitely needs surge protection. The owner's manual may also help. Many manufacturers recommend protection in the fine print.

Low-tech protection: Unplug it

Unplugging electronics during an electrical storm is a poor substitute for permanent surge protection, but it will prevent damage. Also unplug when there's a power outage. As the power grid sputters back into service, it often generates surges. Leave a light switched on so you know when the power is restored.

Understand your electrical system

And restore the power when it goes out

Your home's electrical system is a minor miracle. It takes one of the most dangerous forces in the universe and distributes it safely throughout your home, making every minute of your day more convenient. Here's how it works.

How power gets where you need it

Electricity runs through underground or overhead power lines to an **electrical meter**, which measures your power use and tells the power company how much to charge you. From there, it goes to your **main panel**, which provides an enclosed space where the big incoming wires are connected to dozens of smaller wires that snake throughout your house. Some of these wires form **general-purpose circuits** that branch off to several lights and outlets. Other wires create **dedicated circuits**, each of which serves a single high-demand purpose, such as a fridge, electric heater or the outlets near your kitchen countertop.

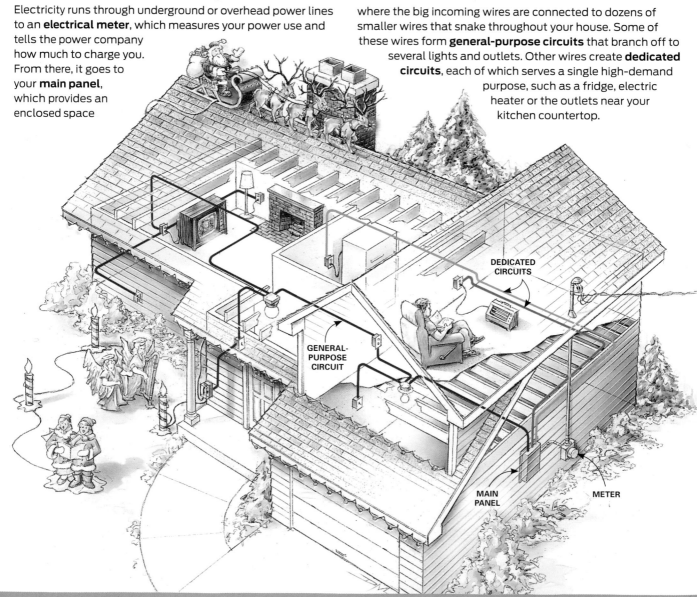

DEDICATED
CIRCUITS

GENERAL-
PURPOSE
CIRCUIT

MAIN
PANEL

METER

The main panel

It's usually a gray metal box located in the utility room, garage or basement. There's no need to worry about opening the panel's door; all the dangerous stuff is safely contained behind a steel cover. Behind the door you'll see a main breaker, which can shut off power to your entire house, and rows of breakers, each controlling an individual branch circuit.

What's a breaker?

Breakers are the most important safety feature of your home's electrical system. Basically, a breaker is a safety switch. When more power flows through a circuit than the circuit was designed to handle, the breaker instantly shuts off. And that prevents fires. Aside from that, breakers allow you to turn off the power so you can safely work with wiring.

Find a tripped breaker

When a breaker "blows" or "trips," the switch lever snaps away from the "on" position. But it doesn't go all the way to "off," so you may have to look closely to find the switch that's not in line with the others. Some breakers have a little window that turns red or orange to indicate a trip.

MAIN BREAKER

MAIN PANEL

BRANCH CIRCUIT BREAKERS

PUSH TO "OFF"...

THEN TO "ON"

Office

M.

Bath

Kit

Reset the breaker

You can't push the switch directly from the tripped position to "on." First push the switch all the way to "off," then back to "on." Don't worry if your hard-wired smoke alarms beep as power is restored; that's normal.

Blown fuses

If you have an older home with fuses rather than breakers, you'll have to peer into the window of each fuse. The difference between a good fuse and a blown fuse can be hard to see, so you'll have to look for the fuse that doesn't look like the others. You'll see that a spring has collapsed or a metal strip has burned, leaving a gap in the strip.

Unscrew the blown fuse and screw in a new one, just like a lightbulb. Make sure to install a fuse with the same "amp" rating. *Never, ever install a fuse with a higher amp rating.*

Voice of experience

Don't trust labels

Inside your main panel, you'll find labels or lists indicating which breaker controls which circuit: "master bedroom lights and outlets," for example. These labels are a good guide, but they're not completely reliable, especially in older homes that have been through repeated remodeling. For example, you might find that all of

the outlets in a room—except one—are on the circuit listed on the main panel. That orphan outlet may be connected to just about any other circuit and not listed on the panel. As every electrician has learned the hard way, you can't trust those labels.

Al Hildenbrand, master electrician and *The Family Handyman* Field Editor

If a breaker trips again and again...

A breaker or fuse that won't "hold" means one of two things: You have a serious problem such as a short-circuited wire, or you've overloaded the circuit by plugging in too many electric devices. First, try to take some load off the circuit by plugging into other outlets that are on other circuits. Appliances that draw lots of power are usually the overload culprits (space heaters, window air conditioners, hair dryers, irons, etc.). If you can't prevent breaker trips this way, there's a good chance that you have a more serious problem. Call in an electrician.

What are GFCIs and AFCIs?

Ground-fault circuit interrupters and arc-fault circuit interrupters detect potentially dangerous flows of electricity and turn off instantly, before they can do any harm. Both can be built into breakers or outlets (a test button on a breaker or outlet indicates that it's GFCI- or AFCI-protected). Electrical codes require GFCIs in areas that might be damp, like kitchens, bathrooms, outdoors or in the garage. AFCIs are required in all living areas, except bathrooms. That doesn't mean you have to call in an electrician to install them immediately. But a remodeling project could trigger these requirements, adding safety to your home—and major expenses to the project.

Eliminate ants

You can safely and easily de-bug your home without pro help

Insecticides keep getting better and better: easier to use, more effective and safer for your family. So you can handle most ant problems yourself, without the expense of an exterminator. But don't hesitate to call in a pro for stubborn infestations. Some ants are more than a nuisance and can damage your home.

I.D. the ant

Take a close-up photo of an invader and e-mail it to your local university extension service (search online for your state's name followed by "university extension service"). The extension service will tell you the type of ant you're dealing with and where it nests. It may give you fact sheets about the ant species and maybe even some advice on getting rid of that particular ant species.

Make poison easy to reach

Place liquid ant bait stations in areas where you've seen ants, like under the sink and along walls, to make it as easy as possible for the ants to take the toxic bait back to the nest. Expect to see more ants (initially) when you set out the bait. That's a good thing. It means more ants are taking the bait back to the colony where they'll share it with the rest of the ants, including the queen.

Don't squish them!

After setting out the toxic bait, resist the temptation to step on ants. Remember that they're working for you now—gathering the poison and taking it to the nest.

> **Caution!**
> Ant poison is also toxic to pets and humans. No matter what product you use, read the instructions completely and follow them carefully.

Kill ants in your yard

Spot-treat ant hills or mounds with an outdoor insecticide. For large-scale ant problems, use a lawn and garden insect killer that contains bifenthrin as the active ingredient. First mow the grass, then spray the insecticide on the entire lawn in the early morning or late afternoon when the ants are most active.

Destroy exterior nests

Look for holes in the siding where ants are crawling in and out. The holes are often located between bricks where mortar has fallen out, under lap siding or in cracks in stucco. Spray the area with insecticide.

Kill fire ants with bait

You need a special bait designed to kill fire ants (check the label). Apply the granules with a broadcast spreader. Fire ants carry the toxic bait back to their mounds where they share it with the colony.

Eliminate ant havens

Trim back bushes, shrubs and trees that brush against your siding or roof. These provide a bridge for ants to reach your house. Keep a 3-in. to 6-in. clearance space between the soil around the foundation and the bottom row of siding to prevent ants from nesting in the siding, and avoid stacking firewood next to the house.

Erase their trails

Ants leave a scented trail that other ants follow. Sweeping or mopping isn't enough to eliminate the scent. Instead, mix 1 part vinegar with 3 parts water in a spray bottle, then spray wherever you've seen ants. By erasing the trail, you'll stop outdoor ants from following the first invaders. But you won't stop ants that have already nested indoors.

Hunt down the nest

The solution to some ant problems (like carpenter ants) is getting rid of their nest. Look for damp areas such as framing or flooring that's soft and spongy from a plumbing or roof leak. Look in attics, bathrooms and exterior walls. When you find the nest, spray it with an insecticide labeled for indoor use.

Spray entry points

Spray an indoor insect killer in places where ants can enter, including windows and doors, holes in exterior walls and cracks in the foundation. Spray a 4-in.-wide band along entry points, just enough to wet the surface. Once dry, the spray leaves an invisible film that repels ants so they won't enter the house.

Spray on a barrier

If you're still getting ants in your house after spraying interior entry points, spray a 12-in.-wide band of insecticide on the foundation and siding. Use an outdoor insecticide that says "barrier treatment" on the label.

Get rid of mice

Trap the ones you have and keep the others out

If you have mice, you need a short-term solution and a long-term defense. Simple snap traps are an effective way to eliminate the intruders. But also take steps to keep out the next wave of invaders.

BACON

PEANUT BUTTER

www.tomca—rand.com

The best bait (it isn't cheese)

Cheese isn't on any mouse's "top-10 list." They'll only eat it if nothing else is available. Plus, cheese hardens after sitting out for a while, making it easier for mice to take the bait without setting off the trap. The perfect bait is actually peanut butter or bacon, or a blend of peanut butter and bacon grease. Mice can't resist the smell and taste. So wipe that on the trip mechanism to get the greatest number of catches.

Are snap traps cruel?

You might think that live trapping and releasing is more humane. But once released into new territory, mice (or other critters) usually die a slow death from starvation or exposure. Poison usually leads to a painful death, too. Snap traps, on the other hand, do the job quickly.

Use the right mousetrap technique

Snap-type mousetraps work—if you use them right.
■ Place traps along walls in areas where you've seen the telltale brown pellets. Mice have poor vision and prefer to feel their way along walls.
■ The best technique is to set two traps, parallel to the wall, with the triggers facing out. Mice sometimes jump over traps, but they can't jump two.
■ Set lots of traps. For an average-size house, two dozen mousetraps isn't too many.

Don't get mouse germs!

Before you sweep up mouse droppings, always spray them with a disinfectant spray such as Lysol. Mice can pass disease to humans through their waste.

Eliminate easy entrances

Mice can slip through gaps as small as 1/4 in. For those gaps, acrylic latex caulk is a good filler. For gaps 1/4 in. up to 1/2 in., use polyurethane caulk. Expanding foam is a fast, convenient filler for anything wider or for areas where appearance doesn't matter. For most cracks, "minimal expanding" foam is the easiest to use.

Check under the siding
Inspect the underside of your siding using a mirror. If you find a gap, mark the location with masking tape so you can seal it later.

Check the dryer vent
Examine dryer vents to ensure the damper isn't stuck open or broken off completely. Also check that the seal between the vent and the wall is tight.

Seal gaps at door and windows
Seal doors, windows and basement sashes with adhesive-backed weather stripping. Clean the surface first so the weather strip will adhere well.

Plug gaps with mesh
Caulk or expanding foam usually keeps mice out. But sometimes, mice gnaw through them. For the ultimate mouse-proof seal, stuff copper scrubbing pads into gaps before sealing with caulk or foam.

Defeat termites

How to deter them, detect them and kill them

Termites are sneaky. They can feast on a home for years and do enormous damage before anyone notices. But there are ways to make your home less inviting, recognize an infestation and wipe them out.

Eliminate easy access to food and water

Termites get water from wet wood or damp soil. Their food source is anything made from wood, including wallpaper, facing on drywall, hardboard siding and cellulose insulation. If you remove the sources of wood and water from around your home, they won't be attracted in the first place.

Caulk gaps in siding

To prevent rainwater from penetrating your walls, fill any holes or gaps in siding and around window or door trim with acrylic latex caulk.

Repair leaky plumbing

Dripping or leaky faucets keep the soil moist year-round, even during dry spells.

Don't store termite "food" on the ground

A crawl space filled with cardboard boxes or anything made of wood set directly on the ground is an invitation to termites. If you must store wood products in a crawl space, store them off the ground on top of bricks or concrete blocks.

Keep bushes trimmed

Heavy vegetation keeps soil moist. And dense branches can keep your siding moist and even lead to moisture inside the walls. Trim your shrubs so sunlight can dry up the soil and siding.

Keep wood away from your home

Firewood stacked next to your house and wood mulch near the foundation can invite termites. Store firewood at least 20 ft. from your home and replace wood mulch with decorative stone or gravel.

Channel runoff away from your home

Limit moisture near your house by adding downspout extensions that are at least 6 ft. long. Fill in low spots that hold water, and slope the soil so water runs away from your home.

Watch for termite swarms, but don't confuse them with flying ants

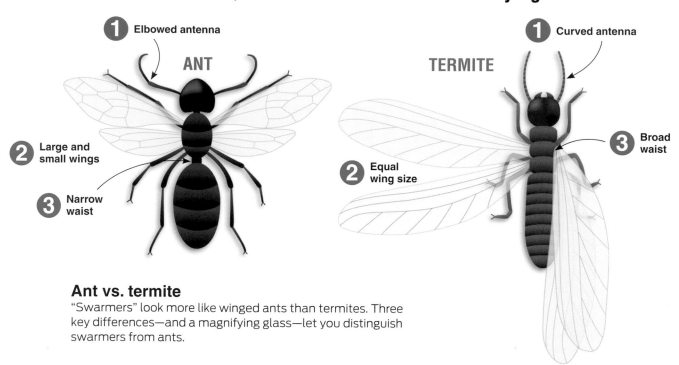

1 Elbowed antenna

ANT

2 Large and small wings

3 Narrow waist

1 Curved antenna

TERMITE

2 Equal wing size

3 Broad waist

Ant vs. termite
"Swarmers" look more like winged ants than termites. Three key differences—and a magnifying glass—let you distinguish swarmers from ants.

FORMER SWARMER

University of Nebraska, Lincoln

MUD TUBE

Swarms in the spring

Each spring, winged termites fly off to start new colonies. If you see swarmers flying around your house, try to spot where they're coming from. If they're coming out of your house or you find them inside, you have a termite colony inside. Also look for piles of wings in corners, on windowsills or caught in spider webs. Collect swarmers (dead or alive) in a jar or plastic bag to help a pro identify the type.

Mud tubes

Termites live in the soil beneath a house and use "mud tubes" to reach wooden structures without dehydrating. Mud tubes are most common on the inside or outside of foundations. You may be tempted to immediately destroy the tubes, but hold off. They can provide clues so pros can diagnose and eliminate termite colonies.

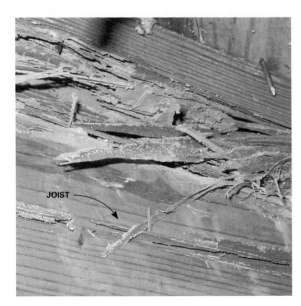

JOIST

Damaged wood

Termites can feed on a house for years without leaving any evidence because they often eat wood from the inside and leave the outside intact. But you can check accessible wood in an open crawl space or unfinished basement for hidden damage. Just stab the wood hard with a screwdriver every 6 in. and check for soft wood.

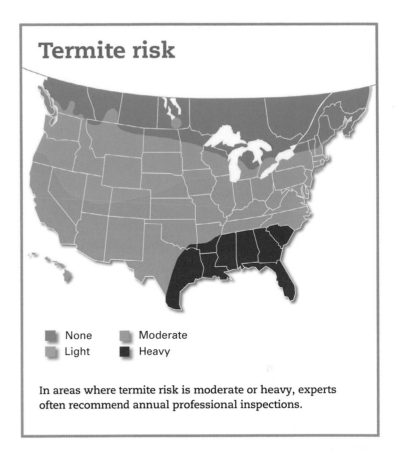

Termite risk

	None		Moderate
	Light		Heavy

In areas where termite risk is moderate or heavy, experts often recommend annual professional inspections.

Hire an exterminator— but do your research first

Think twice before trying to exterminate termites yourself. When it comes to protecting your home from serious damage, professional expertise is worth paying for. Because termites work slowly, you can take your time to find the right extermination service. Get bids from several pest control companies and pay attention to warranties. Some cover the cost of repairs if termites come back while others cover only the cost of treatment.

Exterminators don't just spray pesticides on surfaces. For effective, lasting treatment, they often drill holes and inject chemicals into wood, soil or masonry.

Protect against pet damage

Don't let beloved pets wreck your beloved home

RASCAL

WOOFGANG

SCOUR PAD

Keep them off the furniture

Lay a plastic carpet protector—prickly side up—on seats to train pets to stay off. Carpet protectors are available at office supply stores. Aluminum foil often works, too. Some pets find the feel and sound of foil intolerable.

Prevent clogged drains

If you wash your pooch in a sink, tub or shower, you're begging for a furry drain clog. To avoid that, you can buy a drain screen at a discount store. Or you can simply cover the drain with a scouring pad. It will catch the fur but let water flow down the drain. To protect a tub drain, stuff the pads under the open stopper.

CARPET
EXTRACTOR

HAIKU

Rescue the carpet

If your pet has an accident on the carpet, act fast. Urine can damage fibers and even change the color of carpet. The longer you wait, the greater that risk.

The best tool for the job

If your pet has frequent accidents, buy a "carpet extractor," a small handheld vacuum designed to suck liquids out of carpets. Otherwise, go with the low-tech method shown below.

PUDDLES

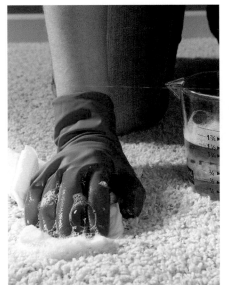

1 Blot the spot right away

Soak up the urine with white paper towels. Printed patterns can bleed color into the carpet. Press hard to soak up as much as possible. Then add about a quarter-teaspoon of dish-washing liquid to a cup of lukewarm water. But don't use the detergent you use with your dishwasher.

2 Apply the soapy water

Soak the area thoroughly with paper towels. Then blot the area with dry paper towels and repeat this wet-and-dry process at least once. Follow up with clear water to rinse out the detergent and blot the carpet dry again.

3 Dry the carpet

Apply one part white vinegar mixed with two parts water and blot the carpet one last time. Cover the damp area with about 20 layers of paper towels and a heavy stack of books. Change the towels again and again until they no longer absorb moisture.

Mask claw marks

Scratches on painted doors and woodwork can be erased with wood filler and a fresh coat of paint. Stained wood isn't quite so easy to fix, but you can make the damage much less visible. The hard part is matching the existing wood tone. You may need to blend two stain colors. Gel stain is more forgiving than standard liquid stain; if you don't like the look, you can immediately wipe it off and start over. Try a lighter color first, then add some darker stain if needed. If the stained area looks dull after the stain dries, add some sheen with wipe-on polyurethane.

CLAW MARKS

FINE SANDING BLOCK

1 Smooth out the scratches

Sand the damaged area lightly with a fine sanding block or sponge. Your goal isn't to completely remove the scratches, but to smooth out the damage.

2 Stain the scratches

Apply gel stain with a brush. Start by applying the stain very lightly and gradually add more until you reach the tone you want.

Perfect lawn patch

Here's how to cut out damaged grass and replace it with a perfect-fitting patch: Lay a piece of sod over the damaged spot and slide through both the sod and the turf below with a spade. Dig out the bad grass and plug in the new sod. Water it daily for a couple weeks and it will blend invisibly into your lawn.

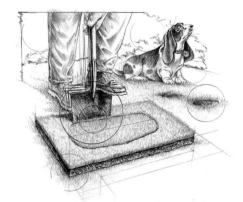

Enzymes really work

Cleaners that contain enzymes aren't like other products. Their key ingredient is harmless bacteria, which eat the organic matter that causes stains and odors. Just spray it on. When the organic matter is gone, so are the stains and smells. And having eaten all their food, the bacteria die.

Time for new carpet?

If your old carpet has the lingering smell of pet urine, there's a good chance that the odor has also penetrated the subfloor underneath. So it's smart to treat the subfloor after the old carpet is out and before the new carpet goes in. Wet any stained areas with a 50/50 mix of water and bleach. After a five-minute soak, wipe up the water and let the floor dry. Then paint over the pet-stain spots with a stain-blocking primer such as Kilz, BIN or 1-2-3.

Voice of experience

Pets and projects don't mix

Home-improvement work zones are dangerous places for pets, with all those tools and chemicals around. Pets pose a danger to your home, too. When I took a break from a recent painting project, my helpful dog fetched my paintbrush for me and carried it across the house, dripping paint all the way.

Dave Jones, *The Family Handyman* **Field Editor**

Don't kill your lawn mower

Stale gas is the No. 1 enemy of small engines

Old gas causes the vast majority of starting problems in mowers, snowblowers and other small engines. The most common fix is a carburetor rebuild, which costs around $100. And that's a waste—because avoiding trouble is far easier than dealing with the consequences.

How to get rid of old gas

Pour doses of it into your car's tank, about a half gallon at a time. Your car can handle stale gas much better than small engines, and small doses won't hurt it. Your city may also have a recycling center that accepts gas.

Buy smaller quantities

Gas has a limited shelf life, so buy only what you need for the near future. If you buy ethanol (oxygenated) gas, buy only enough to last for 30 days. If you buy non-oxygenated gas, limit your purchase to a 60-day supply. With either type of gas, use a container that's sized for the amount you'll buy. Storing 2 gallons in a 5-gallon container leaves you with 3 gallons of air, causing the gas to spoil faster—even if you add stabilizer.

Add stabilizer every time you fill

Many people add gasoline stabilizer when they put the mower away for the winter. That's a good idea, but that's not the only time you should use stabilizer. Stabilizer works best when it's added to fresh gas right at the pump. And, since small-engine gas tanks are vented, pre-stabilized gas can reduce the effects of water accumulation and slow the loss of volatile vapors. Look for a stabilizer product that includes antioxidant protection, corrosion inhibitors, detergent and metal deactivators. (Briggs & Stratton Advanced Formula Fuel Treatment & Stabilizer and STA-BIL are two examples.) If you have a two-stroke engine, buy oil with built-in stabilizer.

Get a new gas container

If your gas container doesn't seal properly, you're going to have gas problems. As the air temperature rises and falls, a poorly sealed container emits gas vapors and pulls in moisture. So you lose the most volatile ingredients in the gas— the ones you need most to start a cold engine. Also, the humidity that gets sucked in condenses on the container walls and falls to the bottom. As you reach the gas at the bottom, you're literally pouring in a blend of old gas and water. If your old container is missing caps, buy a new one.

SPRING-LOADED FILL CAP

INTERNAL VALVE SEALS SPOUT

Filling and storage tips

Let the engine cool after use and then refill the tank to 90 percent. That will reduce moisture condensation and oxidation. Consult your owner's manual for off-season storage recommendations. Most manuals specify "dry storage," which involves draining the tank and running the engine until it dies. Then pull the cord until you get no signs of life from the engine. If the manual recommends "wet" storage, fill the tank to 90 percent with fresh stabilized gas.

Use the right kind of gas

Never use E-85 or E-15 gas in your small engine. Those fuels can cause catastrophic damage. Most small engines operate best with 87-octane fuel (85-octane in high altitudes). Unless specifically recommended by the manufacturer, never use a higher octane fuel in your small engine.

Is ethanol at fault?

Everybody blames oxygenated fuel (gas with ethanol) for carburetor failures. But guess what caused the problems before we started adding ethanol? Yup—stale gas. Whether you buy oxygenated or non-oxygenated gas, operator error is really the root cause of carburetor corrosion and gunk buildup. Gasoline simply goes bad, and it goes bad faster if it's improperly handled and stored.

Voice of experience

Thanks for using bad gas

I just want to say "thanks" to all of you who use stale gas. It keeps me and my fellow small-engine repairmen in business. We especially appreciate our repeat customers who ignore our warnings and visit us every spring.

Pete Novak, *The Family Handyman* **Field Editor**

OUR FAVORITE STORAGE TIPS

Quick, easy ways to get organized

Like all homeowners, readers of *The Family Handyman* magazine fight a never-ending battle against clutter. And when they find a winning strategy, they share it with fellow readers. Here are some of their best tips.

Pocket storage

Hang-up shoe organizers are the fastest way to add easy-access storage just about anywhere. Find them at discount stores.

Mobile tool rack

If you see an old golf bag at a rummage sale, grab it. It will make a great tote for lawn and garden gear.

Measuring cup hang-up

Screw a couple strips inside a cabinet door, add some hooks and you've got a perfect roost for measuring cups. Just make sure your cups won't bump into the shelves.

Hang ladders low

Most people hang ladders high on the wall. But often, lower is better. It makes ladders easier to grab and, since ladders are skinny, leaves floor space open for parking cars, bikes or the mower.

Tight-space shelves

Wire pantry shelves aren't just for pantries. They're perfect for any wall where full-depth shelves won't fit: garages, laundry rooms, utility rooms....

Closet nook shelves

Don't let the recessed space at the ends of a closet go to waste. Install wire shelving to hold blankets, towels or bedding.

More shower shelves

Those shelves that hang from a shower pipe are fine, but you have only one shower pipe. To hang more shelves, mount cabinet knobs on the wall using No. 8-32 hanger screws and screw-in drywall anchors.

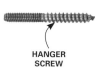

HANGER
SCREW

SCREW-IN
ANCHOR

S-hook hang-up

Pick up a pack of S-hooks at a home center and turn wire shelving into a rack for cleaning gear.

Instant mini bins

Plastic junction boxes for electrical work are cheap and easy to mount anywhere. Get them at home centers.

Toilet paper shelf

Buy a deep "shadow box" picture frame at a craft store, paint it if you'd like and hang it around your toilet paper holder.

Fast shelves

Those plastic crates sold at discount stores make great (and colorful!) shelves. Mount them on walls, using screws and fender washers at the upper corners. Screw to studs where you can; use screw-in drywall anchors where you can't.

Junk drawer in a bag

Heavy-duty zip-top bags are a versatile solution for miscellaneous junk. Unlike a drawer or coffee can, they let you instantly find just the thing you're looking for.

CLOSET ORGANIZER RACKS

ATTACH SCREWS TO BACK SIDE OF FACE FRAME

Can rack

Wire shelving installed upside down in a cabinet makes an easy-access rack for canned goods. No more digging through cans to find the cream of mushroom soup.

Add-on closet rod

Eye screws, carabiners and a couple chains let you hang a second closet rod from the existing rod. Everything you need is available at home centers.

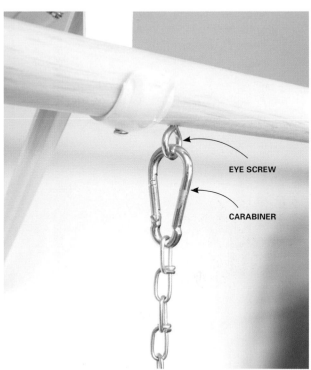

EYE SCREW

CARABINER

Store on a door

A door that opens into a closet or utility room provides a handy surface for hang-up storage. The trouble is that most doors don't offer a flat, solid surface for fastening hooks or racks. The solution is to screw 3/4-in. plywood to the door. (On a hollow-core door, use screws *and* construction adhesive.) Then you can mount as many hooks or racks as you like.

Vertical cabinet space

Cookie sheets and pizza pans are easier to store and easier to access if you store them standing on edge. To create vertical space, install a vertical panel and shorten the existing cabinet shelf.

VERTICAL PLYWOOD PANEL

CUT SHELF TO NEW LENGTH

DRILL HOLES FOR SHELF PINS

SELF-STICK HOOK-AND-LOOP STRIPS

CLOSET POLE AND SHELF BRACKET

Closet bracket bike rack

Brackets designed to support closet rods make a brilliant bike rack. Add some adhesive-backed felt or hook-and-loop strips to prevent scratching your bike.

Simple storage spools

Cut up cardboard to make handy spools for holiday lights, string or cords.

Under-sink archives

Don't file away the manuals and spare parts that came with your kitchen and bath fixtures. Instead, put them right where you'll need them, in zip-top bags hung on hooks at the back walls of cabinets.

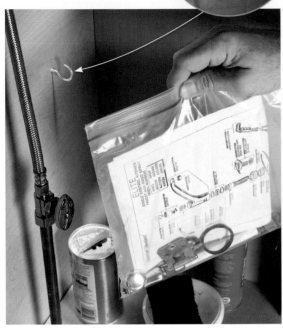

SCREW

DRIP TRAYS

Stay-put balls

Screw flowerpot trays to shelves so balls can't roll off. Cheap plastic trays come in sizes to suit all kinds of balls.

FOAM WEATHER STRIPPING

Instant drawer dividers

Stick strips of adhesive-backed foam weather stripping to the inside of the drawer. Then cut 1/4-in. plywood strips and wedge them into place.

Overhead ladder

A rarely used ladder doesn't have to take up valuable storage space on the wall. Build simple racks by screwing 2x4s together, then screw the racks to the ceiling joists. Be sure to position the racks where they won't interfere with the garage door. Secure the ladder with an elastic cord so it can't fall off.

Joist space storage

Mount a section of wire shelving to the undersides of joists and you've got a row of neat storage nooks. Unlike solid shelving, wire lets you see what's up there.

Preserve lawn supplies

Lawn products like seed and fertilizer soak up moisture in damp garages. To keep them fresh, store them in giant zip-top bags (available at discount stores).

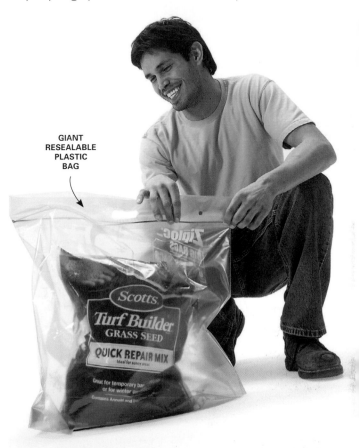

GIANT
RESEALABLE
PLASTIC
BAG

Hang a bike on the wall

Need to hang a bike but can't reach the ceiling? Bike hooks meant for ceilings work on walls, too. Just drive the hook in at 45-degree angle.

Cabinet slots

A metal file organizer is perfect for storing flat kitchen gear like cutting boards or cookie sheets. To keep it in place, set it on a pad of rubbery shelf liner.

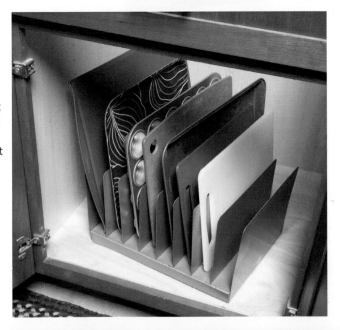

Guard against carbon monoxide

It's deadly and it's in your house—but staying safe is easy

Carbon monoxide, or CO, is a colorless, odorless gas that first makes you feel sick, then puts you to sleep and then kills you. It's a normal byproduct of combustion, so it's produced by anything that burns fuel. Unless your home runs entirely on electricity, it's in your house. Here's how to protect your family.

Sources of carbon monoxide

CO is produced by anything that runs on fuel: gas water heaters, oil furnaces, wood stoves, gasoline engines, kerosene heaters... if it burns, it emits CO.

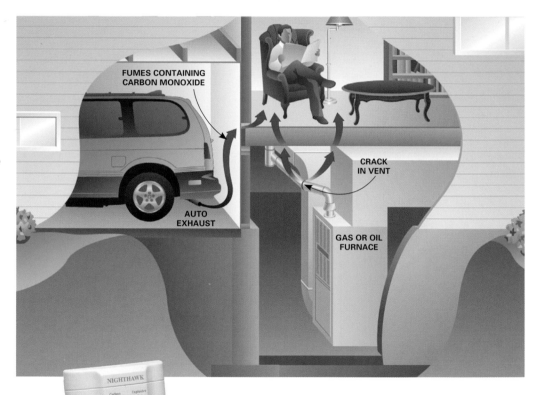

FUMES CONTAINING CARBON MONOXIDE

AUTO EXHAUST

CRACK IN VENT

GAS OR OIL FURNACE

CO detectors are mandatory

Most things that burn fuel vent exhaust gases outside. But exhaust systems can fail, so CO detectors are the best way to stay safe. Install one on each level of your home.

Locate them in hallways near bedrooms but at least 15 ft. away from fuel-burning appliances. CO is roughly the same weight as air, so it neither rises to the ceiling nor sinks to the floor.

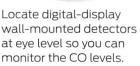

Install a combination combustible gas/CO detector in areas heated by natural gas space heaters.

Locate digital-display wall-mounted detectors at eye level so you can monitor the CO levels.

Install wall-mounted detectors anywhere on the wall, but at least 15 in. below the ceiling.

Replace detectors regularly

CO detectors only have a five- to seven-year life. Listing a build date or an expiration date on the label is a fairly new practice. If there's no date on yours and you can't remember when you bought it, you're probably due for a new one. Some models have a digital readout and a "peak level" memory retention feature. That's helpful to emergency personnel if they suspect CO poisoning. If you have small children, consider buying a talking CO detector. A voice warning is more effective than a horn at waking children.

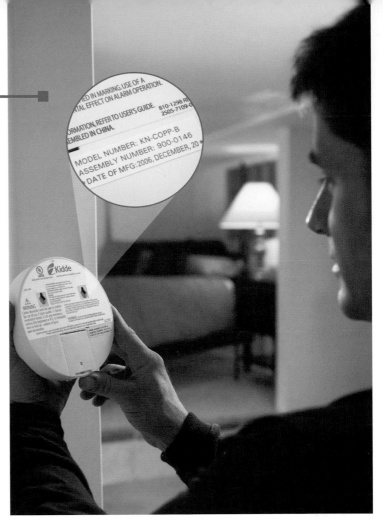

The signs of CO poisoning

The early symptoms of carbon monoxide poisoning resemble those of the flu. If the CO detector alarm sounds and anyone is experiencing headaches, dizziness, fatigue or vomiting, get everyone out of the house and call 911. Never ignore the alarm: Don't assume all is well if no one feels ill. Open your doors and windows to thoroughly ventilate the house. Turn off all potential sources of CO. Have a pro inspect your fuel-burning appliances and chimneys to make sure they're operating correctly and that there's nothing blocking the vents that let fumes out of the house.

Power outages lead to CO deaths

In the aftermath of natural disasters, more people die from CO poisoning than from Mother Nature's fury. When the power grid goes down, people fire up grills, generators and camp stoves—sometimes in garages or indoors. Bad idea. Use outdoor equipment outdoors only and keep generators at least 10 ft. away from your house.

Radon kills

But don't panic—just do a simple test

Radon is a colorless, odorless gas, naturally occurring in almost all soils. Long-term exposure can cause lung cancer. Radon is also unpredictable. One house may have sky-high levels, while the house next door is nearly radon-free. Levels are usually highest in basements, but homes without basements aren't immune. Even in low-radon regions, a few homes have dangerous levels. So testing is the only way to know if your home is safe.

■ Cover soil in crawl spaces with 6-mil plastic sheeting. Run the sheeting up foundation walls, then fasten and seal it at the top.

■ Caulk around pipes or wiring that penetrates walls or floors.

■ Install an airtight cover on the sump pump basin.

How it gets in—and how to block it

Most radon enters homes through gaps and cracks. So sealing entry points is the best first step. Then test again. In most cases, sealing won't yield major results. But it may lower radon levels that are slightly elevated and will make a fan-powered mitigation system more effective.

■ Caulk cracks in concrete floors and basement walls. You can also seal concrete floors with coatings, but researchers disagree about the effectiveness of this.

3 ways to test

Test in the lowest area of your home that's occupied at least 8 to 10 hours per week. If, for example, your basement is used only for storage, test on the main floor. If the results are 4 pCi/L (picoCuries per liter) or higher, take steps to lower radon levels.

■ **SHORT-TERM TESTS** (around $20) are less accurate than longer tests and are used mostly for quick results before a home sale. Most consist of a charcoal canister that you expose for a few days then send to a lab.

■ **LONG-TERM TESTS** (around $25) are conducted like short tests. But the longer time period (90 days or more) provides results that aren't skewed by daily weather fluctuations.

■ **CONTINUOUS TESTING MONITORS** constantly measure radon levels and display a running average. Monitors cost around $130 online.

Voice of experience

Always try simple solutions first. Once, I brought radon levels way down just by clearing some blocked vents in a crawl space.

Matt Haun,
The Family Handyman
Field Editor

The ultimate solution

A radon mitigation system consists of a special fan and plastic pipes. The fan draws radon and other gases from under concrete floors and exhausts them outside. The pipes and fan can be mounted inside your home or out. These systems typically cost $1,000 to $2,000, depending on the difficulty of installation. Your state radon office can provide a list of qualified contractors.

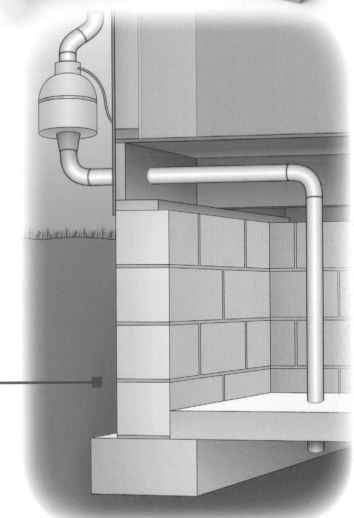

Test for lead paint

If you know it's there, you can live with it safely

About half of homes in the U.S. have lead paint, which is a serious health risk, particularly if you're pregnant or have small children. But you can safely live with lead paint. Knowing if you have it is the first step.

Homes built before 1940:
90 percent contain lead paint.

Homes built between 1940 and 1959:
80 percent contain lead paint.

Homes built between 1960 and 1978:
62 percent contain lead paint.

How to test for lead paint

Most lead-paint poisoning occurs by exposure to lead dust. Testing the dust will determine if you have a lead hazard. The test kits are available at home centers and hardware stores and include step-by-step instructions for collecting the samples, bags for the samples, plastic gloves and an envelope to send the samples to an EPA-certified lab for analysis. Results, mailed back in about two weeks, will tell if the samples contained a potentially harmful level of lead dust. If you have a dust hazard, contact your local health department for remediation guidelines or contact the Environmental Protection Agency at epa.gov/lead.

Take a sample and send it in

Wipe the test area in a backward "S" pattern with a moist cloth, picking up dust to use as a sample.

Living with lead

Lead paint can only hurt you if it gets into you. Usually that happens when you breathe the dust or get dust on your hands before eating. So the key to living with lead paint is to prevent it from flaking, wearing down or otherwise breaking down into dust or flakes. Lead paint that's in good condition or covered with coats of non-lead paint generally isn't a threat.

However, before remodeling or otherwise disturbing painted surfaces, it's best to have a professional lead inspection and risk assessment done. This will tell if your home has lead-based paint, where it's located and if it's hazardous. Find certified inspection firms through your state or local health department.

Stop mold and mildew

It's ugly and sometimes unhealthy—but you can beat it

The air around us is filled with mold spores looking for a nice place to start a family. And when they find a place, they take over fast, causing ugly growth, stains, odors and possibly even health problems. So here's how to prevent your home from becoming their home.

First, understand this: Mold needs moisture

Fighting mold is much easier if you know that mold can't live without a damp environment. Controlling the moisture source is usually the best way to control mold.

Three biggest causes of mold

 Water leaking into the house from the roof, walls or ground.

 Water leaking from plumbing or appliances.

 Condensation produced when warm, moist air contacts a cool surface.

Voice of experience

Mold can be a warning sign

When I tore into this wall during a remodeling job, the mold told me that there was trouble outside. Sure enough, I found that there was no flashing above the window, so water was leaking into the wall. That repair cost the homeowner a few bucks, but she was lucky. If not for the telltale mold, that leak would have eventually cost her thousands in damage.

Mark Petersen, contractor and
The Family Handyman **editor**

Look for leaks

If you see mold near water pipes, waste lines, icemaker lines or plumbing fixtures, chances are the mold is feeding off a nearby leak. Let the water run while you check the pipes and surrounding area for damp spots. If you see mold on or near ceilings, suspect roof leaks. Remember that water can travel in any direction—down, sideways or even up when it wicks into absorbent material like drywall—so the actual leak may be some distance from the mold.

MOLD   DECK FLASHING LEAK

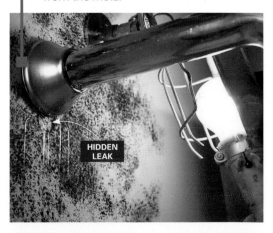

HIDDEN LEAK

Prevent bathroom mold

With three moisture-producing fixtures—sink, tub and toilet—packed into a small space, a bathroom is the perfect home for mold and mildew. Here's how to reduce the dampness that feeds fungi:

Squeegee after showering

Squeegee water off the shower walls after every bath or shower. That eliminates at least three-fourths of the moisture that supports mold and mildew growth.

Seal the grout

Grout absorbs water and supports mold growth for days after a shower. But you can lock out water. First, clean tile and grout thoroughly, then spray on an antimicrobial treatment (such as Concrobium Mold Control). Finally, seal the grout with two coats of grout sealant to keep water from penetrating the grout and wall.

Run the bath fan

Flip on the fan just before your bath or shower and keep it on for 15 to 30 minutes afterward. Better yet, install a timer switch so you don't have to remember to turn off the fan. For the ultimate in convenience and effectiveness, install a humidistat switch, which will turn on the fan whenever it detects high humidity. Some fans have a humidistat switch built in.

Attack closet mildew

Closets are often cool, damp and dark—fungus paradise. Here's how to deal with mold and mildew in closets or on other walls.

Remove mildew

Clean and kill mildew with a mix of three parts water and one part bleach. Scrub thoroughly, but don't worry if the stains don't completely disappear.

Prime the area

Mildew stains can bleed through paint, so coat the area with a stain-blocking primer before painting.

Anti-mildew weapons

- Add mildewcide to paint or use paint that already contains mildewcide (check the label).
- Run a dehumidifier in damp rooms.
- Cut closet humidity. Chemical dehumidifiers are nontoxic products that absorb moisture from the air.
- Leave closet doors open or replace solid doors with louvered doors to increase airflow.

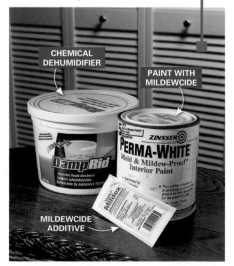

CHEMICAL DEHUMIDIFIER

PAINT WITH MILDEWCIDE

MILDEWCIDE ADDITIVE

Is it mold or dirt?

Most mold is unmistakable, but sometimes it just makes a surface look dirty. For a quick test, dip a swab in diluted bleach (1 part bleach, 16 parts water) and dab it on the wall. If the spot quickly lightens (or keeps coming back after cleaning), assume it's mold.

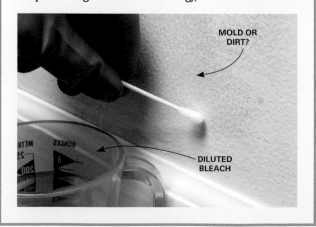

MOLD OR DIRT?

DILUTED BLEACH

Prevent home fires

Avoid a few common mistakes to drastically reduce your risk

Most fires are caused by ordinary things like stove burners, candles and space heaters. Combine these things with a moment of carelessness and you've got a deadly disaster. But prevention is just as easy.

PAPER TOWELS TOO CLOSE TO STOVE

FLAMMABLES OVER STOVE TOP

TOWEL TOO CLOSE TO STOVE

GREASE FIRE

The statistics:
23% of fires, 9% of deaths are caused by cooking

Cooking fires

They mostly occur on the cooktop, usually in the first 15 minutes of cooking. A common scenario is the grease in an unattended frying pan catches on fire and ignites nearby combustibles, which in turn ignite curtains, cabinets or anything else in the vicinity.

Prevention:

■ Never leave the kitchen while something is cooking on the stove.
■ Keep combustibles at least 3 ft. away from the cook-top. This includes curtains and wall hangings.
■ If a fire starts, slip a lid over the flames. Don't carry the pan outside; many grease fires become full-scale house fires when a pan is carried through the house, dripping a flaming grease trail all the way to the door.

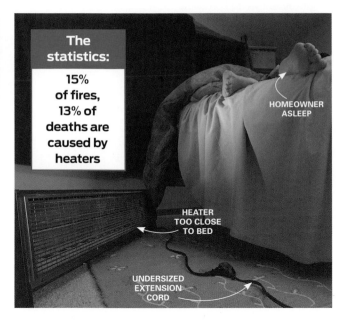

The statistics:

15%
of fires,
13% of
deaths are
caused by
heaters

HOMEOWNER
ASLEEP

HEATER
TOO CLOSE
TO BED

UNDERSIZED
EXTENSION
CORD

1,500-WATT HEATER
ON AN UNDERSIZED
EXTENSION CORD

Heating equipment

Most deaths occur when wood stoves and space heaters are in use and ignite nearby combustibles while everyone's asleep. Wood stoves also cause fires when embers in discarded ashes smolder and ignite other trash. Creosote buildup and sparks can cause a chimney fire that ignites combustibles located too close to a wood stove.

Prevention:

■ Keep space heaters at least 5 ft. away from drapes, bedding and other flammables.
■ Plug space heaters directly into outlets, not into extension cords.
■ Don't use space heaters while sleeping.
■ Empty wood-stove ashes in a metal container and store them outside away from combustibles for at least a week before dumping them into the trash.
■ Have your chimney inspected and cleaned every year.
■ Keep any and all combustible objects at least 5 ft. away from the stove or fireplace.

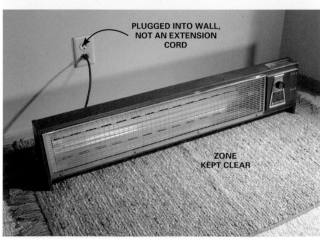

PLUGGED INTO WALL,
NOT AN EXTENSION
CORD

ZONE
KEPT CLEAR

Electrical equipment

Electricity and heat caused by overloaded extension cords, hidden electrical shorts, bad connections and oversized bulbs in fixtures can ignite nearby combustibles such as wood framing, rugs or even the insulation around the cord or wire. Here are telltale clues that can tip you off to dangerous concealed wiring hazards:

The
statistics:

9%
of fires,
10% of
deaths are
caused by
electrical
equipment

■ Electrical cords that are warm to the touch can signal overloading.
■ Charred or plastic burning odors may indicate oversized bulbs and light fixtures.
■ Warm switch or receptacle plate covers may mean a poor electrical connection.
■ Frequently tripping circuit breakers may be caused by a defective breaker or possibly a short in the cables buried in walls or ceilings.

Prevention:

■ Replace extension cords that are undersized or frayed.
■ Never run extension cords under rugs.
■ Replace undersized cords with larger-gauge ones or plug appliances directly into outlets.
■ Call an electrician to track down hidden problems causing frequently tripping circuit breakers.
■ Call an electrician to open up and troubleshoot electrical boxes that have warm covers.
■ Check all the lightbulbs in your home to make sure bulb wattages don't exceed the fixture's recommended maximum.

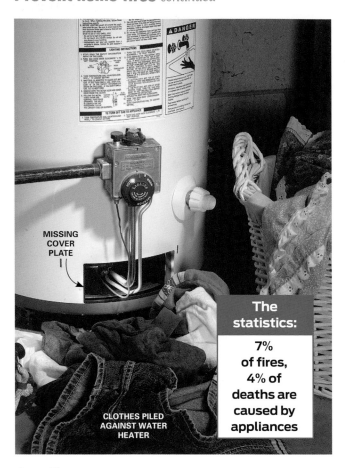

MISSING COVER PLATE

CLOTHES PILED AGAINST WATER HEATER

The statistics:

7% of fires, 4% of deaths are caused by appliances

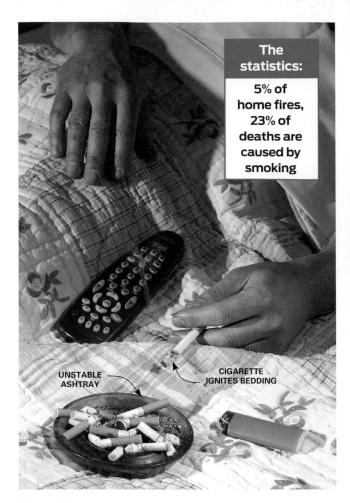

The statistics:

5% of home fires, 23% of deaths are caused by smoking

UNSTABLE ASHTRAY

CIGARETTE IGNITES BEDDING

Appliances

The biggest culprits are lint buildup in dryers and combustibles near gas water heaters. Since water heaters are often in the same room as the laundry, clothes tend to get piled up against the water heater near the flame. The problem is worse when that flimsy cover plate falls off the burner access. Dryer vents catch on fire when built-up dust and lint ignite from either the burners or the heating elements and create a fire path to built-up lint within the vent hose. Especially dangerous are dryers that are vented with flexible vinyl hoses. The vinyl then catches on fire and lights anything near it.

Smoking

Smoking kills more people than any other cause of fire because the fires usually start when everyone's asleep. If a cigarette smolders in the bedding or drops on the carpet when the smoker falls asleep, the gases from smoldering fabrics will actually lull the smoker into a deeper sleep. Live butts that fall between cushions or are tossed into trash cans can take hours to ignite, and when they finally do, everyone is in bed asleep.

Prevention:

COVER PLATE

3'

■ Make sure the water heater cover plate is in place.
■ Replace vinyl dryer vent lines with smooth-walled metal ducts.
■ Mark a "combustible-free" zone 3 ft. away from your water heater with masking tape.
■ Clean lint out of dryers.

Prevention:

■ Don't smoke in bed.
■ Use large ashtrays on tables.
■ Douse ashtrays under the faucet before throwing butts in the trash.

FLAME TOO CLOSE TO COMBUSTIBLES

TIPPY HOLDER ON UNSTABLE SURFACE

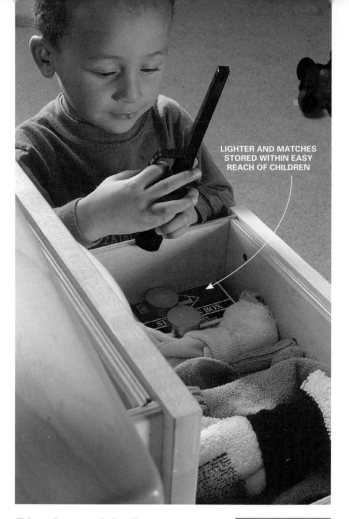

LIGHTER AND MATCHES STORED WITHIN EASY REACH OF CHILDREN

Candles

Like cooking fires, most candle fires occur when candles burn unattended near combustibles—usually in bedrooms. Using candles safely calls for attention and care. They'll often get soft and fall out of a holder and ignite nearby combustibles or even ignite an underlying wooden holder or shelf.

The statistics:
5% of fires, 3% of deaths are caused by candles

Prevention:

■ Use only tip-proof containers.

■ Burn candles only while you're awake and in the same room with them.

■ Keep candles at least 3 ft. away from combustibles.

■ Never burn candles that have combustibles (flowers, leaves and potpourri) cast into the wax.

■ Don't use candles during a blackout. Use LED flashlights and lanterns instead.

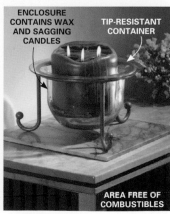

ENCLOSURE CONTAINS WAX AND SAGGING CANDLES

TIP-RESISTANT CONTAINER

AREA FREE OF COMBUSTIBLES

Playing with fire

Children often start fires while hiding in places like closets or under beds, where they're surrounded by combustibles. Their first reaction is often to hide from you or the fire after it starts. There, they become overcome by smoke and/or make it difficult for firefighters to find them. It's obvious that you shouldn't leave matches and lighters lying around, but you also have to be vigilant around burning candles.

The statistics:
5% of fires, 8% of deaths are caused by children

Prevention:

■ Store matches and lighters up high, well out of the reach of children.

Replace smoke alarms

Basic know-how saves lives

If you knew you could drastically reduce your risk of death and destruction just by installing and maintaining a few cheap gadgets, you would do it—right? Well, lots of people don't. About 60 percent of house-fire fatalities occur in homes with missing or neglected smoke alarms. To avoid becoming a statistic, you just need to know—and do—a few simple things.

Where to put them

Install at least one alarm on each level of a home, including one in each bedroom and one in each hallway leading to bedrooms. That's not just good practice; it's required by most building codes.

Smoke rises, so alarms must be close to the ceiling, but not too close. Place wall-mounted alarms 4 to 12 in. from the ceiling. Keep ceiling-mounted alarms at least 4 in. from walls.

Wrong
DETECTOR PLACED TOO LOW

Right
CEILING-MOUNTED SMOKE ALARM
4"
ALARM PLACEMENT ZONE
12"

They don't last forever

After 10 years or so, alarms become unreliable and should be replaced. To check an alarm's age, just remove it from its mounting plate (usually by turning it counterclockwise). On the back, you should find a manufacture date. If not, replace the alarm. And don't forget to change the dead batteries!

There are two types

Before you replace an alarm, you have to know how it's powered. Some alarms are powered by batteries only. Others are "hard-wired" to your home's power supply and have batteries for backup power. Hard-wired alarms are usually interconnected; if one detects smoke, they all scream. To tell what kind you have, remove it from the mounting plate. If it's connected to wires, it's hard-wired. If it's connected to three wires, it's an interconnected model. In that case, you should replace it and all of its neighbors with identical alarms.

Replace a hard-wired alarm

Even if you're a wiring rookie, consider doing this job yourself. It's is one of the easiest electrical projects there is, and you'll save the cost of hiring an electrician. The key to doing it safely is to first turn off the power at the main panel and then make sure it's off by touching wires in the junction box with a voltage detector (about $5)—it will beep or light up if power is present.

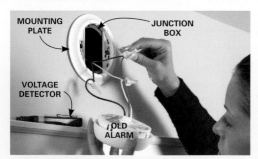

MOUNTING PLATE
JUNCTION BOX
VOLTAGE DETECTOR
OLD ALARM

HARNESS
NEW ALARM

1 Remove the old alarm
Rotate the alarm to remove it from the mounting plate. Disconnect the wires by unscrewing the connectors. Then unscrew the old mounting plate from the junction box.

2 Install the new alarm
Screw on the new mounting plate, connect the new wiring harness to wires coming out of the wall and plug the harness into the alarm. Mount the alarm on its plate and you're done.

Be ready for fire

An extinguisher can save your home

A fire extinguisher can make the difference between a minor fire and total destruction. Experts recommend that you have one on each level of your home. Just remember that household extinguishers are meant for small fires. With a larger or fast-spreading fire, forget the extinguisher and get out of the house.

Choosing is easy

Don't get bogged down in the details of the fire extinguisher classification system. Most extinguishers sold at home centers are labeled "A, B, C"—and that's exactly what you need to put out the most common types of home fires. You'll find several models that fit nicely in a drawer or under the sink and even smaller spray-can versions.

The basic technique

■ Stand a few feet from the fire, start blasting and move toward the fire. The instructions will tell you how far away to start.
■ Move the extinguisher's stream in a sweeping motion.
■ Aim at the base of the fire. Spraying the flames does no good.

They empty fast

Most extinguishers have a very short "discharge time" before they run out of fire suppressant (10 seconds is typical). That means you can't waste time or suppressant. Aim carefully before you pull the trigger.

They make a mess

Extinguishers blast the area with chemicals. So don't use one unless you have to. In the case of a small stovetop fire, for example, a pot lid will usually smother the flames—and won't leave you with cleanup chores.

They don't last forever

If you have an old extinguisher, look for an expiration date on the label. Also make sure the pressure gauge reads "full."

Clean your dryer vent

Prevent fires, save energy and get faster drying

Lint buildup in a dryer and its vent cuts the dryer's efficiency. Clothes take longer to dry and your energy bills go up. But the biggest reason to clean out lint is this: Lint buildup is one of the most common causes of home fires. Lint near the motor, gas burner or electric heating element can catch fire, ignite lint in the vent duct and then spread to the rest of your house.

How to prevent a dryer fire:

■ Empty the lint trap after every load.
■ Vacuum behind the machine regularly.
■ Keep flammables away from the dryer.
■ Clean lint from inside the dryer cabinet and vent duct once a year.
■ If your dryer has a plastic duct, replace it with metal.

1 Clean out the cabinet
Unplug the dryer, turn off the gas valve and pry off the access panel. Vacuum inside the cabinet, especially around the motor and the gas burner or electric heating element.

MOTOR

CLEAN INTERIOR
OF CABINET

ACCESS
PANEL

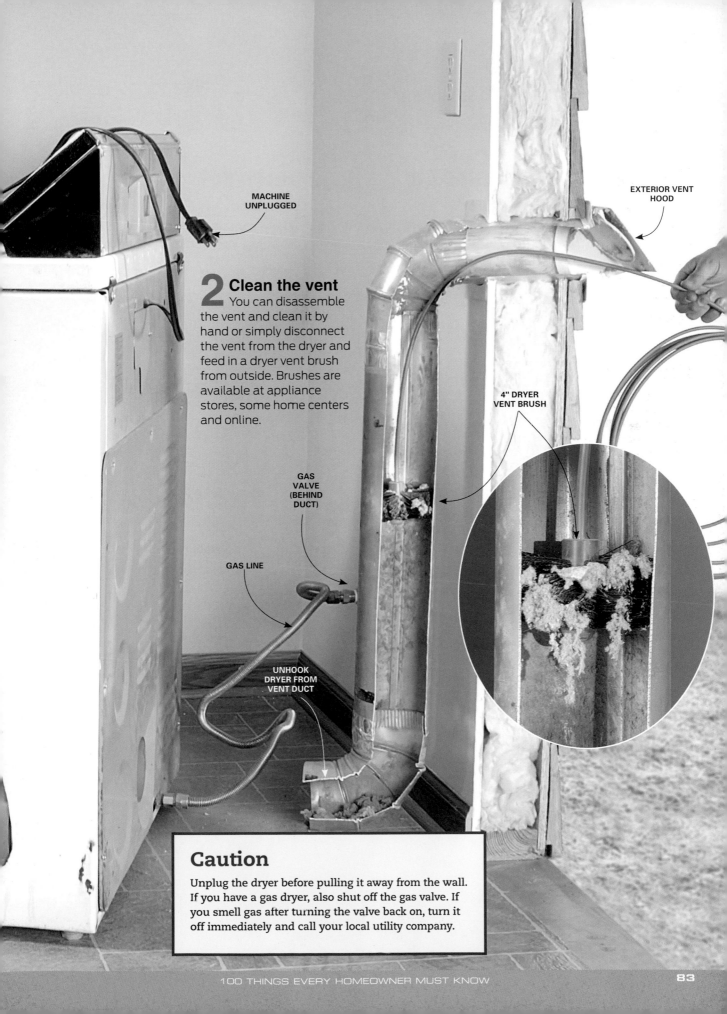

MACHINE
UNPLUGGED

EXTERIOR VENT
HOOD

2 Clean the vent

You can disassemble the vent and clean it by hand or simply disconnect the vent from the dryer and feed in a dryer vent brush from outside. Brushes are available at appliance stores, some home centers and online.

4" DRYER
VENT BRUSH

GAS
VALVE
(BEHIND
DUCT)

GAS LINE

UNHOOK
DRYER FROM
VENT DUCT

Caution

Unplug the dryer before pulling it away from the wall. If you have a gas dryer, also shut off the gas valve. If you smell gas after turning the valve back on, turn it off immediately and call your local utility company.

Keep crooks out

Small security upgrades are a huge deterrent

Most burglars aren't criminal masterminds seeking professional challenges; they just want to steal stuff with minimal time, effort and risk. Unfortunately, there are lots of easy targets in any neighborhood. But that's good news for you. If you make your home just a little harder to get into, you greatly increase the odds that crooks will bypass your house and look for an easier job.

Focus on windows and doors

All the usual security advice (install exterior lighting, ask the neighbors to watch your house, etc.) is worth following. But above all, know this: The vast majority of break-ins occur through ground-level windows and doors. So strengthening them is priority one.

Daytime is crime time

Most of us think of burglary as a nocturnal activity. That used to be true. But these days, most burglaries occur between 10 a.m. and 5 p.m. In many cases, the crooks get in through unlocked doors or windows.

What about window bars?

They're almost impossible to get past, so bars are the toughest type of window security. But before you install them, ask the local police if they're necessary. In many areas, crooks avoid breaking glass. It makes a racket and is dangerous to the thief. As one cop put it, "When we find broken glass, we usually find drops of burglar blood."

Reinforce a door

Burglars don't usually pick locks. That takes too long. Instead, they kick or pry the door open. The dead bolt usually survives that brute force, but the door or strike plate gives way. Here's how to beef up those weak spots:

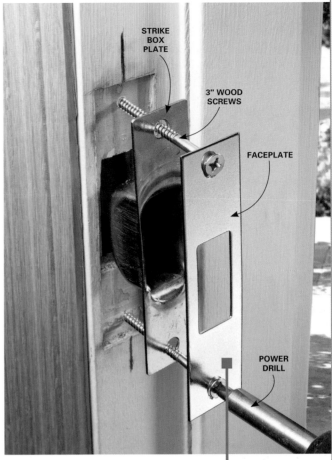

Strengthen the door

When kicked or pried, doors often split. Even steel doors are surprisingly easy to split. To prevent that, install an edge guard (available at home centers). Just remove the dead bolt, slip the guard over the door, screw it on and reinstall the dead bolt. Larger models back up both the dead bolt and the doorknob.

Strengthen the strike plate

A bigger strike plate is better than a small one, but the key factor is the strike plate's screws. It's critical that they penetrate not only the doorjamb, but also sink deep into the wall framing behind the jamb. To check, just remove one of the screws. If it's less than 3 in. long, replace the screws. For even better protection, install a larger strike plate that allows for more than two screws.

Secure windows

The latches on most double-hung windows are no match for a burglar with a pry bar. But cheap pin locks are much tougher. To install one, all you have to do is drill a hole. If you want to lock the window in a partially open position, drill a second hole. Most crank-open "casement" windows are a little harder to pry open, but it's a good idea to add locks to them, too. You'll find special casement locks and latches online.

Protect patio doors

There are two easy ways for burglars to get past a sliding patio door. Sometimes, they pry open the door; many patio door latches are wimpy. In other cases, they pry the door upward, lifting it off its track, and simply remove the door. Here are defenses against both attacks:

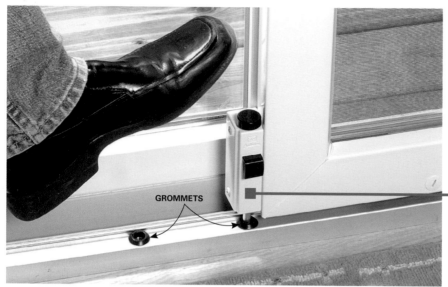

GROMMETS

Add a lock or bar

At home centers and online, you'll find various locks for patio doors. Some, like this one, allow you to lock the door partially open for ventilation. There are also bars available that jam against the door and prevent opening from outside. Some people simply lay a board or broom handle in the lower track to prevent opening. That's OK, but a crook can slip a coat hanger through the door's weather stripping and push the broom handle out of place.

Keep the door down

To prevent the door from being lifted off the lower track, just drive two 3-in.-long screws through the top track. Leave them protruding so the door can slide, but can't be raised. This trick also works on many types of sliding windows.

Do alarm systems work?

Yes, all the experts agree that most crooks shy away from homes with security systems. But you have to advertise; if thieves don't know you have a system, they won't be deterred. Post the yard sign and windows stickers where they can't be overlooked.

If they do get in...

■ Immediately notify credit bureaus, your bank and credit card companies.
■ Inspect your checkbook. If any checks are missing, close the account.
■ Make your home more secure. Crooks often come back about six weeks later to steal the new stuff you bought with the insurance payout.

Don't live with a broken dead bolt

A dead bolt is the key component of door security. The doorknob latch is no substitute. So if your dead bolt no longer works, replace it now. It's a surprisingly easy job. Just remove two screws in the thumb latch, then remove two screws to remove the bolt. Install the new dead bolt the same way. Try to find a new dead bolt with a bolt plate of the same size. Otherwise, you'll have to either enlarge the recess in the door or live with an ugly gap around the plate.

BOLT

BOLT PLATE

THUMB LATCH

Install a peephole

Never open the door unless you know who's on the other side. Whether that door is wood, steel, fiberglass or composite, installing a peephole is easy.

LENS

SLEEVE

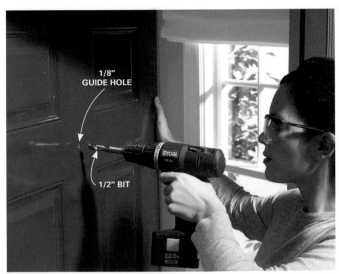

1/8" GUIDE HOLE

1/2" BIT

SLEEVE

1 Drill the hole
Drill a small (1/8-in.) guide hole through the door. Then drill the full-size hole (typically 1/2 in.). Stop about halfway through and then drill from the other side.

2 Install the peephole
Screw the lens and sleeve together. There are notches in the sleeve, so you can tighten it with a stiff putty knife.

Burglar-proof your garage

It's a security weak spot—and a favorite target for crooks

When it comes to security, too many homeowners overlook their garages. But crooks don't. To them, it's often an easy score—or worse, the perfect path into your home, where they can work on your entry door, unseen by neighbors. In about 20 percent of house burglaries, crooks enter through the garage. That's a shame, because boosting garage security is pretty simple.

Don't leave your remote in the car

A thief who breaks into your car can grab the remote for easy access to your garage. This isn't just a problem when your car is parked in the driveway; the registration card in your glove box gives a crook your address. So get rid of the remote on your visor and buy a keychain model. You can easily take it with you every time you leave the car. Home centers stock only a small selection of remotes, but you'll find many more online.

Don't forget to close the door

Lots of garages get looted simply because someone forgot to close the door. A garage door monitor is a good reminder. Just stick the sensor to the door and set the monitor in a conspicuous spot like your nightstand. The brand of your door or opener doesn't matter; any monitor will work. An automatic door closer provides even more security, since it closes the door whether you're home or not. Installation requires some simple low-voltage wiring and takes less than an hour. To find a monitor or an automatic garage door closer, search online.

Garage door monitor

The sensor sends a signal to the monitor, telling you whether the door is open or closed. Both units are battery-operated—no wiring is required.

Automatic door closer

This device allows the door to stay open for a set amount of time, then closes it. You can override it on those summer days when you're working in the garage.

Cover windows to hide the loot

Don't let crooks window shop for the valuable tools or toys in your garage. Install curtains or blinds. Or, if you don't want to block light, apply translucent window film; it's quick, easy and inexpensive.

PLASTIC
WINDOW
FILM

Lock the overhead door

Some people "lock" the door when they go on vacation by unplugging the opener. That's a good idea, but physically locking the door is even better. An unplugged opener won't stop a burglar who has entered through the house from opening the garage door from inside, backing in a van and using the garage as a loading dock for his plunder. Make a burglar's job more difficult and time-consuming by locking the door itself. If your door doesn't have a lockable latch, drill a hole in the track just above one of the rollers and slip in a padlock.

How to choose a dead bolt

Just look for the "ANSI Grade" on the label. Don't even consider a Grade 3, despite the tempting price tag. A Grade 2 model is adequate, but spend an extra 10 bucks and get a Grade 1. Aside from higher security, you'll get a better-built lock that will give you years of trouble-free service.

Hide your valuables

Secret spaces that foil thieves

Your house is full of hideaways that most people wouldn't think about. And most crooks wouldn't either. Just make sure that your family knows your secrets, so they don't donate or toss out your treasure container.

Vacuum vault

The bag compartment inside an old vacuum provides a handy spot for valuables. Lots of other household items work too: an old printer or computer tower or kids' toys.

Paint-can safe

No crook will bother to open paint cans looking for loot. Before you use a can, leave it open for a few days so the leftover paint can thoroughly dry.

Buried treasure

Roll up some cash, stick it in a medicine bottle or any other watertight container and bury it in a potted plant. If you want to avoid digging for your treasure, cover it with a pinecone or stone.

Secret slot between cabinets

Between almost every pair of upper cabinets, there's a 1/2-in. gap. Hang a cash-filled envelope in that slot, using binder clips that are too large to fall in. This only works if you have open space above cabinets, of course.

False-bottom drawer

Pick a deep drawer so the depth change won't be obvious. Cut 1/4-in. plywood 1/16 in. smaller than the opening and rest it on a couple wood strips that are hot-glued to the drawer sides. Then hot-glue some item you'd expect to find in that drawer to the false bottom to provide a handle to lift the false bottom and reveal the booty.

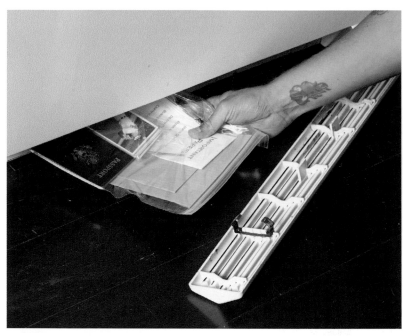

Counterfeit containers

Food containers offer endless possibilities. For example, spray the inside of a mayonnaise jar with cream-colored spray paint so it looks full.

Appliance hideaway

Fridges and dishwashers have cover plates or grilles that hide a large open space. But don't place large items under a fridge. Blocking the airflow will make the fridge work harder and possibly even damage it.

LB FITTING

CONDUIT

Outdoor key safe

Plastic LB fittings and conduit are used to enclose wires entering a building. So a phony fitting will look perfectly normal outside any house. Just stick the LB fitting on a piece of conduit, then plant it in the ground and screw it to the house. You'll find everything you need in the electrical aisle at any home center.

Beware of mice

Mice love to chew on any type of paper, including cash or important documents. So don't hide valuable papers where mice might get them.

Be ready for blackouts

What you need when things go dark

Due to an aging power grid, blackouts are more common than they used to be. And things won't get better anytime soon. So here are some tips to help you survive an electrical outage.

Fill the tub

When the power grid goes down, your city water supply may soon follow. So fill up buckets and bottles. Fill the bathtub, too. But most drains are not all that tight, and in a few hours all that precious water may be gone. To prevent that, seal the drain with duct tape before you fill the tub.

Tompkin Lee, *The Family Handyman* Field Editor

Get cash

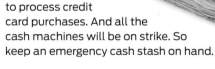

In a blackout, cash is king. Some stores may stay open, but they probably won't be able to process credit card purchases. And all the cash machines will be on strike. So keep an emergency cash stash on hand.

Turn your car into a generator

A power inverter, which turns DC current from your car into AC current for electric gadgets, is the next best thing to a generator when it comes to surviving a blackout. Small units can recharge your computer or phone. Larger ones can power a fridge or power tools.

Conserve batteries

LED flashlights and lanterns have a huge advantage over incandescent models: They allow batteries to last much longer (typically about six to 10 times as long).

Stay tuned

If phone and Internet systems go down along with the power grid, a battery-powered radio may be your only source of weather and emergency information. You could listen in your car, but a portable radio lets you listen anywhere. Some models have a solar panel or a hand crank for recharging, so you don't even need batteries.

Fill the grill tank

During a three-day outage, I fed dozens of friends and neighbors by grilling everything in my fridge and freezer. Without power to keep food cold, it all would have gone bad anyway.

Arthur Barfield, *The Family Handyman* **Field Editor**

Ice saves food

A couple of days without power can cost you a few hundred bucks as food spoils in fridges and freezers. Fill locking freezer bags with water and keep them in the freezer. During a blackout, they'll help the freezer stay cold longer. Or you can transfer them to the fridge or a cooler. When they thaw, you've got drinking water.

A CO detector is essential

Blackouts often lead to carbon monoxide deaths. Here's why: To get heat during outages, people crank up fireplaces, gas stoves and all types of heaters—and anything that burns produces carbon monoxide. So I get out a battery-powered CO detector whenever I use an emergency heat source.

Kevin Yochum, *The Family Handyman* **Field Editor**

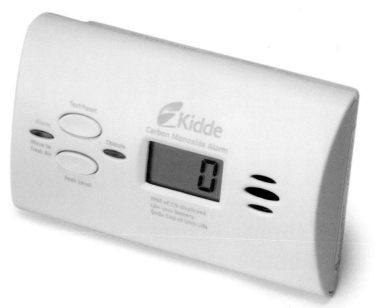

Don't wreck your TV

When the power grid sputters back to life, it will probably create power surges, which can destroy sensitive electronics in TVs, computers and appliances. So unplug anything that may contain electronic components. Leave one light switched on to let you know when the power is restored. And if you have a generator, check the manual. Most inexpensive models churn out "dirty" power that can harm electronics.

Gas up

Your car is a critical part of your survival kit. It's your emergency transport, your charging system for cell phones and maybe even the only heated space you'll have. So keep your tank full before storms. If you have gas cans, fill them, too. When the power is out, gas stations can't pump gas from their tanks into yours.

After the power goes out

■ Don't use candles. Flashlights produce more light and won't burn your house down.

■ Bring solar landscape lights inside. Don't forget to put them out for recharging during the day.

■ Keep the fridge closed. The less you open fridge and freezer doors, the longer your food will stay cold.

■ Tap your water heater. It's your built-in emergency water supply. Let the water cool before you open the drain valve at the bottom of the tank.

■ Don't take chances. Power outages mean packed emergency rooms and delayed ambulance service; it's the worst time to get injured.

Flush with a bucket

Even if a power outage stops your well pump or the city water supply, you can still flush the toilet. Dump a couple gallons into the bowl or fill the toilet tank. This works just as well as the usual flush, but won't refill the bowl.

Can you count on your sump pump?

Test it now—before your basement floods

A sump pump is one of the most important disaster-prevention devices in a house. It's also one of the most ignored; most homeowners don't discover problems until their basements flood.

The bucket test

Remove the basin cover and dump in a few buckets of water. If the pump doesn't run or doesn't eject the water, you've got trouble.

Troubleshooting

IF THE PUMP DOESN'T RUN...
■ Make sure the pump is plugged in (sounds dumb, but this a common oversight).
■ Plug a radio into the pump's outlet and make sure it's live.
■ If the outlet is dead, check the breaker in the main panel. If the outlet is a GFCI, push the "reset" button.
■ If the pump is getting power but won't run, you need a new pump.

IF THE PUMP RUNS
but the water level doesn't drop...
■ Check the discharge pipe outside the house. Frozen or plugged pipes block the water flow.
■ If the pipe is clear, then replace the pump.

Dead pump alarms

For less than $20, you can get a simple battery-powered alarm that howls if water reaches the top of the basin. But that only helps if you're at home, so there are also systems that make a phone call or send a text message if the pump fails.

Keep a replacement on hand

Three days of heavy rain caused a pump-failure epidemic in our region. Every home center and hardware store was sold out. So when our sump pump died, all we could do is watch while our basement filled up. Since that nightmare, I've always kept a replacement pump on the basement shelf.

Steve Weller, *The Family Handyman* Field Editor

The pump is part of a system

Perforated pipes along basement walls carry water to a basin. Rising water in the basin lifts a float, which switches on the pump to force water outside. A check valve in the discharge pipe prevents water from flowing back into the basin.

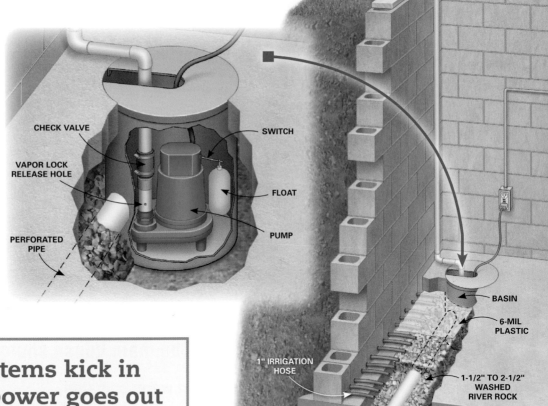

CHECK VALVE

VAPOR LOCK RELEASE HOLE

PERFORATED PIPE

SWITCH

FLOAT

PUMP

BASIN

6-MIL PLASTIC

1" IRRIGATION HOSE

1-1/2" TO 2-1/2" WASHED RIVER ROCK

4" PERFORATED PIPE

Backup systems kick in when the power goes out

Wet weather and power failures often go together, so some homes have backup systems. This is an expensive option ($200 and up), but cheap compared to a flooded basement. A backup system will also take over if the pump breaks down.

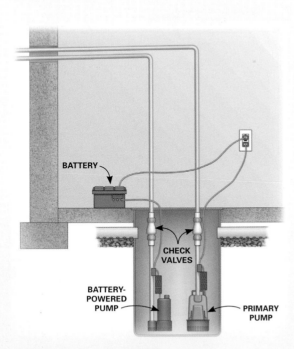

BATTERY

CHECK VALVES

BATTERY-POWERED PUMP

PRIMARY PUMP

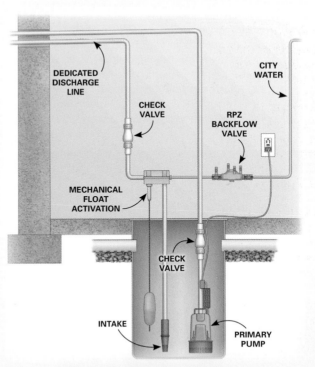

DEDICATED DISCHARGE LINE

CHECK VALVE

CITY WATER

RPZ BACKFLOW VALVE

MECHANICAL FLOAT ACTIVATION

CHECK VALVE

INTAKE

PRIMARY PUMP

Battery backup

A battery—similar to a car battery—powers a second pump in the basin. A "maintainer" plugged into an outlet keeps the battery at full charge. Typically, the battery will need replacement every five years.

Water-powered backup

The backup pump siphons water out of the basin using water pressure from the home's water supply. This will drive up your water bill, but it's better than a basement flood.

Find your shutoff valves

They're the difference between a small puddle and a huge flood

Your home's water supply system is dangerous. In just minutes, a cracked pipe, burst hose or leaking ice-maker line can do thousands of dollars in damage. But if you know the basics about shutoff valves, you can stop the flow instantly and limit the harm.

Find them, test them

Shutoff valves are located near any device that uses water. Most of them are easy to find; they're typically under sinks and toilets, behind the washing machine and above the water heater. Shutoffs for tubs or showers are often hidden behind a wood or plastic "access panel," though some tubs and showers don't have shutoffs. Your main valve—which shuts off water to your entire house—may be indoors or out. Usually, there are actually two valves flanking the water meter and you can turn off either one.

Shutoff valves go unused for years, and mineral deposits can make them impossible to close. So it's a good idea to make sure yours work. If you have standard valves, just turn the handle clockwise. If you have ball-type valves, crank the lever one-quarter turn. Ball valves rarely fail, but it's good to check them anyway.

The main house shutoff

In warm climates...
The main shutoff is typically outside, attached to a wall or underground.

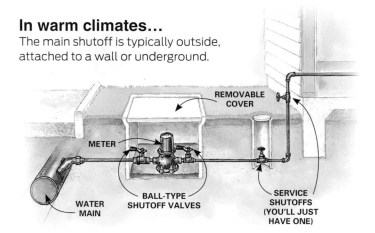

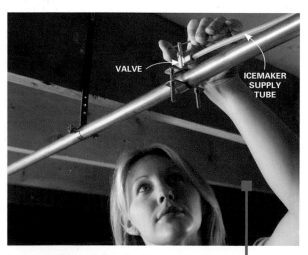

Icemaker shutoffs can be anywhere
Valves for icemakers may be under the kitchen sink, in a utility closet or in a basement or crawl space.

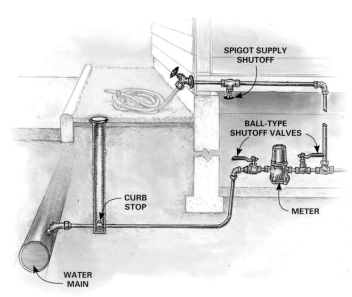

In colder climates...
The main shutoff is typically in the basement. There is also a "curb stop" shutoff that requires a special tool to operate.

Voice of experience

The cost of not knowing

A few weeks after moving into my first home, a washing machine hose burst, releasing a geyser in my laundry room. I knew enough to try the valve behind the washer, but it was ancient. And stuck. What I didn't know about was the main valve, which could have shut off the water to the whole house. So I just stood there like a dummy, waiting for a plumber to show up while water flowed from the laundry room into adjoining rooms. Insurance covered most of the damage, but I paid the deductible, plus higher insurance premiums for years afterward.

Andy Carson, *The Family Handyman* **Field Editor**

Solution for stubborn valves

When a valve won't budge, sometimes it helps to loosen the packing nut just a little. Turn it counterclockwise while holding the handle steady with your hand or pliers. If you ever notice a leak around a valve stem, tighten the packing nut.

STEM

PACKING NUT

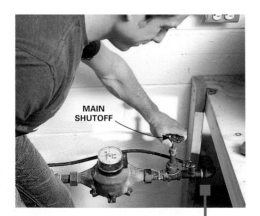

MAIN SHUTOFF

The smartest move you can make before a vacation

Every insurance adjuster has a hundred stories like this one: The homeowners left town Friday and returned Sunday evening to find thousands of dollars in water damage. The moral of these stories is simple: Before going on vacation, turn off the main valve. In less than a minute, you can eliminate the most common cause of home damage.

Insist on ball valves

If you have any plumbing work done that requires replacing valves, ask for ball valves. That may add ten bucks to the cost of the project, but it's a bargain. Unlike other valves, which rely on screw mechanisms and rubber seals, ball valves have a simple ball inside, which rotates to open or close. That simplicity means reliability; ball valves almost always work when you need them.

BALL

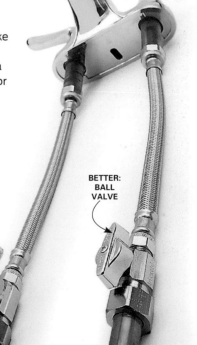

GOOD: STANDARD VALVE

BETTER: BALL VALVE

Work safely

Routine chores can lead to ER visits

When it comes to homeowner hazards, it's the minor jobs that lead the list of major injuries. A homeowner cleaning gutters or even changing a ceiling lightbulb is more likely to get hurt than the electrician working with high-voltage cables. So here are some ways to stay safe while caring for your home.

Protect your brain

Fumes from solvents, adhesives and paints can make you nauseated or dizzy. But it gets worse: Those fumes can also damage your brain or lungs. Occasionally, they even kill users. Good ventilation— open doors and windows—is your first defense. Also wear a respirator with replaceable carbon filters.

Protect your eyes

Of all homeowner hazards, eye injuries are the easiest to prevent. Just wear safety glasses. They're so cheap that you can keep pairs handy anywhere you might need them: the garage, basement and shed. And don't just wear them when using power tools. Eyes get injured in surprising circumstances—while trimming bushes, spray painting, blowing leaves....

NOISE REDUCTION OF 25dB OR MORE

NOISE REDUCTION OF 30dB

NOISE REDUCTION OF 25dB OR LESS

Protect your ears

Sure, the risk of hearing damage is highest for those who use loud equipment every day. But if you use a shop vacuum, leaf blower or circular saw without hearing protection, you're doing permanent damage every time. And that's just dumb because protecting your ears is so easy. The goal is to reduce noise levels to 90dB. All forms of hearing protection—earmuffs, disposable foam earplugs, reusable plugs—are adequate for most noise. With super-loud equipment like chain saws, it's smart to use both plugs *and* earmuffs.

Protect your lungs

Dust isn't just a sneeze-inducing nuisance—heavy repeated doses can lead to severe allergic reactions and even harm your lungs. You can buy a dust mask for as little as 50 cents, but don't. Instead, spend a few bucks on one with an "N95" certification. You'll get a mask that's more comfortable and truly effective at keeping dust out of your lungs.

LOOK FOR N95 CERTIFICATION

Safe ladder setup

Ladder safety starts with careful setup. Sloppy setup leads to falls, even if you climb cautiously.

Set the angle

Setting a ladder at the correct angle is the key to stability. Too steep and it can slide sideways or tip backward. If not steep enough, the feet may slip. To get it right, put your toes against the ladder's feet. Stand straight up and extend your arms. Your palms should just reach the ladder's rung.

EXTEND ARMS

PALMS TOUCH RUNG

LADDER AT CORRECT ANGLE

TOUCH TOES TO LADDER BASE

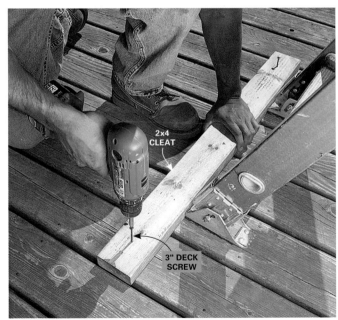

2x4 CLEAT

3" DECK SCREW

MOVE LADDER BACK

SHOES FLIPPED UP

SPUR

DIG UNDER HIGH SIDE

Anchor the feet

Make sure the ladder can't slip out from under you. Sweep off hard surfaces and make sure the ladder's shoe pads are clean. On a deck, screw down a cleat to lock the ladder in place. On concrete, you can often secure the ladder against something heavy like a lawn tractor. On soft ground, flip up the shoes so the spurs can bite into the soil.

Stand it straight up

A ladder that's leaning left or right on uneven ground can slip sideways and take you for a life-threatening ride. Don't straighten a leaning ladder by setting one foot on bricks or blocks. Instead, dig a shallow hole to level the feet. Then, before you climb, jump hard on the lowest rung a couple times to make sure the ladder doesn't tilt.

Voice of experience

Heat makes you dumb

Building a deck on a 100-degree afternoon, I stood on an overhanging joist as I cut it off. When the joist went down, I went down. How could I do anything so incredibly stupid? The ER doctor explained that heat doesn't just make you miserable—it also bakes your brain. Along with dehydration, it impairs your judgment, slows your reaction time and greatly increases your odds of injury. Take frequent water breaks, or better yet, wait for cooler weather.

Peter Karpf,
The Family Handyman
Field Editor

Don't get zapped

House chores—especially outdoors—often bring water and electricity together. The best way to make those situations safer is to use a GFCI (ground-fault circuit interrupter). Newer homes have GFCI protection in bathroom, kitchen, garage and exterior outlets, but those GFCIs may no longer offer protection after 10 years or so. To be safe, plug your leaf blower into a GFCI extension cord before you venture into the wet grass.

Don't fall off the roof

If you get on your roof every fall to clean the gutters, consider buying a personal fall arrest system (aka "roof harness"). For around $100, you can buy a kit, install permanent or temporary anchors in key spots and tether your harness to them for the ultimate in roof safety.

ROOF HARNESS

ANCHOR

Don't blow up the house

The flammable fumes that evaporate from some adhesives, solvents or paints will ignite if they reach a flame. Check the label. If you see warnings about flammable vapors, don't use the product near gas water heaters or other appliances with pilot lights. Candles, small engines—anything that might flame or spark—can also trigger an explosion.

Voice of experience

Call 811 before you dig

That's all it takes to get your utility lines marked. And it's absolutely free. Think about it: Hitting a power or gas line can kill you (or leave you with a huge bill from the utility company). Slicing through a cable TV line can also be life-threatening, as I learned one Super Bowl Sunday.

Jeff Gorton,
The Family Handyman
Associate Editor

Stay safe in a storm

Natural disasters bring unexpected dangers

You already know the obvious dangers of a natural disaster: collapsing buildings, downed power lines, flying debris.... But in most disasters, more people are injured by things that don't seem all that dangerous—things most people wouldn't even think of.

Lightning: Don't get hit indoors

Your home is probably the safest place to be in an electrical storm. But lightning can still get to you through the conductive paths in your house: your wiring, your plumbing and water. Talking on a corded phone, taking a shower or bath, working on your desktop computer and handling power tools during an electrical storm aren't much safer than standing outside. Stay away from all water and appliances until the storm passes.

Don't use candles for emergency lighting

When the power goes out, lots of people light lots of candles. And lots of people burn down their homes. There's no good reason for this. Today's LED flashlights and lanterns burn brighter and last longer than candles, without the risk of fire.

Stay out of gushing floodwater

Six inches of floodwater doesn't look dangerous. But if it's moving fast enough, it's enough to sweep you off your feet and carry you into the hereafter. Rushing water also erodes roads and walkways, creating drop-offs that you can't see under the torrent. The smartest move is to stay out of flowing water.

Don't get shocked in a flooded basement

The water in a flooded basement probably isn't electrified by your home's electrical lines. But it could be. So instead of finding out the hard way, just consider it an energized pool of instant death until you call your utility company to disconnect the power. And after the water is gone, remember that anything electrical in the basement may still be wet, damaged and dangerous. Leave the basement power off until your utility company or an electrician gives you the OK.

Keep your wheels on dry land

Driving through a few inches of water seems safe enough, but more than half of flood-related drownings involve a vehicle. In just 6 in. of water, some cars partially float and become hard to control. Even a monster SUV will become a rudderless barge in 2 ft. of rushing water. When you find a flooded road, better to turn around than risk drowning.

Stay out of toxic waters

Furniture isn't the only stuff floating in your basement. Chances are, the water contains chemicals stored downstairs and a dose of sewage that backed up through basement drains. That's not just disgusting, but also a toxic soup that can make you sick. Before you go down there, gear up with rubber boots and gloves to prevent skin contact. Also wear gloves when cleaning up the polluted sludge left by the flood.

Turn off the gas

Floodwater and floating junk can lead to damaged gas lines and malfunctioning gas controls. Leaked gas then bubbles up through the water, giving your basement an explosive atmosphere on top of the flood. And the smell of gas may be masked by other floodwater odors. So call the utility company to shut off your gas even if you don't smell it. If you do smell gas, get out of the house before you make the call.

Keep your generator away from the house

A generator is the best thing to have in a blackout. But it can make you black out (or die). Hurricane Katrina led to more than 50 cases of carbon monoxide poisoning. A generator engine exhausts carbon monoxide gas, which can give you a headache, knock you out or even kill you. Don't run a generator in your garage or porch, and keep it at least 10 ft. away from your house.

Be prepared for roof damage

When water is flooding in, you can't wait for a pro

Minor roof damage can lead to major water damage inside your home. But if you keep a few simple materials on hand, you can seal most roof injuries in just a few minutes.

First aid kit for your roof

A 9 x 12-ft. tarp is big enough to cover a large area but small enough for one person to manage. If you have a large roof, keep two or three of them on hand. A 14-in. x 10-ft. roll of aluminum flashing is perfect for small holes.

Roofs are dangerous!

Emergency roof repairs often mean walking on a wet roof and wrestling with tarps, which can catch the wind like a sail. We strongly recommend you wear a roof harness (available at home centers and online).

Voice of experience

Trimming trees protects your roof (usually)

In my heavily wooded neighborhood, almost everyone has had serious damage after windstorms. Falling branches have wrecked cars, crashed through windows and punched holes in many roofs. But that never happens to me. I'm always on the lookout for dead or dangerous branches and trim off any threatening limbs right away. That protects against falling branches and reduces the wind load on the tree, so a storm is less likely to bring the entire tree down. I always enjoyed doing the trimming myself, until I felled a big log onto my roof. It tore up the shingles, knocked down my ladder and left me stranded on the roof for two hours. After that, my wife took my chain saw away and called a pro to finish the job.

Drew Butler, *The Family Handyman* **Field Editor**

Tarp large areas

For larger areas, a tarp is the best bandage. But before you spread a tarp, screw plywood over large holes in the roof. Left unsupported, a tarp will sag into a hole, fill with rainwater and possibly leak. If shingles have blown off but there are no holes in the roof, you can lay the tarp directly over the roof sheathing. Stretch the tarp so it lies smoothly over the roof and batten down the entire perimeter; just a few inches of loose tarp will allow strong winds to rip the tarp. Use screws and any type of lumber you have on hand to secure the tarp. Whenever possible, extend the tarp over the roof ridge so water won't flow down and under it. If there's no way to run the tarp over the ridge, slip sections of flashing under shingles and over the upper edge of the tarp. Then drive nails through both the flashing and the tarp.

Patch a small hole

A section of flashing is the perfect patch for smaller holes—often caused by blown-down tree branches. Slide the flashing under the shingles above the hole and nail down the exposed corners of the flashing. Don't forget to caulk around the hole. Special roof sealant is best, but any type of caulk is better than nothing.

A 1-in. hole can let in a gallon of water every minute. And a few gallons can cause thousands of dollars of damage.

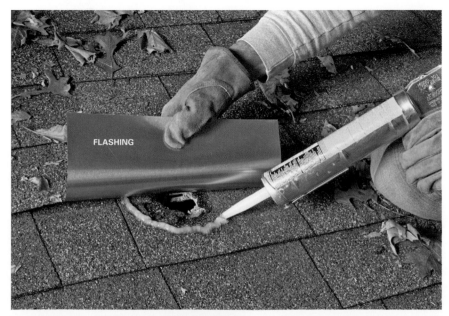

FLASHING

BEST HOME HINTS

Ingenious solutions for common household hassles

Over the past 50 years, readers of *The Family Handyman* magazine have shared thousands of clever tricks with their fellow homeowners. Here are some classics.

Revolutionary door painting

Here's how to paint a door without waiting for one side to dry before flipping it over: Drive one lag screw into the center of the top edge and two near the bottom corners. Set the screws on sawhorses, paint, flip and paint the other side.

3/8" x 4"
LAG SCREW

Luminous light switch

A dab of glow-in-the-dark paint means no more groping for the light switch in the dark. You can buy glow-in-the-dark paint at hardware stores and home centers.

No-slip seat cushions

The rubbery mesh designed to keep rugs from sliding works on chairs, too.

Long-reach shears

Slip PVC pipes over the handles of your pruning shears and tape them in place to extend your reach and clip high branches without a ladder.

Phone shield

When you're painting or gardening, keep your phone clean and dry by sealing it inside a zip-top bag. You can still work the buttons right through the bag.

EXTRA CURTAIN ROD

Extra towel bar

Not enough space to hang towels in your bathroom? Add a second shower curtain rod and you'll have plenty of room. Plus your towel will be within easy reach.

HOUSE KEY

Self-selecting key

Drill a second key ring hole near the edge of your house key and it will stand out from the others. No more fumbling with your keys in the dark.

Flash finder

When your drop something small and can't find it, turn out the lights and shine a flashlight across the floor. Transparent items like a contact lens will glimmer. Other objects will cast a shadow marking their location.

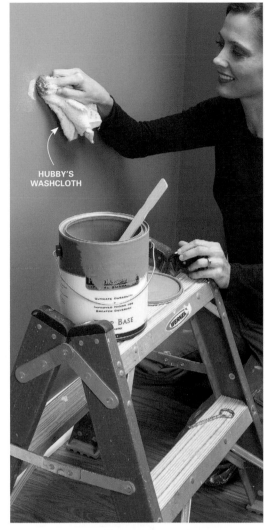

HUBBY'S WASHCLOTH

Touch-up without cleanup

No need to mess up a brush to fix a wall wound. Just dip an old washcloth in the paint and throw it away when you're done. A washcloth leaves the same texture as a paint roller, so your repair will blend nicely.

Trunk bumpers

Keep a couple sections of pipe insulation in your trunk to protect both the car's paint and your oversized cargo.

Tarp trailer

With a big, cheap plastic tarp you can drag leaves, branches or mulch around your yard.

Dust catcher

Before drilling or cutting into a wall, tape a bag below the work zone and it will catch the falling dust.

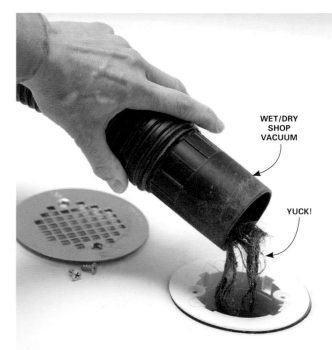

WET/DRY SHOP VACUUM

YUCK!

Suck out drain clogs

A wet-dry vacuum slurps clogs out of plugged drains. Even plumbers use this trick sometimes. If you need to increase suction, seal around the nozzle with a wet rag.

Keep pictures level

A pinch of mounting putty (that sticky stuff used to hang posters) prevents picture tilt without harming walls.

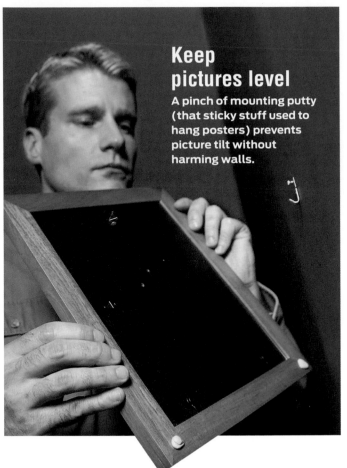

Stop losing socks

Stuff a strip of foam pipe insulation into the space between your washer and dryer or along the wall. That way, socks can't slip into the abyss.

Monetary measurements

A dollar bill is 6.14 in. long. But you don't have to memorize that; just remember that a buck is about 6 in. long and you'll always have an approximate measuring tool in your wallet.

Solid cord connection

A knot keeps cord ends from pulling apart as you drag them around.

Find a flashlight

When the power goes out, you'll be groping in the dark for a flashlight—unless you wrap one with glow-in-the-dark tape. The tape glows for about eight hours after exposure to light.

Hidden remotes

Adhesive-backed hook-and-loop strips let you stick remote controls under an end table. They'll always be handy when you're ready to watch TV but won't clutter up tabletops.

Gutter inspector

Time to clean the gutters? You don't need a ladder to find out. Attach a hand mirror to the end of a PVC pipe. Cut the pipe at a 60-degree angle so the mirror reflects an inside view of the gutter.

Clog claw

Every homeowner should have a flexible-shaft pick-up tool for grabbing stuff out of hard-to-reach spots. They're also great for yanking clogs out of drains!

Tennis ball parking guide

To park your car in perfect position every time, hang a tennis ball from the garage ceiling so it just touches the windshield. It will show you precisely where to stop. No guesswork!

Downspout blowout

A leaf blower lets you clear downspouts without climbing a ladder. If you're using an electric model, make sure all the water has drained out of the downspout before you do this. And be ready for a mucky shower of gutter sludge.

Prepaint lotion

Coat your face and arms with lotion before painting and the splatters will wash off effortlessly.

Secret lock code

If you have trouble remembering your combination, try this: Pick a secret number and add it to each of the combination numbers. Mark the resulting higher numbers on the lock. When you need to unlock, just subtract your secret number from the listed numbers to determine the combination.

Heat up sticky stuff

A hair dryer softens the adhesive under tape or bumper stickers and makes them easy to pull off.

Perfect keyhole template

When you're mounting something on the wall with keyhole slots, lay paper over the slots and make a template by rubbing with a pencil. Then level your template on the wall and you'll know precisely where to position the screws.

No-mess epoxy mixer

For quick, thorough mixing of two-part epoxy, put the components in a bag and knead them together. Punch a small hole in the bag to make a neat dispenser.

Remodel without regrets

When planning, don't rely on your imagination alone

When planning a remodel, most homeowners rely on their own imagination, aided by sketches, blueprints or computer modeling. Those are all good, but nothing can preview a remodeled space like life-size, real-world models. Mock-ups aren't always possible, of course. But when they are, they pay off big in long-term satisfaction.

Build a scale model

A quick, crude model of a kitchen island, cabinetry or even furniture is the best way to determine if it's too big or small. Leave it in place and live with it for a few days before you decide whether it's a convenience or a curse.

Preview a fence

Will a privacy fence really deliver privacy—or hide your neighbor's junk collection? Finding out is easy with a big sheet of cardboard. Along with a helper, you can determine the best location and height.

Design on the wall

Some projects are just too big for full-scale models. But with some tape, chalk and paper, you can create a full-scale layout on walls and floors.

Landscaping layout

Planning a pond or patio? A retaining wall or planting bed? Lay down a rope or garden hose to map the footprint. When you're happy with the shape, mark it with spray paint.

Voice of experience

My favorite modeling material

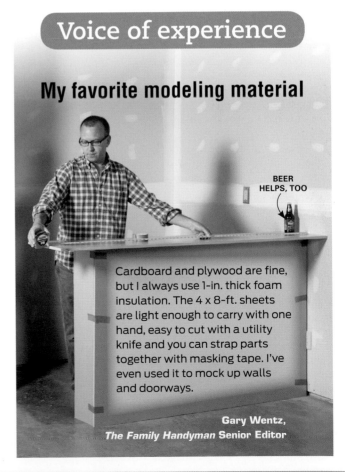

BEER HELPS, TOO

Cardboard and plywood are fine, but I always use 1-in. thick foam insulation. The 4 x 8-ft. sheets are light enough to carry with one hand, easy to cut with a utility knife and you can strap parts together with masking tape. I've even used it to mock up walls and doorways.

Gary Wentz,
The Family Handyman **Senior Editor**

Cut remodeling costs

Your choices can save money or squander it

A major remodel requires hundreds of decisions. And every one of those decisions affects the cost—some in big ways, some in small ways. Here's some pro advice for making cost-conscious choices.

Get bids during the slow season

Most building trades cycle through busy seasons—and busy periods are the worst times to get bids. You'll get less attention and higher quotes. Slow periods, on the other hand, often bring better service and lower costs, even if the work isn't done during that period. Here are some slow seasons for various trades:

■ Roofing: Cold or rainy months
■ Heating: Late summer, before fall
■ Air conditioning: Late winter, early spring
■ Architects and designers: Fall and winter
■ Remodeling contractors: Winter and rainy months

Avoid moving the plumbing

Plumbers are expensive. And since their projects often require tearing into walls or floors, they create more work for other trades, too. So moving the sink to the other end of the bathroom may cost you dearly. Changing the layout of a kitchen is even more expensive because moving appliances means running new gas and electrical lines as well as plumbing.

The BIG mistake

Too many homeowners plan a remodel with special occasions in mind and neglect the practical day-to-day considerations. The result is a home that impresses guests, but isn't convenient for everyday living. This usually means expensive materials and higher up-front costs, followed by regrets later.

Keep the old fridge, but...

Keeping your appliances is a great way to defer costs until your wallet is replenished. But talk to your contractors and appliance pros to make sure you're prepared for replacements. A cabinet installer, for example, can include a movable shelf and wide filler strips so you can install a larger fridge with only minor alterations.

Leave measurements to the pros

Measuring mistakes are costly and common, especially for cabinets, countertops and windows. So if you find a bargain at an outlet center, remember this: If you measure and buy yourself, you alone will bear the cost of mistakes. And often, those bargain cabinets ended up at an outlet store because someone else mismeasured.

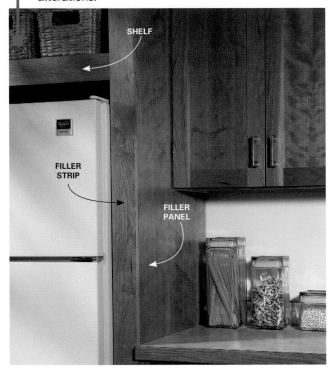

SHELF

FILLER STRIP

FILLER PANEL

Set up a temporary kitchen

Ordering pizza while your kitchen is out of commission might blow your remodeling budget. Instead, set up a kitchen in your laundry room. You already have a sink there, so all you really need are a few small appliances: a microwave, coffeemaker, maybe a hot plate or "dorm room" fridge. Add some shelving and a towel bar and you'll have a functional place to prepare those cost-cutting mac-and-cheese dinners.

Renew cabinets

Cabinets are the largest single item on many kitchen remodeling bids. But most cabinets can be refreshed, even if they're in terrible shape.

Paint

A good painting contractor can make old cabinets look great, often for about one-tenth the cost of new cabinets. If you're willing to do some research and tedious prep work, you can do it yourself and save much more.

Reface

Refacing starts with a layer of real wood veneer applied to the frames. Add new doors and drawer fronts, and the cabinets look entirely new. The bill is typically less than half the cost of new cabinets.

Decorate smart

Designer advice for sensible style

The first law of decorating: Start with limited-choice items

Paint comes in a million colors, so you'll have no trouble finding a color that works with the new sofa. But finding a sofa to complement your paint may be a hopeless quest. So choose a sofa first. This philosophy applies to all decorating choices, from flooring to light fixtures and everything in between.

White works now, and later

Bland colors—shades of white, gray or beige—are a wise choice for permanent, hard-to-change items like toilets, tile, tubs and countertops. They don't provide much drama, but you can add pizzazz with paint or simple, inexpensive accents like rugs or pottery. And as fashions change, you can update the look without costly remodeling.

Home décor database

Get a cheap plastic bin and toss in samples of all the materials you've chosen: Wallpaper, fabrics, paint chips—leftover hardware, too. When you need new curtains or carpet, you'll have everything you need to make a match.

Preview tile

Choosing tile colors and patterns based on a few samples is risky—and you'll live with the results for years. So here's a worthwhile exercise: Make photocopies and tape them in place. When you've found a layout you like, snap a photo to guide the tile installer.

Permanent paint record

Before you put the switch or outlet covers back in place after a paint job, jot down the paint color. You may misplace your paint sample, but you'll never lose this reminder.

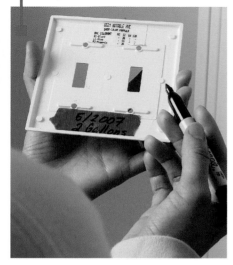

Voice of experience

Blinded by the light

One sunny afternoon, my husband and I selected tile for our bathroom floor and vanity top. The two complement each other beautifully—but only on sunny afternoons. On cloudy days or evenings, the vanity takes on a blue tone and the floor is green. Looks awful. Now we always examine color combinations in different light conditions, natural and artificial, in fair weather and foul.

Amy Hooper, *The Family Handyman* Field Editor

Choose the best flooring

They all look good at first—but some look better longer

Flooring is a big deal. It's a major expense and a long-term commitment. And few things can make or break your home's appearance like flooring can. Here's some expert orientation to put you on a path that will lead to satisfaction rather than regrets.

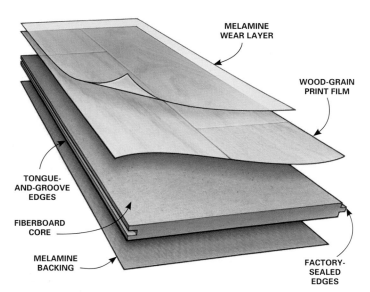

MELAMINE WEAR LAYER

WOOD-GRAIN PRINT FILM

TONGUE-AND-GROOVE EDGES

FIBERBOARD CORE

MELAMINE BACKING

FACTORY-SEALED EDGES

Plastic laminate

Plastic laminate is one of the toughest floors available; it's almost impossible to stain and only ceramic tile is more resistant to scratches. It also resists moisture and spills fairly well, so it's a good choice for basements and kitchens. Plastic laminates vary widely in price and quality. Here's what you'll typically get when you pay more:

■ **BETTER LOOKS:** Some laminates are hard to distinguish from real wood. Others are obvious fakes.

■ **TIGHTER JOINTS:** All plastic laminates are floating floors, locked together with tongue-and-groove joints. But some are manufactured to higher standards and lock together more reliably.

■ **A THICKER, TOUGHER WEAR LAYER:** Ask about the AC rating (abrasion class). AC3 floors are best for high-traffic areas. An AC1 floor costs less but will stand up well in a bedroom.

■ **BETTER MOISTURE RESISTANCE:** Better laminates are treated to repel moisture coming from below or between the joints. Cheaper versions will quickly swell or buckle.

High-quality plastic laminates are ideal for high-traffic areas because they won't stain, burn, scratch, easily scuff or fade.

Luxury vinyl

Luxury vinyl flooring is similar to sheet vinyl, but it's thicker, tougher and much easier to install. It's economical too, with lower materials and labor costs than most other types of flooring.

Looks like wood
Luxury vinyl planks (LVP) imitate wood and form a "floating" floor that simply lays on the subfloor without any fastening.

Looks like ceramic tile
Luxury vinyl tile (LVT) can include grouted spaces between tiles—or not. A thin layer of adhesive fastens it to the subfloor.

It stands up to water
Luxury vinyl is an excellent choice for laundry rooms, bathrooms and other areas where moisture is a concern. Some manufacturers actually refer to their products as "waterproof" rather than just "water resistant."

It's soft and pliable
LVP flooring feels softer and warmer underfoot than most other flooring, which makes it especially nice in bathrooms. It comes in a wide variety of patterns and styles designed to look like wood, granite, tile and other materials. Don't confuse LV products with the lower-priced (and lower-quality) vinyl composition tile (VCT). LV is made with more solid vinyl, which makes it more durable (and more expensive). LVT can be glued down or installed as a floating floor depending on the type.

Solid wood

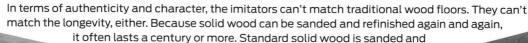

In terms of authenticity and character, the imitators can't match traditional wood floors. They can't match the longevity, either. Because solid wood can be sanded and refinished again and again, it often lasts a century or more. Standard solid wood is sanded and finished after installation. Prefinished versions come with a factory finish that's tougher than on-site finishes. The chief drawbacks of solid wood are durability, stability and cost. Even factory finishes will eventually dull with normal wear. Wood inevitably moves with changes in humidity, so gaps sometimes develop at joints. And solid wood is one of the most expensive flooring choices.

UNFINISHED

PREFINISHED

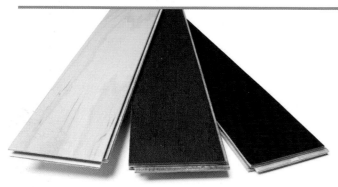

Engineered wood

Engineered wood floors are a lot like plastic laminate, but they're surfaced with real wood. That's an advantage in terms of natural looks and long-term life span. Once it wears, engineered wood can be refinished to look like new, so an engineered floor can have a much longer life than plastic laminate. Wood is also quieter to walk on than plastic. But engineered wood doesn't match the surface toughness or moisture resistance of plastic laminate. It also costs about twice as much as plastic laminate.

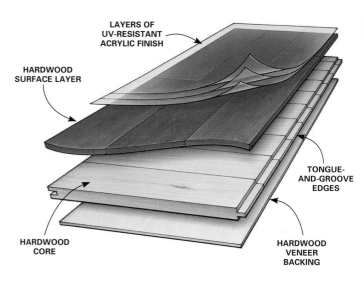

LAYERS OF UV-RESISTANT ACRYLIC FINISH

HARDWOOD SURFACE LAYER

TONGUE-AND-GROOVE EDGES

HARDWOOD CORE

HARDWOOD VENEER BACKING

Tile

Tile is the most diverse category of flooring. Most versions are extremely durable, but some (like marble or limestone tile) are fairly easy to scratch or stain. Tile can be the most expensive type of flooring, but inexpensive tile combined with DIY installation can give you a low-cost floor that looks great. But there is one thing that applies to all types of tile: Proper installation is critical. Before you hire a contractor, gather some basic knowledge. Familyhandyman.com is a one-stop source for understanding tile backers, adhesives, grout and other keys to an attractive, lasting tile job.

Carpet

Check the density

Bend the carpet sample backward. If you can see the backing easily, it's a low-density, lower-quality carpet that will crush more easily.

Buy quality pad

The right pad will extend the life of your carpet, and the wrong pad can cut the life of your carpet in half. The quality of carpet pad is determined by density, not thickness. A good-quality pad will be 3/8 to 1/2 in. thick and have a density/weight rating of at least 6 lbs. (the residential standard). In most cases, cheap, low-density pad will only last a few years before it needs to be replaced. For high-traffic areas, get a thinner pad with a density of 8 lbs. or more.

Nylon is tough

Nylon outperforms other fibers in durability, resilience and easy maintenance. It's a good choice for high-traffic areas like hallways or busy family rooms, and in homes with kids and pets. It costs $10 to $45 per sq. yd.

Triexta resists stains

Triexta (brands include Smart-Strand and Sorona) is a newer fiber derived partly from corn sugar. It has excellent, permanent anti-stain properties (nylon must be treated with stain protectors over its life span). It also has good resilience, but it's too soon to tell whether it will match the long-term durability of nylon in high-traffic areas. Expect to pay $20 to $45 per sq. yd.

Polyester is comfy

Polyester (also called PET) is stain resistant, very soft and luxurious underfoot, and is available in deep and vibrant colors. However, it's harder to clean, tends to shed and isn't as durable as nylon. It's best used in low-traffic areas (like bedrooms) and in households without kids or pets. It costs $8 to $18 per sq. yd.

Olefin is economical

Olefin (polypropylene) is inexpensive but tough and fade-resistant. It's most often made into a looped Berber with a nubby weave that conceals dirt and is often selected for high-traffic "clean" areas such as family rooms and play areas. It costs $8 to $25 per sq. yd.

Choose the best faucet

Style matters, but don't ignore the practical factors

Most people choose a faucet based on looks alone. And that's a mistake. Style does matter, but you can usually get the look you want without compromising on other things.

Ceramic valves are better

Standard faucet valves usually last for years. But eventually, the rubber parts inside wear—and that means a drippy faucet. Ceramic valves, on the other hand, go drip-free for decades, whether they're in kitchens, bathrooms, tubs or showers. Faucets with ceramic valves come in a huge variety of styles and cost about the same as those with standard valves.

Maybe you don't need a new faucet

Years of mineral buildup, especially in crevices, make a faucet look worn out and beyond help. But with a thorough cleaning, most faucets can look as good as new (or almost). Clean with a product that's formulated to dissolve minerals (CLR is one brand) and scrub with a toothbrush. You'll be amazed how good your old faucet looks! Warning: Powerful cleaners might damage surrounding surfaces, so be sure to check the label.

> ## Voice of experience
>
> The problem with ceramic faucets is that we don't get to sell many repair parts.
>
> **Gray Uhl,**
> **trends director,**
> **American Standard**

Consider a simpler stopper

Most bath faucets come with a stopper for the sink. Most of those stoppers are the standard type found in the vast majority of bathrooms. The trouble with that old, standard design is that the linkages are hard to adjust just right and often need readjustment to open or seal properly. So consider a faucet that comes with an improved stopper. American Standard's SpeedConnect and Pfister's Push & Seal are two examples.

Ceramic parts are tiny, but tough. Friction and particles in water slowly destroy other valves, but have no effect on ceramic, which is about five times harder than steel.

Spend enough, but not too much

Plan to spend at least $65 for a bathroom faucet and $100 for a kitchen faucet. You might get a great faucet for less, but it's more likely that you'll get low quality. If you spend much more, you're paying for extra features or style rather than reliability or durability.

Watch the spout height and reach

Faucet spouts vary a lot in height and reach, and most of the time you can just choose the look you like best. But if you have a shelf above the sink, a tall spout may not fit. With a three-bowl kitchen sink, a spout with a short reach may not extend to all the bowls. A bath faucet with a short reach might cause you to slop water behind the spout when you wash your hands.

Pull-down sprayers are better

If you've ever had a "side" sprayer (a spray handle mounted in the sink), you've probably had dribbles or leaks. And you might assume you'd have similar (and more expensive) trouble with a faucet mounted sprayer like the one shown here. Probably not. All of our experts told us that "pull-down" sprayers have proven much more reliable than the old side sprayers.

Count the holes in your sink

If you want to switch from two handles to one, you have to think about the number of holes in the sink. Most sinks have three holes: one for the hot handle, one for the cold and one under the spout. Some single-handle faucets include a cover plate to hide the extra holes. But some don't, so check the label. If you currently have a "wide spread" bathroom faucet with two handles far from the spout, you can't switch to a single-handle model. If you want a kitchen faucet with a pull-down sprayer mounted in the spout, there will be an empty sprayer hole. But the solution is simple: Install a soap dispenser. Your new faucet may even include one.

Some finishes are tougher than others

Choose a finish that matches nearby cabinet hardware, towel bars, etc. Mismatches look bad. The majority of faucets have polished chrome, satin nickel or bronze finishes. All of these finishes are durable and keep their good looks for years. But some are more durable than others. Chrome is the most durable finish and the easiest to keep clean—that's why it's always been the favorite for commercial kitchens and public bathrooms. Nickel finishes are usually labeled "brushed," "satin" or "stainless steel" and have a dull shine. They're durable but prone to fingerprints and water spots, so they're harder to keep clean. Some have a coating that reduces stains and smudges, but that coating isn't as durable as metal. Bronze faucets have a brownish tone and are often called "oiled" or "rubbed" bronze. But the surface is a coating (such as epoxy) rather than metal. This coating is tough stuff, but will chip or scratch more easily than metal.

A single handle is more convenient

Two-handle faucets have a stylish symmetry that suits many bathrooms, especially traditional ones. But in practical terms, single-handle faucets have all the advantages. They're just plain more convenient; water temperature adjustment is easier and there's one less handle to clean.

Move furniture the smart way

Protect your back, your house and your furniture!

Whether you're relocating or just rearranging, moving furniture is a big job. But heavy lifting doesn't have to be back-breaking, especially if you use your brain instead of your back. Here are simple techniques for moving heavy, awkward items without wrecking your body or anything else.

Stand sofas on end

If you ever have to maneuver a couch down a hallway and through a door, you may find it almost impossible to carry it horizontally and make the turn into the room. Before you enter the hallway, place the couch on its end and slide it to the doorway. You'll almost always be able to hook it through the door. If it's a bit taller than the door opening, start the top away from the door and gain several inches of clearance.

'Hook' chairs around corners

Follow the example of pro movers and "hook" large chairs around corners. Turn the chair on its side so it looks like an "L" and move it back-first through the doorway. Then curl it (hook it) around the door frame and slip it through.

Plan where it lands

If you're moving to a new house, decide beforehand which furniture will go where. Before you move, sketch a floor plan with the correct measurements of each room, measure your furniture and create your layout. Then, as you move things in, you (or your helpers, if you're not there) can place your furniture in the correct spot and not have to touch it again. To make it easy on the movers, tape a copy of the plan to the wall of each room so people can tell at a glance where things go.

Carry tall items high and low

A tall dresser, filing cabinet or shelving unit is awkward to handle. Make it a two-person job. Tip the item backward at an angle and have one person carry the top while the other carries the bottom. This centers the weight and keeps the item from swinging out of control. Transporting the item up or down stairs is easier too, since the carrying angle will roughly match the slope of the stairs.

Voice of experience

Measure first!

Before you buy anything big, measure the item and the pathway into your home. Don't forget about small things that might block the path: You may have to remove doorknobs or wall-mounted light fixtures, for example. And don't forget about turning corners. We measured doorways and determined that our new shower enclosure woud fit through. But we didn't think about turning it around corners, so we had to cut a hole in the wall. That method worked, but I don't recommend it.

Carolyn Burdge,
***The Family Handyman* Field Editor**

Protect furniture with blankets

You can rent moving blankets or, for a few bucks more, buy them at home centers or moving outfitters, and always have them on hand. To prevent damage to furniture, walls and trim, wrap the item completely with moving blankets and secure the blanket with stretch film. Find 20-in.-wide rolls of stretch film at home centers and moving outfitters.

Don't carry it—slide it

You can buy furniture slides in many shapes and sizes at home centers and online. It's also easy to make your own sliders from plastic container covers, Frisbees, bedspreads, moving blankets, towels and carpet remnants. Use hard plastic sliders for carpeting, and soft, padded sliders for hard flooring.

Make a mattress sling

Handling a heavy, floppy mattress is tough. Make it easier with a simple homemade sling. Just slip a 5-in. piece of 1-in. PVC pipe over the rope ends and then loop and tie each end to create a comfortable sling grip. Thread the rope through the mattress handles and you're on your way.

Cut and fold a box spring

Is your box spring too big to fit around a tight corner? You could buy a two-piece "split" box spring (and pay several hundred bucks) or cut your existing box spring and fold it so it fits. Sound extreme? There's actually a simple, ingenious way to cut and fold your box spring without wrecking it.

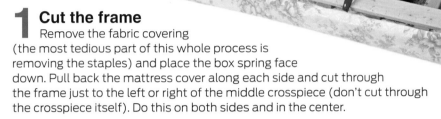

1 Cut the frame

Remove the fabric covering (the most tedious part of this whole process is removing the staples) and place the box spring face down. Pull back the mattress cover along each side and cut through the frame just to the left or right of the middle crosspiece (don't cut through the crosspiece itself). Do this on both sides and in the center.

2 Fold it

You can now fold the box spring like a book and move it. Secure it with a strap to prevent it from springing open.

3 Put it back together

Screw a 1x2 along the center crosspiece cuts and against the inside of the outer frame to reinforce them. Then staple the fabric covering in place.

Pick up some 'hump straps'

Moving and lifting straps (aka "hump straps") take the weight off your back by relying on leverage and large muscle groups. They also leave your hands free to maneuver awkward items. However, they can be tricky to use on stairs because the weight shifts completely to the downhill mover. Look for lifting straps that can be adjusted for different-length objects as well as for different-size movers. The lifting straps shown here are great for moving on flat surfaces. Over-the-shoulder lifting straps give you better control on stairs.

Hang pictures straight and level

Perfection is possible—if you know a few tricks

Hanging a single picture is as easy as nailing a hook to the wall. But when you want to hang two or more aligned with each other, things get complicated. Here's how pros achieve perfection fast and frustration-free.

CENTER MARK

LASER LEVEL

PAPER PATTERN

1 Level and align

Make paper patterns identical to the pictures, then establish a level line on the wall. An inexpensive laser level is perfect for this project, but a standard level will also work. When you've arranged the patterns perfectly, mark the top center of each with the corner of a sticky note as a reference point.

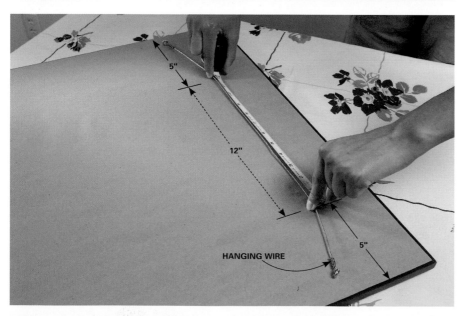

5"

12"

5"

HANGING WIRE

2 Find the hanger locations

Use two hangers for each picture for extra support and to help keep the picture from tipping. Stretch the hanger wire with two fingers spaced equally distant from the edges of the picture frame. Keep the wire parallel to the top of the frame. Measure the distance between your fingertips.

3 Find the distance from the top edge

Leave one finger in place and measure from the wire to the top. Use this and the previous dimension to position the picture hangers on the wall.

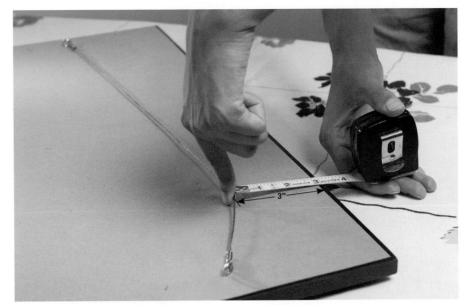

4 Transfer the hanger measurements to the wall

Find the hanger positions by measuring down from the sticky note and to each side from the center. An inexpensive level with inches marked on it makes this much easier. Keep the hangers level.

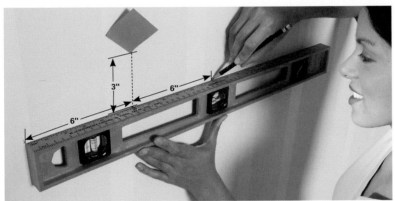
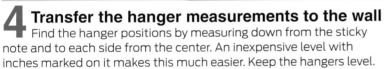

5 Nail the hooks

Then line up the bottom of the hooks with the marks and drive the picture-hanger nails through the angled guides on the hooks.

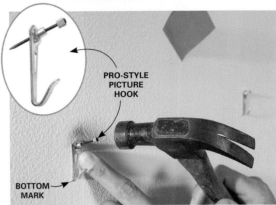

PRO-STYLE PICTURE HOOK

BOTTOM MARK

6 Hang the picture

Slip the wire over both hooks. Slide the picture sideways across the wires until it's level. Use the same process to hang the remaining pictures.

Hang a heavy mirror

Safe, secure and exactly where you want it

A heavy mirror hung the wimpy way is just plain dangerous. If it comes down, it will damage the baseboard and floor and might send glass shards flying. But there's really no reason to worry about it; hanging a mirror securely is easy. First, deal with the hardware on the back of the mirror. If it has a hanging wire, remove the wire and instead screw D-rings to the frame. Locate the D-rings an equal distance from the top of the frame, about one-third of the total height down. Then you're ready for the next steps:

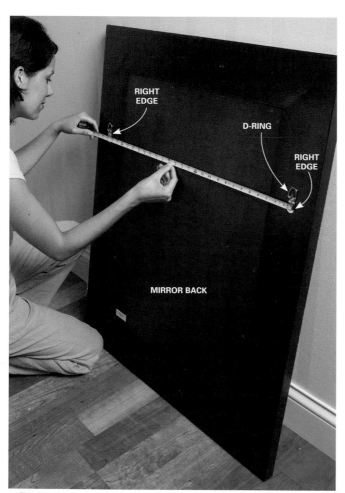

1 Find the center

Measure the exact distance between the centers of the D-rings by hooking your tape measure on one edge of a D-ring and measure to the same edge of the second D-ring.

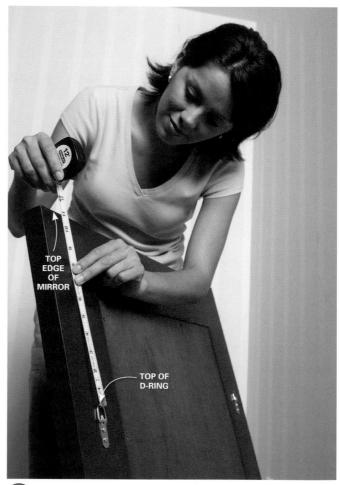

2 Find the distance to the top

Measure from the top of the D-ring to the top of the frame to determine the distance down.

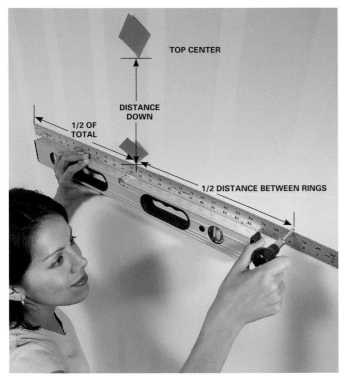

TOP CENTER

DISTANCE DOWN

1/2 OF TOTAL

1/2 DISTANCE BETWEEN RINGS

WALL ANCHOR

3 Transfer the measurements to the wall

Hold the mirror up to the wall and choose the best position. Start with the center of the mirror at about 60 in. from the floor. When you like the position, mark the top center with a sticky note. Use a level and a ruler to plumb down the correct distance. Mark the spot with the corner of a sticky note. Then use the level and ruler to find the exact anchor positions.

4 Drive in the anchors

Screw in the anchors with a screwdriver or drill. If you hit a stud, no problem—just drive a 2-in. screw into the stud.

Match the anchors to the mirror

Before you buy anchors for this project, set your mirror on a scale. The weight will help you select anchors. Screw-in anchors like the one shown here usually carry weight ratings from 40 to 75 lbs (check the label). If you have a super-heavy mirror, choose toggle-style anchors; they're often rated at 100 lbs. or more.

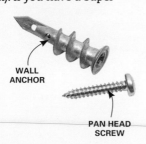

WALL ANCHOR

PAN HEAD SCREW

5 Hang the mirror

Screw a pan head screw into the anchor. Leave the screw sticking out about 1/4 in. Hook the D-rings onto the protruding screws. If the top isn't level when you're done, wrap a few turns of electrical tape around the D-ring on the low side to raise that side slightly.

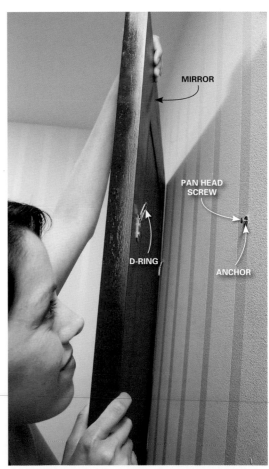

MIRROR

PAN HEAD SCREW

D-RING

ANCHOR

Pick a paint color you'll love

You'll live with it for years, so don't rush the decision

When the time comes to paint, too many homeowners dash off to the store, grab some tiny samples and spend just a few minutes selecting a color. And sometimes that works out just fine. Other times, it leads to years of regret. Here's how to avoid those regrets.

Hang up samples

It's difficult to tell what a color is going to look like on your wall from a small paint sample chip, so many manufacturers offer sample containers of their colors. Depending on the manufacturer, you can buy sample containers in quarts, pints or even smaller sizes. They're a wise investment that will prevent you from wasting money on a color that isn't right. Because colors can change dramatically under different lighting conditions, roll the sample onto a white tagboard instead of onto the wall. That way, you'll be able to move the sample to other walls and view it under all the different lighting conditions in the room.

Consider the neighbors

You may think a purple house with red trim would be really groovy, but your neighbors will hate you. And no color choice is as important as good relations with your neighbors.

Work with your permanent colors

Base your color choice on the permanent furnishings in the room or the features on the exterior of your home. Inside, the flooring, rugs, artwork, blinds and upholstery will suggest a color direction. Outside, factory-finished materials like the roof, gutters, fascia, soffits and brickwork are existing elements whose colors rarely change but should play a role in determining your paint colors. The landscaping is another important factor. Select colors that fit in with the surrounding palette. If you have brilliant-colored spring blooming trees or a sea of green foundation plantings, choose colors that will complement them.

Don't get creative before selling

The best investment I've ever made was to buy a house with a pink garage door. Really, it was PINK! And the owner thought it looked great! But it killed the home's curb appeal and my realtor estimated that it knocked about ten thousand bucks off the sales price. My friends gave me a lot of grief, but a quick coat of white paint solved that problem.

Ed Martin, property investor and *The Family Handyman* Field Editor

Use color collections

Paint companies carefully assemble colors into "families" or "collections." Basically, these are combinations of complementary colors that may not occur to you until you see how well they work together. Take advantage of all this research already done for you by color experts. Find brochures at paint stores or go online to paint manufacturer Web sites.

Lighten the ceiling color

Because ceilings are seen in shadow, the color often appears darker than the same paint on walls. If you want the ceiling to match the wall color, buy ceiling paint one or two shades lighter than the wall color. Or instead of buying another gallon of a lighter shade, save money by diluting the wall color with 50 percent white paint.

Pick other décor first

Paint is available in any color you can imagine. So it will be easy to find a color that works with your new curtains or furniture. But if you choose a paint color first, your search for matching curtains won't be so easy.

Store leftovers upside down

Paint can lids don't always seal perfectly. But stored upside down, the paint will form an airtight seal. Before you reopen the can, give it a long, hard shaking so that the solids in the paint fall off the lid.

Virtually paint your house

Many manufacturers offer opportunities to "paint" your home virtually— you upload a photo of your home or a room and try out different colors and painting schemes. You can also search for homes similar to your own and try "painting" with various combinations and products. There are also apps that allow you to take a photo of a color you like and have it matched with a manufacturer's color or suggested palette. Just be aware that your computer monitor, phone or iPad screen will affect the color of the paint you see.

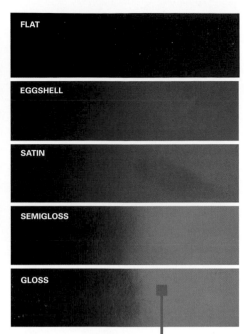

FLAT

EGGSHELL

SATIN

SEMIGLOSS

GLOSS

Sheen matters as much as color

When you choose a color, you have to choose its sheen, too. Most paint companies offer flat, eggshell, satin, semigloss and gloss as options. Glossier finishes offer greater durability and are easier to clean, but they emphasize any wall imperfections. Flat paint will do a much better job of hiding imperfections, but it's easier to damage than gloss. Flat finishes are generally best for ceilings and low-traffic areas like living and dining rooms where all you'll need to do is wipe them down with a damp sponge. If they do get scuffed, they're easy to touch up. Glossier finishes—including satin and semigloss—can withstand moisture and grease so they're good for trim and cabinets and high-traffic areas like kitchens and bathrooms.

Repair bad walls

Your walls may look fine with their existing coat of flat, white paint. But with glossier paint or a dark color, every little bump and crater will show up. So if you're set on using a dark color or a glossy sheen, inspect your walls first. Most walls can be smoothed out with a combination of filling holes and sanding down rough spots. Really bad walls may require "skim coating," a thin coat of joint compound covering the entire wall.

Don't paint the walls only

Just as paint accentuates features, you can use it to hide unappealing elements too. Paint exposed plumbing, radiators, gutters and other components the same color as the walls to make them blend in. You can also do that with light fixtures, switches, outlets and just about anything else.

Vivid colors fade faster

The more intense or dark a color is, the more likely it is to fade and show dirt. After a few years, vivid blues and deep reds will become subdued, and you may see streaks and splotches of dirt more readily. Dark colors can also absorb heat and sustain more moisture problems than lighter shades. And because dark paint fades, it can be difficult to match exactly when you do small touch-ups. On the plus side, dark colors can give your house an air of dignity or drama. Generally, organic colors like red, blue, green and yellow tend to fade more quickly than earth tones like beiges, tans and browns, which are more stable.

Beware of dark colors in bathrooms

Extremely dark colors don't handle the moisture in a bathroom very well; they can become blotchy or chalky.

Pick the best paint for the job

Get better-looking, longer-lasting results

On painting projects, there are two keys to success: careful preparation of the surface and using the right products. Prep work is usually tedious, but simple. Choosing paints and primers, on the other hand, is confusing. Even small stores carry dozens of types, and the labels often add to the confusion. So here's a guide:

Acrylic latex: Usually the best choice

Most of the paint and primer cans on store shelves contain acrylic latex paint. And there's a good reason for that. On most surfaces—wood, masonry, metal, drywall—it's a proven performer, indoors and out. It's also reasonably priced and water-based for easy cleanup.

Are expensive paints worth it?

Prices for paint and primer vary widely. One can of acrylic latex, for example, might cost four times as much the acrylic latex on the next shelf. Some designer-brand paints give you medium quality at a high cost. But generally, higher cost means better coverage, a smoother finish and longer life.

Fight mildew

Got a mildew zone? Choose a paint that contains mildewcide or add mildewcide to the paint. Be sure to clean the area with 1:3 mix of bleach and water first.

Primer tips

■ Use primer and paint from the same manufacturer. Many primers are formulated to work best with certain paints.
■ Paint within 48 hours of priming. Many primers bond physically and chemically with the topcoat. But that bonding power diminishes quickly.
■ Tint it. For no extra charge, the paint store can add some pigment to primer. That will get you one step closer to the final color you want and possibly eliminate one coat of paint. Primers are often tinted gray rather than the color of the topcoat.

Smooth finishes on woodwork

For cabinets, doors or trim, you want a smooth finish. But some paints, even high-quality paints, just aren't formulated for that. Smooth paints are usually labeled "enamel" or "door and trim." Most are acrylic latex, but another category beats acrylic latex for smoothness: Water-based alkyds level out and dry smooth just like old-fashioned oil-based paints, but clean up with water. They're also among the most expensive paints on the market. But when you consider all the time you'll put into a first-class paint job, spending $20 more doesn't seem so bad. Water-based alkyds are available at paint stores.

The best paint for plastic

Making paint stick to plastic was a problem for decades. But now spray paint manufacturers offer formulas just for that job. These paints don't just stick; they fuse with plastic surfaces to form a nearly unbreakable bond.

Block stains

Some stains—from smoke, water, crayons or markers—bleed through standard paints and primers no matter how many coats you apply. Some woods, especially cedar and redwood, contain natural pigments that bleed through paint. The solution is to start with a primer that's formulated to seal in stains. Some come in spray cans, convenient for quick spot priming. Most pro painters report best results with oil-based products, but water-based primers are also available. Most stain-blockers also seal in odors such as tobacco smoke.

Smoother finishes on rough surfaces

If you want a smooth finish, check the label. Some metal primers are formulated to fill pockmarks and scratches. Some are also sandable, so you can smooth out rough spots after the primer dries.

Prep for a neater paint job

Protect against slop, splatter and spills

It's a great feeling: the satisfaction of a newly painted room transformed by a fresh color. But hasty prep and accidents can erase that satisfaction, leaving you with messy regrets. Here's how to goof-proof your next painting project.

Bag light fixtures

Painting a ceiling is a cinch—except for the light fixture. Here's how to get it out of your way: First remove any glass parts, including the bulbs (make sure the power is off). Unfasten the fixture, usually by removing a couple of screws. Then hook one end of a wire through the fixture and the other to the junction box. Make sure your hanging wire—not the electrical wire—supports the fixture. Then slip a plastic bag over the fixture.

   Dealing with chandeliers and pendants is even easier. The decorative plate at the ceiling is usually held up by a ring nut. Just unscrew the nut and the plate will slide down over the chain or tube. There's no need to support the fixture with wire.

TEMPORARY HANGING WIRE

Sheet over doors and windows

Paint rollers throw off a mist of paint that speckles everything below. Here's the quickest way to protect doors and windows: When you tape around door and window trim, use tape that's wide enough to project at least 1/2 in. from the trim. That way, you can stick light plastic to the protruding tape—there's no need to tape the perimeter of the plastic separately. For doors, slit the plastic with a utility knife so you can slip through.

Cover carpet with canvas

Canvas dropcloths are the best coverings for carpet. They're easy to spread out, and unlike plastic, they stay put without tape. Just bunch them up a bit along walls and they'll stay where you want them. Good dropcloths aren't cheap, but you don't have to cover the entire floor. Many pro painters use a long, narrow "runner" that they drag around the room as they go. Normal drips and splatter won't soak through canvas, but heavy spills might, so clean up major spills immediately.

Stack up the furniture

Cramped working conditions lead to messy accidents. If you can't move furniture completely out of the room, stack it up. Set upholstered chairs upside down on the sofa. Cover the dining room tabletop with cardboard so you can set chairs on top of it. But don't let your stack become an obstacle. Maintain a generous workspace of at least 3 ft. between the stack and the walls. Cover your furniture stack with plastic.

Spend more on painter's tape

When buying masking tape, let price be your guide. More expensive tapes block paint better and release easier without harming surfaces. You might save $3 on a cheaper roll of tape, but you'll regret it.

Protect hard floors with paper

Both canvas and plastic dropcloths are slippery when laid over wood, vinyl or tile. For protection that stays put, you can't beat rosin paper (available at home centers). Just tape sheets of it together and then tape the perimeter to the floor. Be sure to clean wood floors before laying down the paper; grit trapped underneath can lead to scratches. A single layer will protect against paint drips, but wipe up any spills before they can soak through.

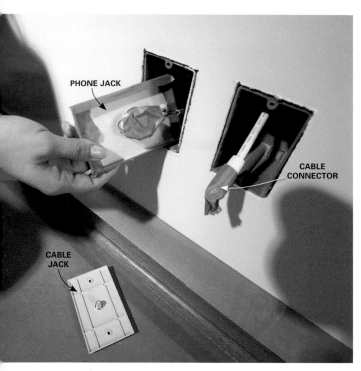

PHONE JACK

CABLE
CONNECTOR

CABLE
JACK

Mask off sensitive wiring

A little paint in the wrong place can cripple the connections that serve your phone, TV or computer. To protect phone jacks without disconnecting all those tiny wires, unscrew the faceplate and cover the front with masking tape. Then mask the terminals on the back of the plate. Slip the plate into the junction box. Disconnect coaxial cable from its plate and tape the cable's connector.

Tape over switches and outlets

Don't try to paint around electrical cover plates. Removing them takes just a few seconds and makes for a faster, neater job. Unscrew cover plates and then shield each switch or outlet with 2-in.-wide masking tape. Also remove curtain hardware, picture hooks, grilles that cover duct openings and anything else that might get in your way. The thermostat is one exception—it's easier to wrap it with masking tape than to remove and reinstall it.
Caution: Turn off the power before removing cover plates.

Shelter baseboard with tape

Don't waste time by completely covering baseboard with several strips of tape. A single overhanging strip of wide tape will catch roller splatters just as the roof overhang on your house keeps rain off the siding. Use 1-1/2-in. tape for narrow baseboard, 2-in. tape for wider baseboard. Tape won't stay stuck to dusty surfaces, so wipe down all your trim before masking. To minimize paint seepage under the tape, press the tape down hard by running a flexible putty knife over it.

Don't make tracks

Remember that when you're walking on dropcloths, you're walking on paint spills. Always check your shoes before walking away. My habit is to kick off my shoes before leaving the work area.

Jim Peterson, pro painter

Spill-proof paint can

After an ugly accident, I bolted a large bucket to my ladder. That gives me a safe place to set my paint can.

Russel Durrwachter, *The Family Handyman* Field Editor

Not just for the kitchen

Painters love Glad Press'n Seal self-stick kitchen wrap because it goes on fast and stays put. Line paint trays to eliminate cleanup later or use it to shield any surface.

Lou Taylor, pro painter

Preserve picture holes

A fresh coat of paint can fill and hide small nail holes. So if you plan to hang pictures in the same locations after painting, stick toothpicks or large-headed pins in the holes. If you leave them protruding just a little, you can roll right over them.

Jim Christensen, *The Family Handyman* Field Editor

Paint like a pro

Essential tips for excellent results

There's more to painting than just slapping it on; it takes some know-how to get great results. Here are some key tips gathered through years of observing and asking professional painters.

Accurate masking

When masking trim, hold the tape tight against the wall as you unroll it. Then lower the tape onto the trim and it will land in perfect position. Drag a putty knife across the tape to "bed" it firmly onto the trim.

Cut before you remove tape

Before you pull off masking tape, give the paint 24 hours to dry. Then run a sharp blade along the edge of the tape to slice through the paint film. If you don't do this, the paint film will tear, leaving an ugly, jagged edge.

KNIFE

DRY PAINT

TAPE

Don't start in corners

When painting trim, unload your brush a few inches from inside corners. Then spread it into the corner. If you unload directly into the corner, you'll end up with a heavy blob that's difficult to spread out.

Set up a staging area

Painting requires a lot of gear. To avoid constantly moving stuff or tripping over it, lay down a dropcloth outside the room and park your supplies there.

Degloss varnished wood

Paint doesn't stick well to clear coatings on wood. So before you paint, treat varnished wood with deglosser. It's faster than sanding and leaves a surface that paint can grab onto.

Prepare for a paint shower

Paint rollers spin off a fine mist that speckles everything below. So before you roll—especially a ceiling—put on a cap and glasses. For easy paint removal from skin, rub on some lotion before you paint.

Don't paint out of the can

A paint can is awkward to hold and easy to spill. Worse, leaving the can open while you paint allows partial drying and the formation of chunks. So work from a smaller container. Any can or jar will do. Some store-bought containers, like the one shown here, have disposable liners to eliminate cleanup.

Bill Zuehlke

Dump the bumps

The bumps along the edge of a textured ceiling make it impossible to get a neat, straight paint line where walls meet the ceiling. So scrape them off with a screwdriver.

Prime every patch

Fillers like spackle or joint compound instantly suck the moisture out of paint. That gives the patched spot a noticeably different sheen and stands out like a sore thumb on a freshly painted wall. A little dose of primer seals patches and prevents those ugly blotches.

CAULKED CRACK

Caulk every little crack

Paint will fill and hide tiny cracks—but only temporarily. Within days or months, even the smallest cracks will come back to haunt you. A bit of acrylic latex caulk prevents that.

Don't land on edges

Think of your brush as a fighter jet landing on an aircraft carrier. If you land on edges, you'll scrape paint off the brush and create a big drip. So take off only; never land.

Super-smooth rollers

With practice, you can achieve a smooth finish with a brush. Or you can get a finish that's almost as smooth with a mini roller. With most paints, microfiber rollers provide the smoothest finish.

Don't open the can with a screwdriver

Sure, a screwdriver works, but it leaves dents in the seal. And that leads to gooey chunks in the paint. Pick up a paint can opener when you buy the paint.

PAINT CAN/
BOTTLE OPENER

Remove mistakes

If you slop some paint on varnished wood, don't despair. Home centers carry liquid paint remover products just for that situation. Let the paint dry and mask off the paint you don't want to remove. Gently scrape off as much paint as you can with a putty knife. Then squirt a few drops of remover on an old toothbrush and scrub away the rest.

Strain out the goobers

A half-full can of paint that sits around for a few days will develop gooey chunks and strands of partially dried paint that can ruin your paint job. To filter them out, buy a pack of paint strainers. These cheap mesh bags catch the goobers and purify the paint. Fussy painters use them even on paint that's fresh off the store shelf.

STRAINER

Roll paint right

Get smooth, even coverage every time

Ask 10 painters how to roll a wall and you'll get 10 answers—some simple, some complicated, some incomprehensible. The method shown here is one of the simpler approaches, easy to understand and master. As you gain experience, you'll develop your own variations and—like a pro painter—you'll determine that your way is the *only* way.

Before you roll

Once you start rolling a wall, you can't stop until that wall is done. If one swath of paint starts to dry before you complete the neighboring swath, you'll end up with differing textures where those two areas meet. So have everything ready to go.

■ Mask all the woodwork. Remember that rollers throw off fine drops of paint that will fall on all surrounding surfaces.
■ Brush paint onto all the areas where a roller can't go: Along trim and inside corners, and around switches and outlets.
■ Screw a long handle into the roller frame. There are special handles made just for this, but a push-broom handle works, too.

Get a good roller

A cheap roller might save you five bucks, but it won't hold much paint, so you'll have to reload more often and the project will take longer. Worse, it will leave hundreds of tiny fibers on your wall. Ugly. Be sure to get a roller labeled "shed-resistant."

What to avoid

The goal is to spread paint evenly, without lightly covered areas or heavy coverage that leaves large, stringy bumps. Above all, you want to avoid ridges created by the edge of the roller. After loading the roller with paint, ridges are inevitable, so the solution is to go back and flatten them after the roller is unloaded.

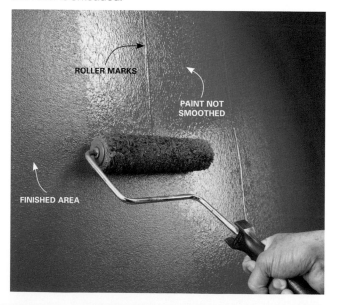

ROLLER MARKS

PAINT NOT SMOOTHED

FINISHED AREA

A 3-step process

FULLY LOADED ROLLER COVER

BRUSH PAINT AROUND EDGES FIRST

1 Get the paint on the wall
Load the roller with paint. Starting about a foot above the baseboard, roll upward. About halfway up, veer over a few inches and continue up the wall. When the roller is about a foot from the ceiling, roll straight down. Continue rolling up and down to spread the paint from baseboard to ceiling.

2 Repeat step one

Reload the roller and cover another swath of the wall. Don't worry about uneven coverage or ridges at this point—just get the wall covered quickly. Water-based paints dry fast. If you move too slow, some areas will become sticky before you can smooth them and you'll end up with texture differences on the paint's surface.

3 Smooth it out

Steps one and two will give you a covered section about 4 ft. wide, but it won't look good. So go back to the beginning—without reloading the roller—and make long up-and-down strokes to even out the paint. Press lightly and overlap your strokes by 3 to 4 in. Repeat this process to cover the entire wall.

Trouble at the top of the wall?

It's not easy to cover the upper end of the wall *and* avoid slopping paint on the ceiling. If you see uncovered spots up there, unscrew the long handle from the roller frame and immediately make a horizontal pass.

Spray paint perfectly

And apply flawless wood finishes, too

Do it right, and a sprayed-on coat of paint is absolutely flawless. Do it wrong, and you've got a sloppy, spattered mess. The same goes for clear wood finishes like lacquer or spray-can polyurethane. Whether you're painting or clear-coating, here are some tips to avoid trouble and achieve perfection.

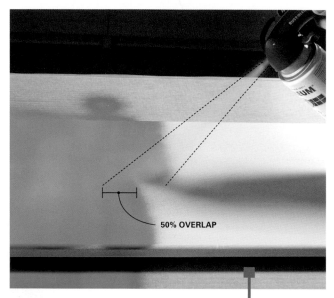

50% OVERLAP

Overlap the spray pattern

If you overlap just a little, you'll get narrow bands of heavy coverage. Instead, overlap the spray about halfway over the previous pass. That way, the entire surface will get the same coverage.

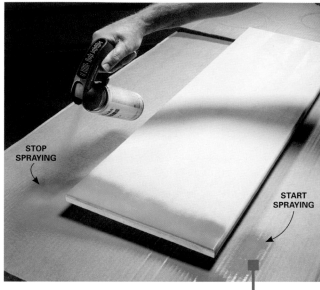

STOP SPRAYING

START SPRAYING

Start before and stop after

Spray nozzles tend to spit out a few large droplets when you start spraying and spit again when you stop. To keep sputter splatter off your project, pull the trigger before you're over the target and release the trigger after you're past the edge.

Get a handle

If you've sprayed a project that required a few cans of paint, you already know about finger strain and pain. For less than five bucks, a trigger handle not only prevents the pain, but also gives you better control of the can.

Don't swing an arc

It's the most natural motion for your arm, but it gives you heavy buildup at the center of the surface and poor coverage at the ends. So instead, move the can parallel to the surface. Concentrate on straight, steady motion for even coverage.

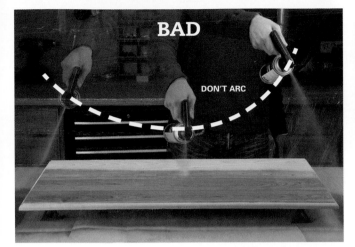

BAD

DON'T ARC

GOOD

KEEP THE CAN PARALLEL TO THE WORK

Go light on vertical surfaces

You've probably heard this many times before, but it's true: Several light coats are better than one heavy coat, especially on a vertical surface where heavy coats mean runs. Nobody has ever regretted going too light, but every experienced spray painter knows the agony of drips and sags.

Wear a respirator

Spray cans fill the air with a fine mist and solvents. Open windows and doors to provide ventilation and wear an organic vapor respirator to protect your lungs. Working outside is the most effective way to avoid breathing fumes, but wind can blow away your paint before it reaches the surface, while bugs and falling leaves wreck your finish.

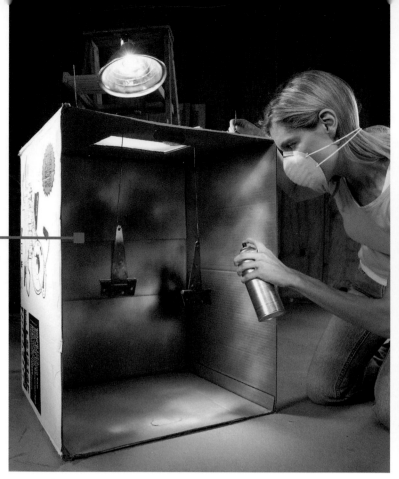

Make a spray booth

Take a tip from pro finishers and contain messy "over-spray" with a spray booth. Yours can be a simple cardboard box. Cut a hole in the top to let in light. The hole also lets you suspend items from a coat hanger and spin the item so you can hit all sides.

Voice of experience

Let it rest in peace

My son and I painted our rowboat perfectly. For faster drying, I started up a fan—and blew dust all over it, creating thousands of tiny "dust whiskers." There are lots of ways to destroy a finish with dust before it dries: Opening the garage door, running a shop vacuum, sweeping the floor... I'm sure you can invent your own method. Or you can just walk away and let it dry in peace.

Mark Hawley,
The Family Handyman
Field Editor

2" DRYWALL SCREWS

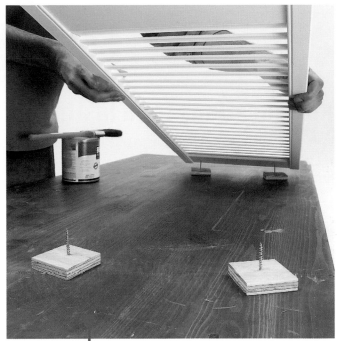

Elevate to avoid sticking

If your project is sitting directly on a workbench or newspaper, it's impossible to paint it without also gluing it to the work surface. So whether you're spraying paint or brushing, find some way to raise the work. Screws driven into furniture legs work great. Scraps of plywood with protruding screws also solve the problem.

Spin and spray

On some projects, you'll walk miles circling the item to spray all the surfaces. So pick up a lazy Susan turntable at a discount store and save some legwork.

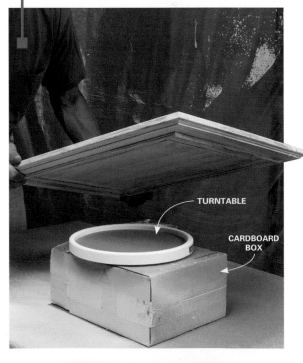

TURNTABLE

CARDBOARD BOX

Unclog a nozzle

When you're done painting, hold the can upside down and spray for a few seconds until only propellant comes out. That almost always works to blast paint out of the nozzle, leaving it clear and open for the next job. If it doesn't, or if you forget, there's a fix: Soak the nozzle in nail polish remover. It may take a few hours to unclog the nozzle.

Hire the best roofer

Key questions for a lasting, leak-free roof

Nailing down asphalt shingles is one of the simplest jobs in construction. It's difficult to do wrong. But the preparation and details—especially where shingles meet dormers, chimneys or vents—aren't so easy. Here's how to find a roofer who will do it right.

Will you replace damaged or rusted flashing?

One of the most common roof leak sites is at the intersection of the roof and a wall, like the sides of a dormer. These areas are waterproofed with step flashing, a series of overlapping pieces of sheet metal that are bent to lap onto the wall. Make sure your roofer is planning to inspect the step flashing and explain your options for replacing or repairing it.

STEP FLASHING

Do you plan to tear off the old shingles and pull the nails?

When you're comparing bids, ask if the roofing contractor recommends tearing off the old shingles. Removing the old roofing materials allows the roofing contractor to inspect the roof sheathing and repair rot or other damage, exposes problems with flashings and provides a smooth surface that's easier to waterproof and roof over.

How will you charge for extra work, like replacing rotted wood?

Regardless of how careful the contractor is to include all the necessary work in the bid, there are bound to be surprises. For example, it's hard to know the condition of the roof sheathing until the shingles are removed, and at that point in the job you don't have much bargaining power. Include an hourly rate for extra work in the contract, or a square-foot price for replacing the sheathing.

Will you replace the roof vents and valley flashing?

It's a bad idea to save money by reusing roof vents, plumbing vent flashing or valley metal. Replacing all of these with new materials only adds a few hundred dollars to the cost of a typical roof, but ensures a leakproof job. For the best appearance, also ask the roofer to use metal that's prefinished to match the color of the shingles.

Once you start, will you stay on the job until it's done?

Less-reputable contractors may take your down payment, start the job, and then disappear for a few days to start other jobs. Make sure your contractor plans to stay until the job is done. And to ensure timely completion, don't make the final payment until every detail is complete.

Where roofs leak

Shingles rarely leak. It's where the shingles stop and meet other things that trouble usually occurs. Those are the areas to keep an eye on and the areas to ask a roofing contractor about. Here are three common trouble spots:

Chimney flashing

A proper chimney treatment includes step flashing, counterflashing that covers the step flashing and possibly a "cricket" to divert water away from the chimney. Be sure to ask your roofer about these details before you sign a contract.

Plumbing vents

Vent flashing has a limited life span. The rubber gasket cracks or the metal eventually rusts. Loose or missing nails also cause leaks. All-metal vent flashing lasts longer, because it doesn't rely on a rubber gasket. A good roofer will replace, not reuse, all vent flashings regardless of type.

Step flashing

L-shaped sections of flashing keep out water where the roof meets dormers, walls or skylights. Missing nails can allow it to slide down and let in water. Over many years, it can also rust away. Flashing that's in good condition can be left in place and reused, but don't trust any roofer who wants to simply slather roofing tar over it.

Voice of experience

Little leaks are a big deal

As a contractor, I roofed more than a hundred houses. So you might think I'd know better, but.... When I suspected a leak in my own roof, I was so busy working on other people's houses that I left it alone. When I finally got to it, I found rotten sheathing. Then I dug deeper and found rotten rafters, plus a thriving mold colony. Had I dealt with the leak early, it would have been quick and easy. But waiting cost me a couple days and a couple hundred bucks.

Travis Larson,
The Family Handyman **Senior Editor**

Hire the best painting contractor

Key questions for long-lasting exterior paint

Anyone can slap paint on a house and make it look good. But a lasting paint job requires tons of tedious prep work, and some painters take shortcuts around those time-consuming steps. Here's how to find one who won't.

What areas are you planning to caulk?

A thorough job of caulking extends the life of the paint job by preventing water from seeping under the paint and loosening it. Your painter should caulk cracks where the siding meets windows and doors, and any other cracks where water could enter (but not the cracks under lap siding).

How will you prepare the surface before painting?

Preparation is the key to a lasting paint job. Make sure your contractor is planning to wash the surface to remove dust, dirt and other contaminants, either by scrubbing or with a pressure washer. The next step should be scraping all loose paint followed by sanding and another wash or wipe-down to remove sanding dust.

What kind of paint do you plan to use?

Good painters use good paint, but they may not plan to use the best paint. Ask the painting contractor to include 100 percent acrylic exterior paint in the estimate. Even if you're charged a little extra, you'll save money in the long run.

Will you prime before caulking and painting?

Primers are absolutely necessary over bare wood and a good idea over old paint too. If there are layers of old paint with exposed edges, ask your painting contractor to use a binding primer on these areas. Binding primers form a flexible seal to help prevent old layers of paint from peeling off.

Find your property lines

It's the first step in any outdoor project

Before you build anything in your yard (a deck, fence, even a doghouse) you have to know where your property lines are. If you build over the line, or even too close to it, local authorities can make you demolish your project.

METAL DETECTOR

STAKE

Locate the stakes

Iron stakes mark property lines in most communities. They're typically located at corners and jogs where property lines meet. To get started, request a plot plan from city hall. You may be able to find the stakes by dragging a rake over the suspected location. But more likely, the stakes will be several inches underground. In that case, your best bet is to buy or rent a metal detector (cheapies cost less than $40). When you've found your target, dig to make sure that it's really a stake and not just a lost quarter.

FENCE LINE

PROPERTY LINE

SETBACK

Voice of experience

Setback regret

Before building my garage, I got the plans and location approved by the city. But during construction, I asked the contractor to extend the eaves by a few inches. When the inspector showed up, he noticed that the eaves went beyond the setback line. The correction cost me almost $1,000. Ouch.

Greg Handler, *The Family Handyman*
Field Editor

Know your setbacks, too

A "setback" is the minimum distance between the property line and any structure. Setbacks vary by community and the type of structure. A privacy fence, for example, can be closer to the property line than a garage or deck. Some cities also have setback rules for tree planting.

GREATEST GOOFS

Learn from the mistakes of others!

The Family Handyman magazine holds the world's largest collection of homeowner horror stories, all of them sent in by readers. Here are some of the most common mistakes homeowners make—and lessons for the rest of us.

The new fandango

I was in a hurry to get the new ceiling fan installed before my wife got home, so I didn't read the red tag attached to it and proceeded with the job. I finished the wiring just as she walked through the door and flipped the switch, anticipating her admiration. The fan spun faster and faster—then crashed to the floor. While cleaning up the broken bits, I found that red tag, which said something about proper support.

Al Michaels

Editor's note: A standard junction box designed to support a light fixture won't support a fan. That's why special support brackets are on the store shelf right next to the ceiling fans.

Topsy-turvy

At the end of the summer, I decided to beat the fall to-do list and remove the window air conditioner units at my law office. I proceeded to remove the screws from the window sash of the first unit and muscle it out myself. Well, it slipped and fell out the window a few feet into a mulched flower bed. My secretary asked if I could use some help with the next one. Stubbornly, I forged ahead by myself. The second unit was much larger and my plan of attack failed even more miserably as the unit slipped from my hands and went crashing to the sidewalk 10 ft. below. Luckily, no one was in its path.

Skip Spurling

Editor's note: Falling air conditioners are one of the most common (and dangerous) goofs we hear about. Get help!

How many DIYers does it take . . .?

I walked into the laundry room, turned on the light switch and nothing happened. Luckily, I had the tools and know-how to solve the problem. I tested the circuit and replaced the switch. When that didn't work, I replaced the fluorescent light's ballast. Still nothing. Then it dawned on me that it must be the bulb. Sure enough, once I replaced the bulb, it worked perfectly.

Gail N. Shultz

Editor's note: As your DIY knowledge grows, beware of the expertise trap: a tendency to look for complicated solutions. Whether you know a little or a lot, always try the simplest fix first.

Big porcelain doorstop

I helped a friend pull out his old water-wasting toilet and install a new one. After finishing, we decided to relax and watch the game on TV. About a half-hour later, we heard laughter coming from the bathroom. We rushed over and found his wife unable to close the bathroom door. The new toilet protruded a few inches farther, blocking the door from closing.

Jason Sheehan

Editor's note: There are two types of toilet bowls: standard and "elongated." A longer model may also block cabinet or shower doors. In a small bathroom, it can also be a shin-bruiser.

Dismantled dryer

When I tossed a load of wet towels into our clothes dryer and pushed the start button, the dryer made an unbearably shrill squealing noise. "Sounds like it's just a belt slipping," said my husband, pleased with his budding home repair skills. Hours later, however, he still couldn't find a way into the dryer to remove the screaming belt. In fact, he was doubly embarrassed because he couldn't reassemble the parts strewn around him on the floor. He declared defeat. A pro came out the next day and made no comment when I handed him the bag of dryer parts.

Larrilyn Lindquist

Editor's note: Whatever you take apart, the best way to avoid reassembly remorse is to take pictures as you disassemble.

Sprayed—and sprayed again

I propped up my new French doors outside and began painting one with my new spray gun. Then I went inside. While I was gone, the automatic sprinklers came on and soaked the doors. To make matters worse, the doors fell onto the newly mowed grass. I had to sand down the doors and start over.

Greg Alderete

Editor's note: Painting outdoors seems like a good idea, but leads to all kinds of trouble. The most common problems are bugs, leaves or dust in the wet paint.

Quick on the thaw!

It was time to defrost the workshop freezer before winter set in. We had already received a dose of cold weather, so my kerosene "bullet" heater was up and running. In a moment of genius, I decided to speed up the thawing process. I was in a hurry to meet my father-in-law (who had purchased the freezer as a gift for me a few years before), so I moved the heater closer to the refrigerator and continued to tidy up the garage.

Well, the bullet heater sure did the job. When I returned just a few minutes later, it had not only thawed all the ice but also melted the plastic liner and shelving!

Rob Weisbarth

Editor's note: Impatience while defrosting often leads to wrecked freezers. The most common mistake is to pry or chip the ice away. That's dangerous because you can easily damage the refrigerant lines inside the freezer.

This side up

When we moved into our new house, my first project was to install a cat door. I did an excellent job, making perfectly straight, accurate, splinter-free cuts. The only problem was that I cut the opening on the top of the door. The cat's name is Magic, but....

Stephen Gray

Editor's note: Doors often get cut or trimmed in the wrong spot. So follow this old carpenter's rule: Label the area that needs work with masking tape before you remove the door from the hinges.

Securely fastened

When our son moved into a new house, my husband built a beautiful oak shelf and screwed it to the wall. It looked great. The next day my son went to close a pocket door. It wouldn't budge. After a few seconds of inspection, he realized that the long shelf screws went right through the door. The shelf is now hanging on a different wall, and the door works fine, but all agree, it looks much better closed!

R. Groeger

Editor's note: When mounting something on a wall, here are three ways to avoid trouble: Ask yourself what might be inside the wall, use screws that are long enough (but not longer) and if it feels like you've hit something unexpected, stop!

Stained with guilt

My father and I decided it was time to stain the 7-ft.-high fence in my back yard. To speed up the job, we used a sprayer and hit the tough areas with a brush. Well, all went fine until the guy next door came over steaming mad. All over his car were specks that seemed to match the color of the fence. Red-faced with embarrassment, we realized the wind had carried our stain over and through the fence, depositing tiny droplets all over his car. The good news is, we didn't have to pay for a new paint job—a local body shop removed the damage for a reasonable $150!

Anthony Misunas

Editor's note: Whether you're spraying with a gun or an aerosol can, remember that paints and stains drift, especially outdoors.

Snap, crackle, poof!

To dampen the noise coming from our washer and dryer, I decided to fill the laundry room door with expanding foam. I drilled holes in the edges of the hollow-core door, inserted the nozzle and injected foam into each hole. Half an hour later, the door bulged and then broke open, releasing a sticky flood of foam.

Thomas Wood, Sr.

Editor's note: The instructions on a can of expanding foam tell you how much foam to use: "fill gaps 50%," for example. Overfilling can cause a huge mess—or destruction.

Master your drill

Bore perfect holes—in anything!

SCRAP WOOD

HOLE SAW

CLAMP

Prevent breakout

Any type of drill bit will bust out slivers as it breaks through the other side of the wood. Usually, that's not a problem. But when you need a neat exit hole, clamp on a scrap to prevent breakout. If you're using a hole saw or spade bit, here's another approach: Bore through until the point of the bit emerges on the other side. Then drill from the other side.

Straight in

When you need a hole that's perfectly perpendicular to the surface, tack two scraps of wood together and use the inside corner as a guide.

The right bit for the job

Twist bit
The standard choice for most holes up to 1/2 in. It bores through wood, drywall and metal.

Modified twist bit
It's like the old standard, but with a reengineered tip for faster drilling, easier starting and cleaner holes.

Brad-point bit
The pointed tip lets you position a hole with perfect precision, and the sharp outer edges eliminate splintering as the bit enters the wood.

Masonry bit
The carbide tip grinds into concrete, mortar, brick, stucco or stone.

Think before you drill

I was in a big hurry to finally hang that shelf above the vanity. With a little luck, I'd be done before kickoff. As I bored through the drywall, I hit something hard. No problem. A hard push broke through the obstruction—which turned out to be a pipe. Never did get to watch the game that day. Every contractor I know has a story with the same moral: When drilling, remember that there may be a surprise on the other side. And if you hit something that doesn't feel right, stop.

Brent Berger, carpenter and
***The Family Handyman* Field Editor**

Hammer into masonry

A standard drill equipped with a masonry bit is fine if you just need to punch a hole or two in soft brick or stucco. But for lots of holes or harder materials like concrete, you'll want a hammer drill. A hammer drill pounds the bit forward as it turns for much faster drilling. Hammer drills come in several sizes. Bigger is faster—and more expensive. But you can pick up a powerful drill at a reasonable price at any rental center.

Tile bit

It bores into ceramic tile and even glass. Some versions work with porcelain tile; others don't.

Spade bit

This is the most economical bit for drilling large holes (up to 2 in.) in wood or drywall. Some models have a screw tip for faster drilling.

Auger bit

The screw tip pulls the bit into wood, for fast drilling of large holes. These bits are worth the higher cost only if you're drilling hundreds of holes.

Hole saw

For really big holes (2 in. or more) in wood, drywall or thin metal, this is the most economical choice.

Drive screws like a pro

How to avoid 'cam-out' frustration

In theory, driving screws is goof-proof. Just turn the screw and it goes in. But there's one common frustration: The bit sometimes slips or "cams out," gnawing away at the screw head. In an instant, you're stuck with a partially driven screw, the head so wrecked that you can't drive it in or back it out. All you can do is turn it out with a pair of pliers. Here's how to avoid all that.

Push hard, really hard

Pressure is the best prevention for cam-out. With enough pressure behind it, the driver bit simply can't skip out of the screw head's slot. So get behind the drill and push. That's not possible when you're reaching overhead or off to one side, so in many cases the best way to prevent cam-out is to get up on a stool or move your ladder to get closer to the screw.

Drill before you drive

In most cases, you can drive construction screws without drilling a hole. But if you're having trouble, grab a drill bit that's slightly smaller than the diameter of the screw. Drill a hole and you'll find driving much easier. You'll also avoid splitting the wood as the screw sinks in.

Get a bit holder

It's possible to mount a bit directly into a drill's chuck. But instead, spend a couple bucks on a magnetic bit holder. The magnet is a handy feature, but the long shaft of the holder is more important. It lets you see whether your drill is aligned straight and true with the screw—and that helps to avoid cam-out.

Toss out battered bits

Over the past 30 years, I've spent countless Saturday afternoons helping inexperienced friends with building projects. Here's a typical scene: I hear the telltale chatter of cam-out, walk over to my friend, scowl, yank the drill out of his hand and insert a fresh bit. Problem solved. As driver bits wear, cam-out becomes inevitable. So keep a supply of new bits and toss out the old ones.

Travis Larson,
The Family Handyman **Senior Editor**

Choose better screws

Phillips-head screws are a lot easier to drive than screws with a single slot in the head. But when it comes to avoiding cam-out, some are even better. "Square-drive" screws, for example, resist cam-out well. For the very best cam-out resistance, use Torx or similar screws. Avoid traditional wood screws; they simply don't penetrate wood as easily as modern "construction" screws that have sharper tips. Some construction screws even have self-drilling tips for easier driving.

TORX CONSTRUCTION SCREW

PHILLIPS WOOD SCREWS

Drive screws at an angle

"Toe screwing" takes some practice, but it's worth the effort. It allows you to make connections you otherwise couldn't and to hide screws under boards where they won't be seen (under a deck railing as shown here, for example). To make it easier, drill a pilot hole before driving. Or try it without a pilot hole, using the same two-step technique.

STRAIGHT STARTER HOLE

1 Start out straight
Bore straight into the surface with a drill bit that's slightly smaller than the screw you'll use.

ANGLED PILOT HOLE

2 Continue at an angle
When you've drilled about 1/8 in. into the wood, keep the bit spinning while you shift the drill to a sharp angle.

Master the jigsaw

Make the most of this incredibly versatile tool

A jigsaw is perfect for any skill level. It's less intimidating than a circular saw and amazingly versatile—lots of projects require nothing more than a drill and a jigsaw. Here's how to do more and do it better with your jigsaw.

Find the right speed

Typically, there's an SPM (strokes per minute) "sweet spot" where the saw cuts fastest and cleanest and with the least vibration. Try different speeds by changing pressure on the trigger. Once you find the best speed, set the adjustable speed dial so you can pull the trigger all the way while maintaining the desired SPM.

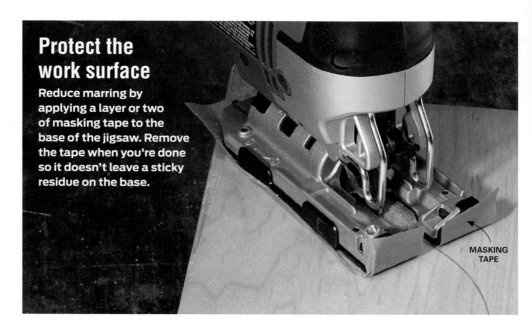

Protect the work surface

Reduce marring by applying a layer or two of masking tape to the base of the jigsaw. Remove the tape when you're done so it doesn't leave a sticky residue on the base.

MASKING TAPE

METAL-CUTTING BLADE

Cut anything

The main mission of a jigsaw is to cut curves in wood, and it's easy to overlook its other abilities. Instead of slaving away with your hacksaw, grab your jigsaw to quickly cut steel, copper or any metal. You can also cut plastics and tougher stuff like ceramic tile. The key to success is to match the blade to the material.

SQUARE

Let the tool do the work

Pushing as hard as you can on the saw doesn't necessarily make it cut faster; sometimes the opposite is true. And pushing too hard into a curve can cause you to veer off your line, burn the material or break a blade. Ease off on the pressure until the saw cuts smoothly with little vibration.

Square the blade

To get a square-edge cut, the blade has to be perfectly perpendicular to the base. So before you make a cut, make sure the blade isn't bent. If it is, just toss it or save it for jobs where a clean, square cut isn't important. With a straight, new blade in the saw, adjust the base to square it up.

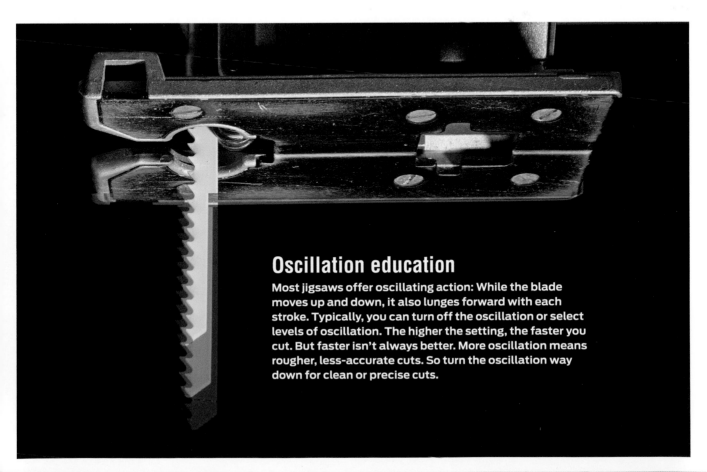

Oscillation education

Most jigsaws offer oscillating action: While the blade moves up and down, it also lunges forward with each stroke. Typically, you can turn off the oscillation or select levels of oscillation. The higher the setting, the faster you cut. But faster isn't always better. More oscillation means rougher, less-accurate cuts. So turn the oscillation way down for clean or precise cuts.

TEAR-OUT

TOP-SIDE TEAR-OUT

Cut with the "good" side down

Most jigsaw blades cut on the upstroke, so chips and splinters occur mostly on the top of the wood. So if you value one side of a board more than the other, make sure you keep the good side face down, and mark and cut the less important side.

DOUBLE-SIDED

FIBER CEMENT

FLUSH-CUT

CERAMIC

Beyond basic blades

There are a couple things to know about blades: The larger the teeth, the more aggressive and rougher the cut. And the narrower the blade, the tighter it can turn. Narrow, double-sided blades are especially suited for sharp turns. There are also specialty blades for various materials and even flush-cut blades that extend the cut to the front of the base.

Drill starter holes

If you need to cut out a hole in the center of the work surface—like a hole for a heat register in a sheet of beadboard wainscoting—drill a hole slightly bigger than your jigsaw blade in two opposite corners. That way, you can make four neat cuts starting from the two holes

ACCESS HOLE

ACCESS HOLE

Smart starting and stopping

Be sure the blade is up to speed before you start your cut. If you start the saw with the blade touching your material, it can grab hold and rattle the material, possibly damaging it. And let the saw come to a complete stop before you lift it. If you don't, you might experience the dreaded "woodpecker effect," when a moving blade bounces off the surface, leaving behind pockmarks and a bent blade.

Make relief cuts for sharp turns

There's a limit to how sharp a curve a jigsaw blade can cut—the narrower the blade, the sharper the turns it can make. If you try to force the blade into a turn tighter than it's capable of, you'll either veer off your line or break the blade. For the tightest turns, make relief cuts. The sharper the curve, the more relief cuts you'll need.

RELIEF CUTS

Measure accurately

Pro tips for perfect precision

Burn an inch

The hook at the end of a tape measure is designed to slip in and out a little. That movement compensates for the thickness of the hook, depending on whether you're taking inside or outside measurements. But a bent hook or worn rivets can lead to inaccuracy. So when you need precision, bypass hook-related errors by holding the tape at the 1-in. mark and making your mark exactly 1 in. beyond the desired measurement.

Longer is better

A 20-ft. tape measure is better than a 10-footer, even if you don't need to measure that far. Longer tapes generally have a wider, stiffer blade that will extend farther without bending and falling to the floor. That means you can measure longer distances without a helper holding one end.

A tape measure can hurt you—really

Sounds crazy, but any carpenter will agree: When a tape retracts from several feet out, it can pick up speed and slam into your finger with painful force. Slow it down by holding your finger against the underside of the blade.

Measure twice for long stretches

When you need to measure a long span and don't have a helper to hold the tape, take two measurements and add them up. This is also a super-accurate way to measure a space that's enclosed on both ends—inside a drawer, for example.

PENCIL MARK AT 5'

1 Measure halfway
Measure to a spot near the center and make a mark exactly at the nearest foot.

THIS MEASUREMENT PLUS 5'

2 Measure again
Measure from the other side and tally up the two measurements

Measure up, not down

When measuring something tall, work with gravity, not against it. To measure ceiling height, for example, butt the tape against the floor and extend it to the ceiling. Bend the tape at the ceiling and "eyeball" the measurement. You'll be able to get within 1/4 in. of the exact height.

Mark, don't measure

Whenever possible, pro carpenters leave their tape measures in their tool belts. Holding an item in place and marking it is often faster, easier and more accurate. Most importantly, it eliminates errors.

JAMB CENTER

SCRIBE FLUSH

Voice of experience

When precision matters

Two tapes may give you slightly different measurements. And sometimes, even a 1/16-in. variation spells trouble. So when I'm building furniture, I pick one tape, label it and use it throughout the job.

Stephen Evans, furniture maker and *The Family Handyman* Field Editor

Master the hammer

You can do more than just pound nails

Nail-pulling know-how

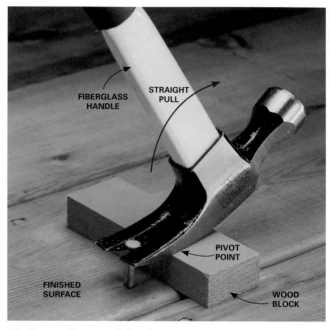

Pull sideways

The usual way to pull a nail is to lever the claw straight up. But when a nail won't budge, yank the handle to the side. That puts the pivot point closer to the nail for more pulling power.

Pull against a block

A small block under the claw does two things: It protects the surface beneath it and provides more pulling power, especially after the nail is partially removed.

Which weight?

For most people and most jobs, a 16-oz. hammer is about right. Avoid hammers with a jagged "waffle" texture on the striking face. When you miss a nail, they do ugly things to surfaces—or your thumb.

The versatile rip claw

If you're in the market for a hammer, buy one with a straight claw. Unlike a curved-claw hammer, a rip hammer—when swung backward—can dig holes, split wood and wreck stuff that needs wrecking.

No. 62

Find a stud

When technology fails, detective work prevails

What's a stud?

Studs are simply the vertical 2x4s (or 2x6s) that form the skeleton inside a wall. For heavy-duty projects, you need to know exactly where they are. When installing stair railings, for example, you need to anchor brackets to something solid like a stud. But for most jobs—like hanging pictures or towel bars—drywall anchors are strong enough.

The high-tech way

You can pick up an electronic stud finder at any home center for less than twenty bucks. Just run the gadget horizontally across the wall and it will tell you when it senses a stud. Stud finders work great on drywall. Sometimes they work well on old plaster and lath walls, sometimes not.

The detective's way

If you don't have a stud finder handy, or it won't work on your plaster walls, don't give up. The builders of your house left some clues:

Nail holes

Baseboards are almost always nailed to studs. Examine them closely and you'll find tiny dots of wood filler that reveal a stud location.

JUNCTION BOX

Switches and outlets

Electrical junction boxes are usually fastened to studs. To determine which side of the box is attached to the stud, you'll have to unscrew the cover plate. Then slip in a business card along the outer side of the box and feel for the stud.

Stud spacing

Studs are usually centered 16 in. apart (or sometimes 24 in.). So if you find one, you can find others with only a tape measure.

Mark studs with tape

There's no need to mark up walls with a pencil; a scrap of masking tape will do. If you need pinpoint precision, stick on the tape, then mark with a pencil.

Be ready for anything

Essential gear for makeshift solutions

Some products have so many uses that you just have to keep them on hand. Even if you don't have an immediate need for them, you will sooner or later. Here are a few favorites.

Stretch wrap

Seal boxes shut, tie down a load or wrap up unruly objects for storage. Keep a roll in the garage and you'll use it regularly. There's a lot of wrap on a roll, so even if you're a heavy user, it will last for years.

Duct tape

Whatever the problem, duct tape is the solution. There are dozens of different versions: light-duty, heavy-duty, transparent, glow-in-the-dark.... If you're only going to keep one roll on hand, get the expensive, heavy-duty stuff. It sticks better. The only thing you shouldn't use duct tape for is ductwork. That was its original purpose, but foil tape works much better.

Eraser sponges

When nothing else works, one of these pads probably will. The material they're made from was originally used for insulation. But it also provides very aggressive, very fine abrasion; that means it scours away surface stains without damaging most surfaces. Mr. Clean Magic Eraser and Scotch-Brite Easy Erasing Pad are two common brands.

Cabinet bumpers

Just keep a little pack of them in your junk drawer and you'll find unexpected uses for them. Shown here, for example, a couple bumpers will silence a toilet tank lid that rattles when kids stomp down the hall.

Pipe insulation

Until you have it, you won't understand how desperately you need it. Aside from insulating pipes, it provides bump protection when storing table leaves—and in a hundred other situations. Pipe insulation's close cousin, the swim noodle, is thicker and better for some tasks, like stopping a hatchback from bashing into the overhead door.

SWIM NOODLE

Zip ties

They're great for holiday decorating and a hundred other fastening jobs. And they're so cheap that you can keep stashes in several strategic locations: garage, kitchen, laundry room. Wherever you put them, they'll get used.

No. 64

Finish wood flawlessly

Pro tips for silky-smooth perfection

Wood finishing is a skill nobody truly masters. Even the pros make mistakes. But with some patience and attention to detail, beginners can do it right. Your best approach is to start on something small and simple before you take on more challenging projects.

The basic process

There are a dozen ways to color and coat wood. But for most DIYers, stain followed by a clear coating of polyurethane is the best combination.

100-GRIT SANDING SPONGE

LIGHT GRIP

1 Sand it smooth
On coarse-grained wood like oak, start with 100-grit sandpaper, then go to 150-grit. On fine-grained woods like cherry, birch or maple, you need to end with a higher grit; 100-150-220 is a good combination.

2 Add color
Apply stain with a brush or rag, then wipe off the excess with a rag. Spread out used rags to dry before putting them in the trash. Stain-soaked rags are a spontaneous-combustion hazard.

3 Apply polyurethane
This is the hard part; you have to work fast and apply the poly smoothly. Before the poly begins to dry, drag a brush lightly over it to smooth it. Apply two to four coats, lightly sanding between coats.

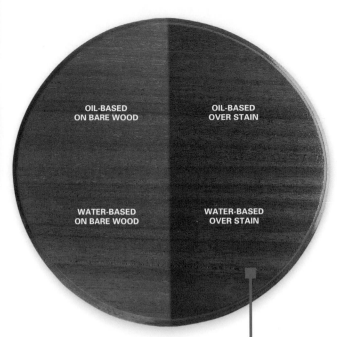

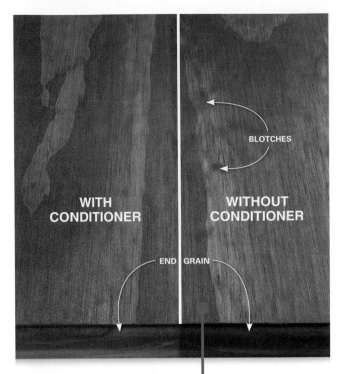

Water-based poly vs. oil: What's the difference?

Water- and oil-based polyurethanes are equally tough, but there are some important differences:

- Water-based poly goes on milky and dries crystal clear. Oil has a warm amber tone.
- Oil-based poly dries much slower, which makes it easier to smooth out before it becomes gummy. This is a big advantage on large surfaces.
- Water-based poly cleans up with water. Oil requires mineral spirits. Oil also emits harmful fumes, so you need good ventilation.

Beware of blotches

Some woods absorb stain unevenly, which causes dark blotches to appear. Birch, maple, pine and cherry can all play this ugly trick on you. It's hard to eliminate this effect, but you can limit it by applying a wood conditioner before staining. Conditioner also prevents wood's end grain from absorbing more stain than the face grain. It's available wherever stains and finishes are sold.

Voice of experience

Test, test, test!

In just 30 minutes, I once ruined a bookcase that took me 65 hours to build. The stain went on blotchy and the color was nothing like I expected. Every woodworker I know has a similar story (or several). I've learned that you can't rely on the stain samples in stores. Actual color varies a lot, depending on the type of wood and how you prepared it for finishing. Now I always do several sample tests. Sometimes I mix stains to get the color I want.

David Radtke,
The Family Handyman **Contributing Editor**

EXTRA-FINE
SANDING PAD

Sand between coats

Even master finishers end up
with a few imperfections in the
clear coating. To remove them,
lightly sand the entire surface
with extra-fine sanding pads or
paper. Be careful not to sand through
the finish, especially along edges. Clean up
the fine dust with a vacuum then a tack cloth
before applying the next coat.

Expensive brushes are worth it

Spend extra for a good-quality brush. Even if you spend $20
or more, you won't regret it. Quality brushes hold more
finish, lay it on smoothly and are less likely to leave lost bris-
tles in your clear coat. If you clean your brush immediately
after use, it'll serve you well far into the future.

If you choose a satin finish...

Multiple coats of satin or
semigloss poly can obscure
the wood's grain. Ugly.
That's why experienced
finishers often start out
with gloss. Then, if they
want less sheen, they add
a final coat of satin.

Wipe-on poly is wonderful

Polyurethane that's formulated for
application with a cloth has some
important advantages over the
brush-on stuff: It goes on thin, so it's
less likely to run, sag or pick up airborne dust. Smooth application with
a cloth is also easier than brushing,
especially on shaped surfaces. The
big disadvantage of wipe-on is that it
forms a very thin coating, so you have
to apply lots of coats to equal one
coat of brushed-on finish.

Spray or wipe the final coat

Brushing is a good way to build up a thick layer of poly, but it's also difficult to apply smoothly. So woodworkers often brush on a few coats, then use spray or wipe-on poly for the final coat or two. Spraying and wiping are more likely to end in perfection.

Wood can go wild

Wood expands and contracts as the humidity changes. And if you finish just one side of wood, the unfinished side will shrink or swell differently from the finished. Years ago, I learned this the hard way when I finished only the top of a table. Over a few weeks, it went from perfectly flat to wild and wavy. The moral of the story is this: Whenever you finish the "show" side of a large piece of solid wood, slap a coat of poly on the hidden side too. That will equalize the effects of humidity changes.

Elisa Bernick,
The Family Handyman
Contributing Editor

Caulk like a pro

Anyone can seal a crack—making it look good is the challenge

Laying a smooth bead of caulk is like playing the piano: You can learn to do it well, but don't expect applause for your first efforts. It's best to start where perfection is less important (exterior window trim, for example), and then move on to high-visibility work like a tub surround.

Clean the tip

Start every bead with a clean tip. Plan to muck up two or three rags over the course of a caulking project.

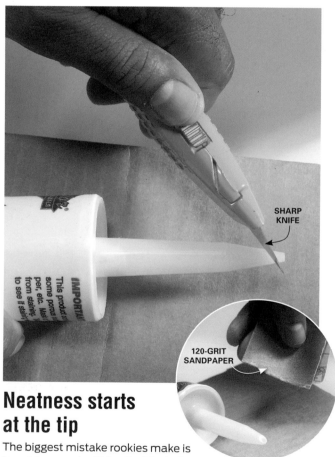

Neatness starts at the tip

The biggest mistake rookies make is to cut too much off the tip. That allows too much caulk to flow out, which leads to a mess. So cut near the end at a sharp angle. You can always trim off more if needed. Smooth and round the cut tip with sandpaper.

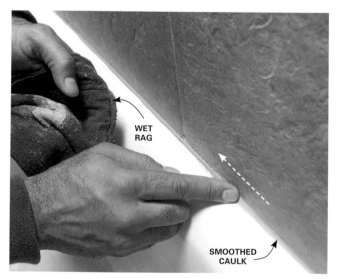

Smooth it with your finger

Immediately after laying the bead, drag your finger across it. In order to slide smoothly, your finger needs lubrication. For acrylic/latex caulk, dip your finger in water. With silicone, slip on a surgical-style glove and use alcohol.

Don't use your wrists

Every golfer knows that the best way to control a putter is with the upper body. The same goes for caulking. Use your upper body, or even your legs, to move the tube, not your wrists.

Meet in the middle

When you have a long bead to run and can't get it done in one pass, don't start again where you left off. It's hard to continue a bead without creating a glob. Instead, start at the other end and meet in the middle.

Nix the squeeze tube

Squeeze tubes are OK at first, but as they empty, it's harder and harder to squeeze out a steady, consistent flow. That means a lumpy bead. Better to spend a few bucks on a caulk gun and use gun tubes.

Install wire shelving

Tips you won't find in the manufacturer's instructions

Wire shelving is fantastic stuff: versatile, inexpensive and DIY-friendly. Manufacturers give you all the details you *need* to know, but here are some pro tips you *should* know for a faster, smoother, stronger installation.

Buy extra parts

Even if you're putting up just one shelf, have extra thingamajigs on hand. Returning a few parts later is better than halting the progress of your project and running to the store.

A bolt cutter works best

Cutting a shelf to length means cutting through four hard steel rods. A hacksaw will do the job just fine. But if you're installing lots of shelves, consider spending $30 or so on a bolt cutter. It will save you time and arm strain.

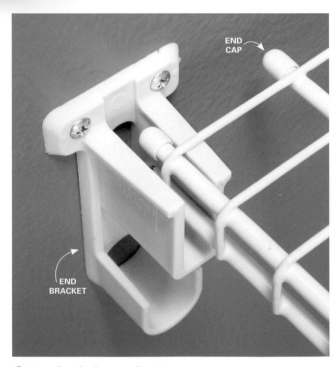

END CAP

END BRACKET

Cut shelving short

Before cutting a shelf, measure wall to wall and then subtract an inch. That allows for the thickness of the end brackets, plus a little wiggle room. Cutting to the exact spacing between end brackets leads to gouges in the wall as you install the shelf. And don't skip the end caps. Without them, clothes will snag on cut ends.

Avoid uplift

Back wall clips will hold the shelf up, but when there are a bunch of clothes hanging on the front of the shelf, the back edge can lift. To hold it down, screw a retaining clip to a stud near the center of the shelf. If the shelf is more than 8 ft. long, install a couple, evenly spaced.

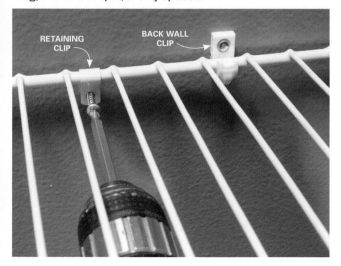

RETAINING CLIP

BACK WALL CLIP

Prevent tipovers

Wire makes great pantry shelving, except for one thing: Small cans and bottles tend to tip into the gaps between wires. To prevent that, pick up some pegboard when you buy the shelving. It's inexpensive and comes with a white coating that's easy to clean. Some home centers will even cut it to size for you.

PEGBOARD

Voice of experience

Buying advice from a pro

I've installed thousands of wire shelves over the past 15 years and have seen two mistakes over and over again. First, too many homeowners pay extra for heavy-duty shelving they don't really need. Standard closet-gauge shelving is fine for most closets. Save the heavy-gauge stuff for garages. Second, consider adding a hanger bar. It's a lot more convenient than hooking hangers on the shelf. My clients sometimes decline this feature because it adds around 30 percent to the cost—then they call me later to add a bar or two.

CORNER HANGING BAR

BAR HANGER SUPPORT

Tim Bischke, closet installer and *The Family Handyman* Field Editor

CLOSET GAUGE

HEAVY GAUGE

Connect coax cable right

Mistakes mean slow downloads and rotten reception

Coaxial cable provides brilliantly simple connections for all kinds of high-tech gadgetry (TVs, routers, cell phone boosters, surveillance systems, etc.). But "simple" doesn't mean foolproof. Coax is, in fact, finicky stuff; minor mistakes can lead to major performance problems. Here's how to avoid trouble and let the data flow fast.

Don't use a cheap splitter

Every time you connect another cable to the main incoming cable, you weaken the signal. But you have to split the signal in order to add another TV. Still, you can avoid poor picture quality. First, buy a splitter that can handle the bandwidth needed by high-definition TV and high-speed Internet. If you get poor picture quality after installing a splitter, call your cable provider (they may increase your signal strength). At electronics stores, you can also install an amplifier to boost the signal from your antenna, cable service or satellite dish.

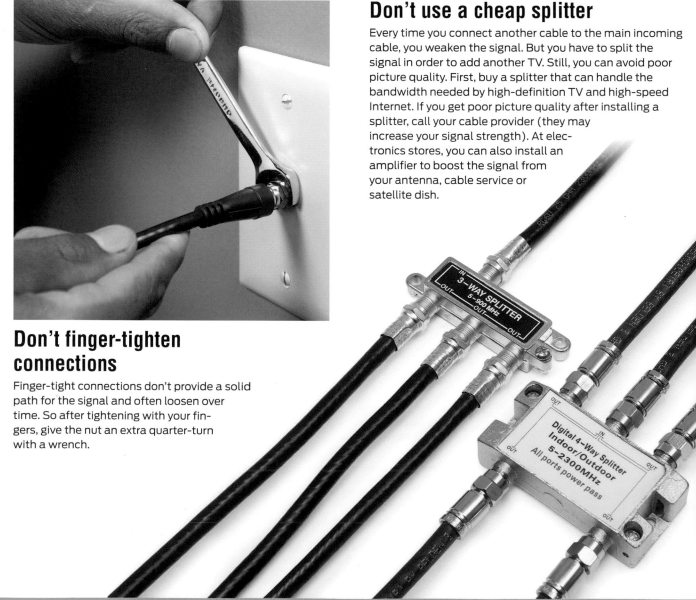

Don't finger-tighten connections

Finger-tight connections don't provide a solid path for the signal and often loosen over time. So after tightening with your fingers, give the nut an extra quarter-turn with a wrench.

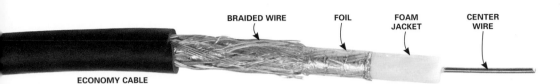

BRAIDED WIRE   FOIL   FOAM JACKET   CENTER WIRE

ECONOMY CABLE

Don't buy cheap cable

Shielding is what counts when it comes to cable quality. It blocks interference and keeps the signal clean. So skip the "dual-shield" or "double-shield" cable and go for a "quad-shield" product; it has twice as much braided wire and foil shielding. After spending big bucks on a TV or computer, it doesn't make sense to skimp on cable.

QUAD-SHIELD CABLE

Don't kink the cable

When you kink coax cable, the center wire gets too close to the shielding. That leads to interference. Once coax is kinked, the damage is done. You can't fix it by straightening the cable.

OUCH

Reception getting worse?

If your TV reception seems to be worse than it once was, it may not be your imagination. Coax connectors outdoors eventually corrode and weaken the signal. This is one of the most common causes of poor reception. Your cable provider can solve the problem by replacing the connectors. You can do it yourself, but you'll have to spend at least $20 on special tools.

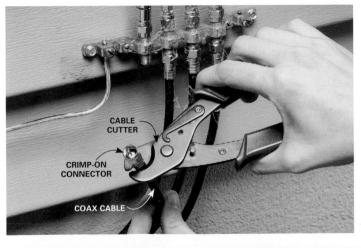

CABLE CUTTER

CRIMP-ON CONNECTOR

COAX CABLE

Replace a light fixture

The instructions cover the basics—here's how to handle complications

It's the perfect job for a rookie electrician. Just disconnect a few wires, take down the old fixture and connect the new one. And while you're at it, eliminate the $100 electrician's charge. But some of the steps aren't quite as easy as they appear. Here are some solutions from professional electricians.

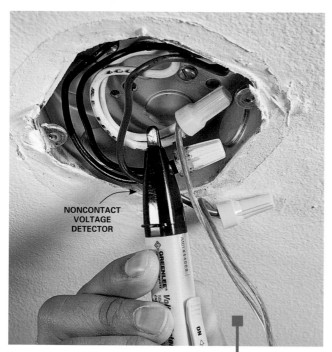

NONCONTACT VOLTAGE DETECTOR

Be sure the power is off

The junction box in the ceiling may contain wires from more than one circuit. So even if the light switch is off and you've turned off power at the main panel, there may be a live wire in the box. So always probe with a noncontact voltage detector before you disconnect any wires.

> **CAUTION!** If the wires in the box are dull gray instead of brown or copper-colored, you have aluminum wiring and need to call in an electrician to work with it.

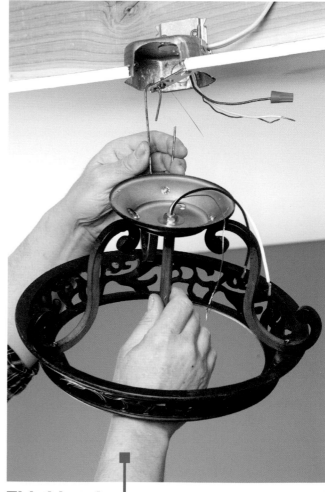

Third hand

Connecting a fixture takes three hands: one to hold the fixture and two to make connections. If you don't have three hands, hang the fixture from a scrap of wire.

Two mounting systems

If you're not familiar with them (or even if you are), light fixture mounting systems can drive you crazy. There are two types, and just knowing what's under the canopy is half the battle. If you see two screws or screw caps on the canopy, you have the type on the left. If not, you have the type on the right.

Mounting with screws and cap nuts

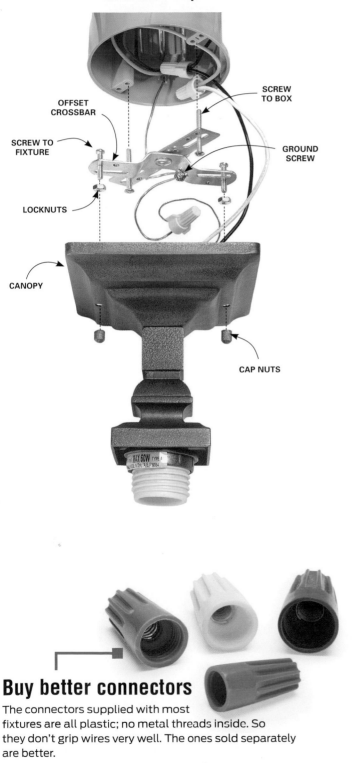

OFFSET CROSSBAR

SCREW TO FIXTURE

SCREW TO BOX

GROUND SCREW

LOCKNUTS

CANOPY

CAP NUTS

MAX 60W TYPE A

Mounting with a threaded pipe

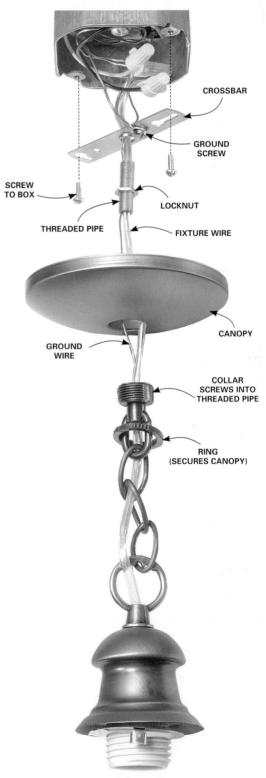

CROSSBAR

GROUND SCREW

SCREW TO BOX

LOCKNUT

THREADED PIPE

FIXTURE WIRE

GROUND WIRE

CANOPY

COLLAR SCREWS INTO THREADED PIPE

RING (SECURES CANOPY)

Buy better connectors

The connectors supplied with most fixtures are all plastic; no metal threads inside. So they don't grip wires very well. The ones sold separately are better.

Voice of experience

Beware of obstructions

Every once in a while, I show up at a home to install a new fixture and run into an obstacle. It might be a hanging fixture that won't allow a door or cabinet door to open or a sconce that blocks the medicine cabinet. The worst part is that I sometimes don't recognize the problem until I install the fixture. Ouch. Measure first.

Al Hildenbrand, electrical contractor and *The Family Handyman* wiring whiz

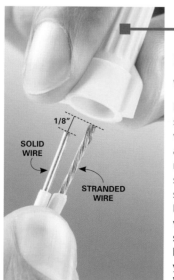

Connecting solid wire to stranded

Light fixtures come with stranded wire, while the wires in your junction box are solid. Twist-on connectors tend to grip the solid wire, but not the stranded. That makes a lousy connection. To prevent that, just extend the stranded wire about 1/8 in. beyond the solid before you twist on the connector. Works every time.

SOLID WIRE

STRANDED WIRE

1/8"

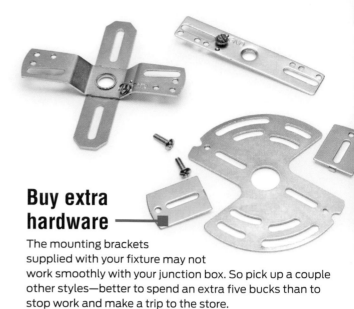

Buy extra hardware

The mounting brackets supplied with your fixture may not work smoothly with your junction box. So pick up a couple other styles—better to spend an extra five bucks than to stop work and make a trip to the store.

Some fixtures are too hot

If your home was built before 1985, it probably has wiring that can't handle the heat generated by many newer fixtures. These hot fixtures carry a warning: "Use wire rated for at least 90 degrees C." The easiest solution is simply to avoid a fixture with this warning in a pre-1985 home. But if just must have that fixture, check your wiring. If you see "NM-B" or "UF-B" on the outer sheathing of the cable or "THHN" or "THWN-2" on the insulation of individual wires, you're OK for hot fixtures.

Short wires, no problem

When the wires in the junction box are too short, connecting them is frustrating. Here's the solution: Buy some "stab-in" connectors. In tight spots, they're much easier to use than twist-on connectors. Cut a couple 5-in. sections of wire (of the same gauge as the wires in the box) and connect them. Then connect the fixture wires to the added wires with twist-on connectors.

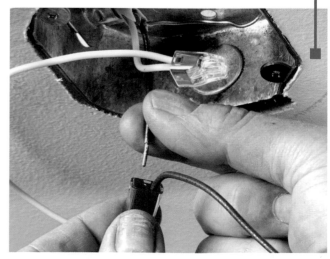

Make home chores easier

Simple upgrades that pay off over and over again

Your home isn't just a place to live. It's also a workplace. And as with any workplace, efficiency improvements pay off big in time and labor savings. Here are a few ideas to get you started.

Voice of experience

Every year, I promise myself that I'll do at least two things to make home tasks more efficient. After 15 years of efficiency upgrades, I have more time for golf than any of my friends.

Frank Anderson, *The Family Handyman* Field Editor

Every home needs a hand cart

A hand cart makes all kinds of jobs easier, indoors and out. Some models cost less than $20 at home centers.

1/2" HOLE

Trash-can vacuum breaker

Ever wonder why a bag is so hard to lift out of a trash can? It's because the bag forms an airtight seal inside the can, which in turn creates a vacuum in the can. Take two minutes to drill a hole near the bottom of the can and you'll never have that problem again.

High-reach vacuum

If you have cobwebs around skylights or chandeliers, there's no need to climb a ladder. Just measure the diameter of your vacuum hose and then buy PVC pipe that's similar in size. Home centers carry sections up to 10 ft. long. Also ask for a rubber pipe coupler to connect the hose to the pipe.

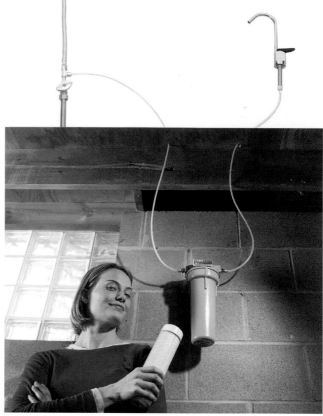

Easy filter changes

Most water filters are installed under the sink. The trouble with that is that you have to clear out the cabinet just to change the filter. So if you're getting a filtration system installed, put the filter in an easy-access spot, like a nearby closet or in the basement below.

Clear closet floors

Cluttered closet floors get bypassed by the vacuum or broom. Clearing out all the junk is just too much work. But if you mount a wire shelf just a few inches above the floor, you can clean floors easily and still have space for stuff that would otherwise clutter the floor.

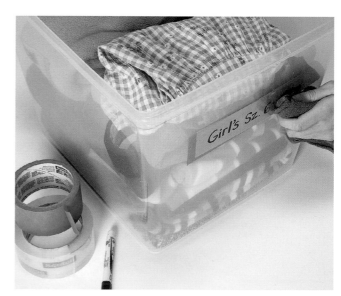

Labels save time

If you don't label storage bins, you're guaranteed to waste time rummaging through them to find stuff. Here's one flexible recipe: a layer of masking tape for legibility, covered with clear tape and then labeled with a dry-erase marker for easy changes. But however you do it, label those bins and boxes.

Raise your dryer

Set your dryer on a box and save your back. All it takes is a simple box made from 2x8 boards and topped off with 3/4-in. plywood. It's a great project for a first-time carpenter. Before you begin, make sure your dryer's exhaust duct, power cord and gas line will accommodate the move up. If you have a rigid duct rather than a flexible duct, you'll have to alter it.

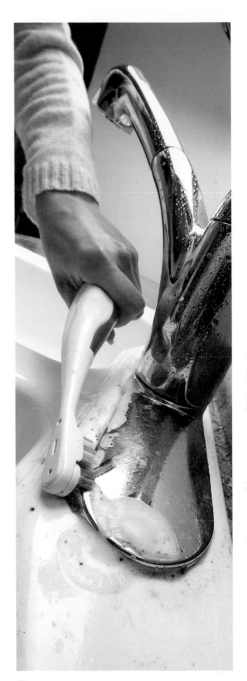

Furnace filter system

Regular filter replacement is the very best thing you can do to keep your furnace in top condition. And here's a way to keep track of that task: Buy several filters and label them. With some systems, monthly filter changes are best. Others can go a few months between changes.

Power scour

Everybody saves old toothbrushes for cleaning jobs, but an electric toothbrush is even better, and you can get one for less than 10 bucks at a discount store.

No. 70

Wash windows like a pro

Squeaky clean in less than a minute

Washing windows is a slow, frustrating, miserable job—but only if you do it wrong. Do it like the pros and it's easy. All it takes is a few basic tools and a simple process.

Start with the right tools

Glass cleaner and paper towels are not the way to go. Instead, stop by a home center and spend about $20 on cleaning gear:

■ A scrubber for large areas, or a sponge if you have divided-glass windows.
■ A high-quality squeegee. Don't go cheap; a good squeegee is well worth an extra five bucks. A 10- or 12-in. model is best for large areas.
■ A microfiber rag or two. Microfiber absorbs more and cleans glass better than other fabrics.
■ A razor scraper for paint specks or other tough spots. If you don't find one alongside cleaning supplies, try the paint aisle.
■ You'll also need rags to wipe off the squeegee, a bucket and dishwashing liquid (1 teaspoon per 2 gallons of water).

SQUEEGEE

SCRUBBER

5 steps to perfection

1 Scrub the glass

SCRUBBER

Dip the scrubber into a bucket of soapy water and squeeze out the excess water. Then scrub. Be sure to cover every square inch of glass.

CLEAN STRIP

TOUCHING GLASS

2 Create a clean strip

Tip the squeegee so that only the end contacts the glass. Then drag the squeegee down along one side of the window. This clean strip makes it easier to start the horizontal strokes.

3 Make the first squeegee pass

Keep the top of the squeegee in contact with the upper edge of the window. Wipe the squeegee on your pocket rag after each pass.

NARROW CLEAN STRIP

POCKET RAG

4 Work your way down

Overlap each pass by about 2 in. Angle the squeegee slightly to direct water down the window.

2" OVERLAP

ANGLE SQUEEGEE

WIPE PERIMETER

MICROFIBER RAG

5 Wipe the perimeter

Wrap a microfiber rag around your finger and run it around the outer edge of the window. That's it—you're done!

Yes, you can squeegee inside, too

The pros do it all the time, even in houses with varnished woodwork. The key is to squeeze almost all of the water out of the scrubber. Wipe up any water that dribbles onto woodwork. If you have divided windows, you'll need a smaller squeegee.

NARROW SQUEEGEE

DIVIDED-LITE WINDOW

Clean faster, clean better

Pro tips for smarter cleaning— and avoiding it

Everybody knows how to clean. But as with any task, some know better than others. So even if you've kept your house spotless for years, you can learn a few things from pros who do it all day, every day.

Minimize scum with synthetic soap

"Synthetic" soaps make cleaning your shower or bath easier because they don't contain the ingredients that create tough soap scum. Any liquid or gel soap is synthetic. Most bar soaps are standard soaps. But a few, including Zest and Ivory, are synthetic.

Use a HEPA vacuum filter

Stop blowing dust all over with an old vacuum. A HEPA vacuum filter captures microscopic airborne particulates. Old-fashioned paper or conventional vacuum bags pick up only about 30 percent of dust and allergens, and blow the rest back into the air.

CHANDELIER CLEANING SPRAY

PLASTIC TARP

Rinse off a chandelier

Cleaning a chandelier the standard way—wiping each part by hand—takes forever. Instead, spread a plastic tarp on the floor and douse the fixture with chandelier cleaner. Spray it on heavy to rinse off the dust. The cleaner that's left on the chandelier evaporates fast and won't leave spots. You probably won't find chandelier cleaner in stores, but it's available online.

Blow out the garage

Forget the broom—just open the door and blast out the dust and debris with an electric leaf blower. Works great on porches, too. Be sure to wear a dust mask, plus eye and ear protection.

Coat shower doors to keep them clean

When the beads of water left on your glass shower door dry out, they leave minerals behind that are at best unsightly and at worst can be tough as nails to remove. You can avoid beading water altogether by coating the glass with an auto-glass treatment. Aquapel and Rain-X are two brands that you'll find at auto parts stores and some discount stores.

Steam-clean a microwave

Just boil water to soften up the baked-on gunk in your microwave. For a fresh scent, add a slice of lemon. Allow the steam to work for 5 to 10 minutes, then wipe everything clean.

FILTER

Vacuum first, then scrub

Do you ever find yourself chasing strands of wet hair or running into dust balls in the corners with your sponge or cleaning rag? You can eliminate this nuisance by vacuuming the bathroom before you get out your cleaning solutions.

For a really thorough cleaning, start at the top, vacuuming the dust from light fixtures and the top of window casings. Then work your way down. And finally, vacuum the floor methodically so you cover every inch. You don't want to leave any stray hair or dust bunnies to muck up your cleaning water. A soft-bristle upholstery brush works best for this type of vacuuming.

Clean your vacuum filter—or else

Bagless vacuum filters are convenient and efficient. But if you don't clean them regularly, the strain of pulling air through a dirty filter can burn out the vacuum's motor. The typical way to clean the filter of a bagless vacuum is to tap it against the inside of a trash can until most of the dust falls off. But that raises a cloud of dust and doesn't get the filter completely clean. For faster, neater, more effective filter cleaning, use a shop vacuum. Clean prefilter screens and post-filters the same way. Just remember to be gentle with the shop vacuum's nozzle. Some filters have a coating that you can scrape off if you press too hard.

Get a doormat

Eighty-five percent of the dirt in a home is carried in on shoes! A doormat helps to prevent that. Better yet, nag your family members to take shoes off.

Microfiber: better in every way

Microfiber fabrics are made from incredibly tiny strands that reach into crevices and form millions of little pockets that hold dirt particles. The strands also have sharp scouring edges, so microfiber cloths often clean effectively without chemicals or even water (you can use cleaners or water if you choose). When used dry, microfiber cloths generate static electricity, which attracts and holds dust. To clean out all that dirt, just toss microfiber items in the washing machine. Find microfiber dust cloths, mops and other cleaning gear at most discount stores.

MICROFIBER CLEANING GEAR

MICROFIBER DUSTING GLOVE

Install a detachable toilet seat

Get the hinges on the toilet seat and everything underneath clean by installing a detachable toilet seat. Most are easy to remove by just twisting two hinge caps about a quarter of a turn. Then you have easy access to clean under the hinges. You'll find detachable seats at home centers.

Use a multipurpose cleaner

Stop using four to six products to clean your bathroom. The pros use one multipurpose cleaner that does it all. Our pros recommend Mr. Clean Multi-Surfaces Cleaner with Febreze.

Make yard chores easier

Quick improvements that save time and toil

Everyone loves a project that takes a little time now and pays off big in time savings later. So here are some upgrades that will speed up chores every summer for years to come.

Mowing borders eliminate trimming

A ground-level row of stones or bricks provides a border that you can mow right over. No need to get out the grass trimmer. This trick works along retaining walls, fences, planters, even buildings.

Garden tool garage

Mount a cheap mailbox in a hidden corner of your garden and you've got a place to store garden gear—right where you need it.

Backyard pipeline

Backyard pipeline

If you have a fence, you can run a permanent water line to a convenient spot far from the house. All it takes is a few pipe or conduit straps (in the plumbing and electrical aisles at home centers).

Slow watering, the fast way

When it comes to watering, a slow trickle is better than a fast flood; water soaks in deeply and evenly instead of running off. But leaving your hose on a slow trickle lets you water only one spot at a time and you have to keep moving the hose. So drill a few 1/8-in. holes in buckets. You can fill the buckets fast and walk away, allowing gravity to do the rest.

Out of your way—instantly

Flip-up downspout extensions won't slow you down while mowing. You can lift them out of your path with your foot. You'll find downspout hinges at some home centers and online. Installation is as easy as driving a few screws, though you may also have to cut the extension at a 45-degree angle.

Grow a great lawn

Smarts—not hard work—lead to lush, healthy turf

You don't need to be a grass fanatic to have the best lawn on the block. It's not how much work you do—it's when and how you do it. Here are the keys to a healthy lawn.

Test the soil

If the soil pH is wrong (too acidic or too alkaline), grass won't thrive even if you do everything else right. Grass grows best in the "pH happy zone," between 6 and 7.2. To determine your pH, collect one table-spoon-size sample a couple of inches under the sod in three different places in your yard. Some garden centers offer testing services, others are online (search for "soil testing"). If the pH is too high, you'll treat the lawn with iron sulfate or sulphur; too low and you'll use pelletized limestone. Whoever does the testing will tell you what and how much to use. Applying the treatment is as easy as walking around the yard with a spreader.

First aid for dog spots

Gypsum granules and plenty of water are the antidote for dog urine. If you treat the spot right away, the grass won't die. If it does die, you still need to neutralize the spot before reseeding.

Water deeply but not often

Heavy watering every few days develops deep roots that tap into sub-surface nutrients. Frequent, light watering does just the opposite, encouraging grass to stay healthy only under ideal conditions. To give your lawn the right amount of water, start with this test: Water for 30 minutes, then dig into the soil with a spade. If the soil is wet to a depth of less than 6 in., you need to water longer. If the moisture depth is more than 6 in., you can water for a shorter period. How often you water depends entirely on your soil and climate. In most areas, two to four times per week is best.

Fertilize on schedule

If you fertilize just once a year, do it around Labor Day. That's when your grass will benefit most. For even better turf nutrition, fertilize a second time in mid-October. That gives grass a dose of nutrients to store through winter. You probably won't need fertilizer in spring or summer. But if you do fertilize in the spring, go light—about half the normal amount. If you fertilize in summer, watch the weather. In hot, humid conditions, fertilizer does more harm than good.

Voice of experience

Don't fertilize when your grass doesn't need it. Grass grows fastest in late spring and early summer. Why promote even more growth with fertilizer?

Joe Churchill, turf expert
and *The Family Handyman* Field Editor

Five great ways to wreck your yard

1. Dethatch when you shouldn't

Dethatching is rarely a good idea. It involves flailing away at your lawn with a powerful, engine-driven steel rake to rake up the old woody stems resting at the base of the grass leaves. It tears up not only the grass but also the roots.

2. Catch the clippings

When you cut the grass, let the clippings lie. They'll release nutrients into the soil and form a mulch to help keep in soil moisture.

3. Ignore the directions on lawn treatments

They are SO important! It's not only the concentration for fluids or the spreader setting for granules. Pay attention to the details like the rain forecast and what temperature ranges the treatments require. Skip them and you'll either wreck your lawn or waste your time and money.

4. Overfertilize!

You'll kill your whole yard in no time. And if you don't kill it outright, it'll turn yellow and take weeks to heal itself.

5. Mow with dull blades

Dull mower blades rip through the leaves, which stresses the plant. Instead, you want to slice them off cleanly. You can always tell a lawn that's been mowed with a dull blade because it's brown on the top.

Lawn photo: Getty Images/James Worrell

Mow smarter

Less time, less effort and a healthier lawn

Everyone *thinks* they know how to mow: Just push the mower back and forth across the yard. But many homeowners harm their lawn every time they mow. Here's how to treat your turf right—and save yourself some trouble.

■ Get the height right

For most types of grass, a mower setting around 2-1/2 in. is best. Warm-climate grasses do best a bit shorter: 1-1/2 to 2 in. To determine the type of grass you have and the ideal cutting length, search online for "grass identification." When in doubt, err on the side of taller. Cutting grass too short weakens the plants.

■ Don't follow the same path

Change mowing direction each time you mow. That will minimize soil compaction from your feet or the tires of a riding mower. Sounds nit-picky, but compaction really does harm grass.

■ Cut higher to crowd out weeds

Every plant has a strategy for competing against other plants. For grasses, that strategy is to crowd out other plants. So if you have a weed problem, set your mower a little higher and let grass smother weeds.

■ Mulch, don't catch

Finely mulched grass clippings become fertilizer for the grass. So bagging grass is both a waste of effort and a missed opportunity for free fertilizer.

■ Don't let grass get too tall

Cutting off a large portion of the total height stresses grass. So avoid cutting off more than one-third of the total height. If the desired height is 2 in., for example, don't let it get taller than 3 in. before you cut.

■ Cut it short in the fall

If you live in a snowy climate, make your final fall cutting a short one: 1-1/2 to 2 in. That will reduce mold growth during the winter.

■ Don't mow wet grass

If you do, you'll have to scrape the inside of the mower deck to remove a thick cake of clippings. You'll also leave big clumps of wet clippings that will smother the grass beneath.

■ Sharpen the blade

A dull blade rips rather than slices. That stresses the grass and leaves a brown, shredded tip on each blade of grass.

Voice of experience

Mow autumn leaves, too

A mulching mower shreds dry leaves into tiny flakes that settle into the turf and decompose into natural fertilizer. Over the years, this shortcut has saved me many hours of raking and provided tons of free nutrition to my lawn.

Cameron LiDestri,
The Family Handyman **Field Editor**

Consider a cordless

Cordless electric mowers have some huge advantages over gas-powered models: You don't have to store gas, pay for tune-ups, change the oil or struggle with starting problems. Some electric mowers are small and light enough to store on a shelf, and all are much quieter than gas mowers. The main disadvantages are cost, and for some models, run-time.

Sharpen a mower blade

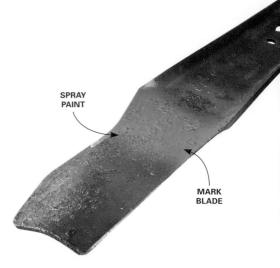

SPRAY PAINT

MARK BLADE

No need to pay someone else; you can do it in about 15 minutes

A sharp blade is better for the looks and health of your grass, so it's best to sharpen it twice during each mowing season. That may take you 30 minutes the first time. But once you've learned how, you'll cut that time in half.

Mark the blade

People often reinstall blades upside down and then go nuts trying to figure out why it won't cut. To prevent that, mark the face-down side with a blast of spray paint before you remove it.

1 Disconnect the spark plug
Yank off the plug wire to prevent accidental firing of the engine. That's unlikely, but possible. Don't forget to reconnect the wire before you try to start the engine.

2 Remove the blade
Turn the mower on its side with the air filter and carburetor side up. That prevents oil and gas from dripping into the air filter. Wedge a block of wood against the deck to lock the blade in place as you unscrew the bolt that secures the blade. A squirt of penetrating oil helps to free a stubborn bolt.

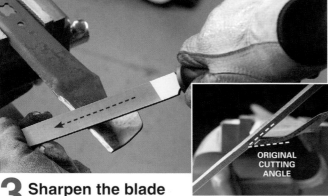

ORIGINAL CUTTING ANGLE

3 Sharpen the blade
Secure the blade with a clamp or vise, top side up. Then get to work with a metal file. Hold the file at the same angle as the bevel on the blade to avoid changing the cutting angle. Apply pressure as you push the file forward; apply no pressure on the backstroke. Don't go for razor-sharp. Butter-knife-sharp is good enough.

NAIL

4 Check the balance
An out-of-balance blade causes vibration and extra wear on bearings. So hang the blade on a nail. If one side dips, file it to remove some metal and balance the blade. Reinstall the blade and cut some grass.

Win against weeds

Wipe them out now and future control will be easy

A few weeds may not seem like an urgent problem, but you can't leave them alone. While you're ignoring them, they're spreading. Wait too long, and your eradication job will soon double, then double again. If, on the other hand, you attack when their numbers are small, you can wipe them out in just a few minutes and future weed control will require only occasional spot treatments.

Identify, then attack

There are three types of weeds. Each type requires different products and application methods. So before you can defeat them, you have to know which type you're up against.

CREEPING CHARLIE

CRAB-GRASS

QUACK GRASS

Broadleaf weeds
Unlike grasses, broadleaf weeds have (surprise!) broad leaves. Some common examples are dandelions, clover and creeping Charlie (ground ivy).

Annual grasses
Grasses like crabgrass reseed themselves near the end of the growing season and then die. The seeds germinate the following spring to grow new plants.

Perennial grasses
Grassy weeds like quack grass go dormant through the winter, along with your grass, only to reemerge in the spring. They spread through the roots and seeds.

The very best weed control
A healthy lawn is an inhospitable place for weeds. Thick, lush grass chokes out existing weeds and prevents new weeds from taking hold.

Voice of experience

Small doses of herbicide will control weeds. But you have to use the products right— and most people don't.

Joe Churchill, turf expert and *The Family Handyman* Field Editor

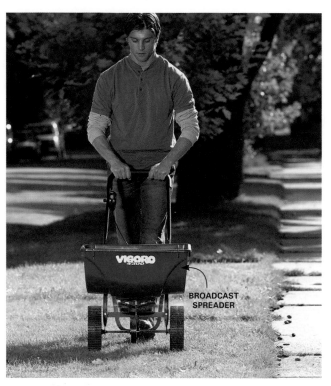

BROADCAST SPREADER

RUBBER GLOVE

CLOTH GLOVE

WIPE UP FROM BASE

Kill annual grasses (and fertilize at the same time!)

The most cost-effective way to control crabgrass is to use a fertilizer with crabgrass preventer added to it. But you have to do this in the spring, before crabgrass seeds germinate. Apply it when you would normally apply your first application of fertilizer, and do it just before it rains to work both the fertilizer and the herbicide into the soil. The fertilizer will help thicken the turf. Thicker turf helps to squeeze out crabgrass plants missed by the herbicide.

Kill perennial grasses one by one

Perennial grassy weeds have sprawling underground root systems. Pulling the grass only gets some of the roots, and the remaining ones will quickly sprout new plants. The only effective solution is to use a "nonselective" plant killer like Roundup. Nonselective products kill all plants, so you have to apply them to the weed and only to the weed. Here's one way: Slip on a rubber chemically resistant glove (they're labeled as such) to protect your skin. Then put on a cheap cloth glove. Dip your fingers in herbicide and wipe the weed. Toss the glove in the trash when you're done.

Don't fight weeds where grass won't grow

If you've tried more than once to nurture grass in an area and failed, it might be time to throw in the towel and treat the area with a landscaping alternative. The obvious choices are stone, mulch and attractive ground cover plants that tolerate the same conditions grass can't handle.

GRASS-UNFRIENDLY AREA

Kill broadleaf weeds

Herbicides formulated for broadleaf control will kill broadleafs only—they won't kill grasses. The key is to use only as much as needed. That saves time and money and keeps you from needlessly introducing chemicals into the environment.

SMALL PRESSURE SPRAYER

Spot-kill weeds with a small pressure sprayer

For a few isolated weeds, spot-treat the weeds with a small, trigger-controlled, pump-up pressure sprayer filled with a mix of herbicide concentrate and water. You can also buy broadleaf killer premixed in spray bottles.

2-GALLON TANK SPRAYER

Treat weed patches with a 1- or 2-gallon sprayer

Patches or clumps of weeds are best treated with a tank sprayer filled with a mix of herbicide concentrate and water. This is faster and more economical than buying several spray bottles of premixed herbicide. After spraying, triple-rinse the sprayer to flush out all the herbicide.

DIAL SPRAYER

ADJUSTABLE DIAL

CONCENTRATED WEED KILLER

Treat large areas with a dial sprayer

If your whole lawn is filled with weeds, use a dial sprayer attached to your garden hose. Add concentrated broadleaf killer to the pot and set the dial at the top to the mixture called for on the herbicide container. Hook up the garden hose and apply an even treatment to the weedy areas. Clear the yard of anything that can get contaminated by overspray. And protect your flowers and bushes with plastic sheeting or cardboard. Broadleaf killers will kill or harm anything with leaves—including your flower bed.

Plant a tree

Do it right today and it will thrive for decades

The key to a thriving, beautiful, mature tree is knowing what you're doing on planting day. Here are the essential tips for planting and caring for your new tree so you can enjoy it for years to come.

Plant in spring or early fall

The ideal time to plant a tree is in early spring before "bud break" or in the fall before the tree goes dormant. Cool weather allows the tree to establish roots in its new location before new top growth puts too much demand on it. Some trees establish better if planted in early spring. These include oaks, pines, dogwoods, American holly, willows and black gum. A tree planted during the hot summer months can get stressed by the heat and will be harder to keep watered properly.

Dig a shallow, broad hole

Dig a saucer-shaped hole three to five times the diameter of the root-ball (or the spread of the roots for a bare-root tree). This allows the roots to easily penetrate the softened backfill and properly anchor the tree. As you dig, place the soil on a tarp to make backfilling easier and to avoid damaging surrounding grass.

Set the roots free

If the roots circle the root-ball, but none are thicker than a pencil, use your fingers to gently tease the root-ball apart to encourage the roots to expand into the surrounding soil. If the tree is severely root-bound and has circling roots larger than a pencil in diameter, use a method called "box cutting." Use a pruning saw to shave off all four sides, creating a square root-ball.

Don't plant too deep

Plant the tree so its root collar—the trunk flare right above the root system—is about 1 in. above ground level. Take the tree out of the container (slitting the container sides) or cut away the wire cage and burlap. Then measure the distance from the root collar to the bottom of the root-ball and dig the hole to that depth. Don't go by the soil level in the container. Dig down into the planting medium to find the root collar so you know how deep to plant the tree. If you're planting a bare-root tree, leave a cone of soil at the bottom of the planting hole and set the root system on top. Place the handle of your shovel flat across the hole from one side to the other to make sure the crown is level with the sur-rounding soil. You should be able to partially see the root collar, or trunk flare, after the tree is planted.

Don't improve the soil

For years, experts recommended adding compost, peat moss or fertilizer to the planting hole. But most now agree that you shouldn't backfill with anything other than the original soil from the planting hole (despite what the plant tag says). Soil amendments in the planting hole can dis-courage the tree roots from spreading into the surrounding soil and can cause poor water drainage. Also, in some instances, fertilizers can kill young roots.

Mulch wide, but not deep

Make a 3-ft. (or larger) circle of mulch 2 to 4 in. deep around the trunk. But don't mulch too deep. This can create surface drainage problems and deprive roots of oxygen. Keep the mulch 3 or 4 in. from the trunk to avoid disease, rot and pest problems. Some good mulch choices are shredded bark or composted wood chips. Don't use woven or plastic land-scape fabric or other weed barriers underneath the mulch. These can cause major problems later on as seeds grow roots down through these materials and anchor themselves into the barriers.

Plant a tree continued

Plant a tree *continued*

Water carefully

For the first few weeks, you may have to water every few days depending on the weather. After that, longer (deeper), less frequent watering is much better than shorter (quicker), frequent watering. To help the tree create deep roots to resist drought and wind, encircle it with a soaker hose a few feet out from the trunk and run it at a trickle for an hour. Stick a popsicle stick (or your finger) 2 to 3 in. into the ground. If the soil is damp down 3 in., you're giving it enough water. If not, water until the soil is damp but not saturated around the root-ball. Allow the soil's surface to begin to dry out between waterings.

Don't plant too close to a building

Plant a tree with its mature size in mind. Many arborists suggest planting a tree no closer to a structure than one half of its expected mature canopy spread. Also, watch out for overhead power lines—most shade trees will grow at least to the height of residential power lines. Choose shorter, ornamental trees for these areas.

Voice of experience

Avoid problem trees

You'll be living with this tree for a long time, so make sure you plant one you won't grow to detest in a few years. Trees to avoid include cottonwoods, which have invasive root systems, messy mulberries and stinky female ginkgoes. Before you buy a tree, research its benefits and potential negatives so you won't resent it later on. Contact your local extension service for a list of recommended trees for your area.

Plant a tree that will grow well given your hardiness zone, existing soil conditions (test if you're not sure), sun exposure and available moisture. One of the best ways to check how trees will do on your land is to observe species growing naturally in the vicinity with the same conditions.

**Jeff Gillman, horticulture Ph.D
and *The Family Handyman*
Field Editor**

Prune like a pro

Healthy, handsome trees and bushes: All it takes is an hour each year

Scraggly, lopsided, overgrown trees and bushes are everywhere. And that's a shame because keeping them attractive is so easy. For a typical yard, all it takes is a half-hour once or twice per year. Aside from looks, proper pruning also prevents disease and encourages flowering and better growth.

Make three cuts

When you're almost done cutting through a branch, the weight will snap the uncut portion of the branch, tear the bark and leave a jagged cut. That doesn't just look bad; it also injures the tree and leaves it vulnerable to disease. But you can avoid that by first lopping off the branch 8 to 12 in. from the trunk (Cuts 1 and 2, at right). That will unload the weight of the branch so your final cut (Cut 3) will be neat and clean.

Don't delay

Pruning is easy to put off. But with every year of delay, trees and shrubs become harder to prune. As branches get bigger, so does the task of trimming them. A job that would take 20 minutes now might consume an hour next year. You may also need bigger tools. Worse, neglected trees or bushes can become so hopeless that you'll have to cut them down and start over.

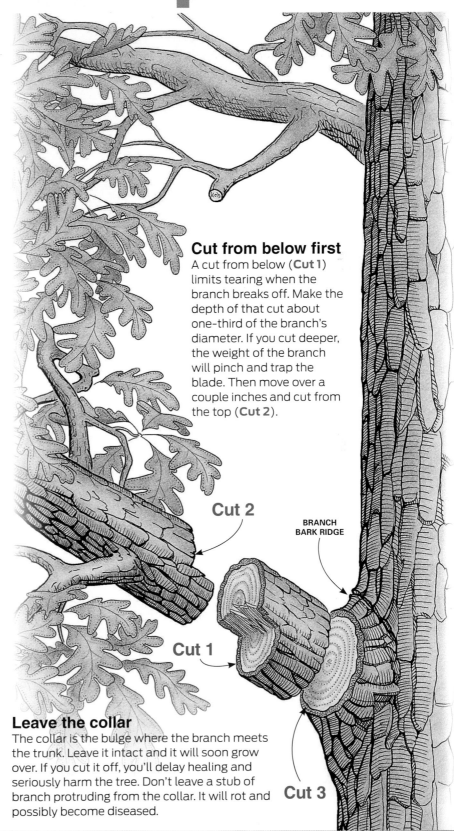

Cut from below first

A cut from below (**Cut 1**) limits tearing when the branch breaks off. Make the depth of that cut about one-third of the branch's diameter. If you cut deeper, the weight of the branch will pinch and trap the blade. Then move over a couple inches and cut from the top (**Cut 2**).

Cut 2

BRANCH BARK RIDGE

Cut 1

Leave the collar

The collar is the bulge where the branch meets the trunk. Leave it intact and it will soon grow over. If you cut it off, you'll delay healing and seriously harm the tree. Don't leave a stub of branch protruding from the collar. It will rot and possibly become diseased.

Cut 3

Cut out 'the four Ds'

Dead, damaged or diseased branches are usually easy to spot. Cutting them off not only makes the tree or bush look better, but also discourages disease from starting or spreading. The fourth "D"—deranged branches—refers to branches that are crossing and rubbing on others, growing in a different direction or just awkward looking.

CROSSING BRANCH

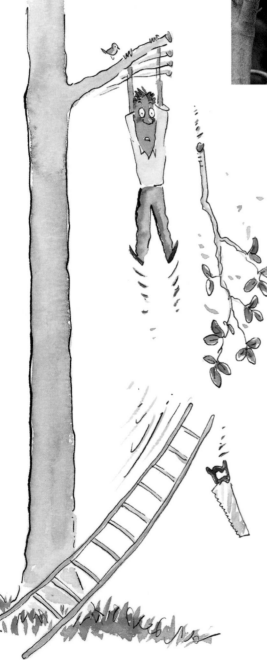

Voice of experience

Two universal mistakes

After 20 years in the tree-trimming business, I've trained dozens of novices. At some point, they all make two mistakes—despite my warnings. First, when cutting a branch from the side or below, they cut too deep. The downward weight of the branch pinches the blade and the saw is stuck. This can happen with any type of saw.

The second mistake is leaning a ladder against the branch they're cutting. Cutting off the branch releases weight and the remaining portion springs up. Usually, this means two seconds of shrieking terror. But sometimes, the ladder and occupant come crashing down.

Al Morgan, *The Family Handyman* Field Editor

Stay safe with a pole saw

A saw mounted on a long pole lets you trim high branches from the safety of the ground. The most basic models are motorless; you provide the power. Others are mini chain saws powered by cords, batteries or gas engines.

Pinch off new growth

When an evergreen tree or shrub reaches the ideal height and shape, it may never again need major pruning. Instead, just pinch off the lighter-colored new growth each spring.

NEW GROWTH

First year

BRANCH TIP

Second year

SIDE BRANCHES

Promote dense growth

Bushes made up of many small branches—rather than a few larger ones—look fuller and more uniform. To encourage this, clip off main branches about 1/4 in. beyond a bud. Several smaller branches will soon radiate from near the cut, resulting in a denser bush.

BEST PROBLEM SOLVERS

Secret weapons for faster, easier fixes

There are lots of products designed to sidestep difficult tasks and make home repairs easier. Some are excellent, some are adequate and a few are just plain dumb. Here are some that *The Family Handyman*'s experts have successfully used over and over again.

Big-job wood filler

Standard wood filler is fine for small, simple repairs, but it doesn't work well for filling larger areas. It shrinks as it dries, so cracks form and you have to apply several layers. Standard filler is also hard to shape to match neighboring surfaces. Epoxy wood filler eliminates those problems. It doesn't shrink, and you can sand, carve, drill or cut it just like wood. Plus, it's much more durable than most fillers, indoors or out. The only downside is that epoxy fillers are two-part products that require some messy mixing. Find them at home centers and online.

Tub and shower makeover

When tub or shower fixtures grow old and ugly, most people go shopping for a new faucet, then call a plumber. But you can skip that expense by leaving the faucet valve in the wall and replacing the visible parts only. Tub and shower "trim kits" come in a huge range of styles; some are available at home centers, many more online. Just make sure the kit you buy will work with the brand and model of your existing faucet.

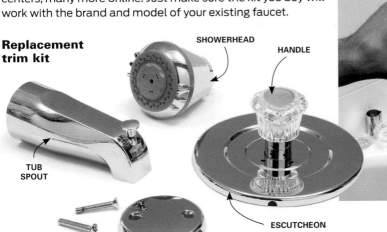

Replacement trim kit

SHOWERHEAD

HANDLE

TUB SPOUT

ESCUTCHEON

OVERFLOW COVER

Instant tub drain replacement

When a tub drain won't hold water or just looks bad, the usual solution is to replace it. But removing the corroded old flange can be a frustrating job, even for plumbers. An easier solution is to cover the old flange with a new flange and stopper. The only drawback is that the new flange stands slightly higher than the old one, so a tiny moat of water remains around the drain after you empty the tub. You won't find an add-on stopper at most stores, but there are a couple styles and several finishes available online. Search for "Nufit stopper."

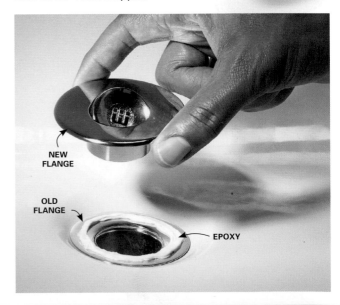

NEW FLANGE

OLD FLANGE

EPOXY

Resurface bad walls

You can patch cracks in plaster walls, but there's a good chance they'll come back. Wall liner, on the other hand, can bridge cracks and flex with seasonal movement. It's basically wallpaper, but much thicker and paintable. Some versions are smooth, others textured. Find it at home centers and online.

Add outlets the easy way

If you're tired of that tangled nest of cords under your desk, "surface wiring" might be the solution. It's a system of plastic or metal channels that lets you add switches, outlets or light fixtures anywhere, without tearing into walls. That saves time and expense, whether you're doing it yourself or hiring an electrician. You'll find surface wiring components at home centers.

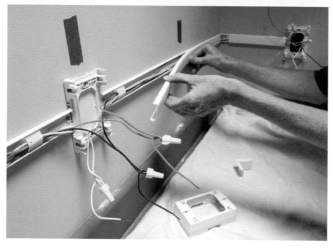

Prevent stuck bulbs

A little corrosion makes a lightbulb hard to unscrew. This is usually a problem in damp areas: outdoors or in garages or basements. The solution is grease. But you can't use just any grease—be sure to use a product intended for bulbs. You'll find it at some home centers and online.

Simple, superb drain cleaner

Before you try the usual drain-clearing methods, slip this barbed plastic strip down the drain and yank out clogs. It works especially well on hair clogs in bathroom sinks, showers and tubs, but often works on other clogs, too. You'll find "drain zippers" at home centers.

Clean out your pipes

The insides of drain lines are coated with a slimy mix of soap scum, grease and other stuff you don't want to know about. This coating builds up gradually and eventually becomes thick enough to slow the flow of sewage and make clogs more likely. So if you're having chronic clog problems, try an enzyme drain cleaner. These products contain harmless, dormant bacteria. Just dump some down your drain and they'll feast on the slime, multiply, and feast some more. Enzyme drain cleaners are available at some home centers and online.

Make carpet damage disappear

If your carpet has a burn or stain, you don't have to live with it. With a "cookie cutter," you can cut out the damaged spot and replace it with a patch cut from a remnant, closet or under the sofa. It's surprisingly easy. With some types of carpet, the patch is visible, but not very noticeable. With others, the repair is almost impossible to see. To buy a repair kit online, search for "cookie cutter carpet tool."

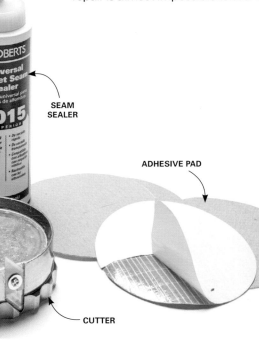

SEAM SEALER

ADHESIVE PAD

CUTTER

ADHESIVE PAD

No-skill pipe connections

Got a broken pipe? Before you call a plumber, consider this: Push-in plumbing connectors let you join pipes instantly just by shoving the pipe into the connector. No skills, knowledge or tools needed. Push-ins work with copper, PEX or CPVC plastic pipe. So if you need to replace a section of copper pipe, for example, you can simply cut out the bad section and replace it with a piece of PEX and a couple push-ins. Even a first-time plumber can manage that. Push-in plumbing connectors of various types and sizes are sold at home centers.

Fix a toilet

Stop constant running—and most other malfunctions—in just a few minutes

Toilet trouble is inevitable. Sooner or later, every toilet will lose flushing power, run constantly or develop a bad habit like making you hold down the lever to achieve a full flush. Luckily, toilets are simple contraptions, so you don't need a plumber to fix most problems.

How it works

When you push the flush handle, you raise the flapper and all the water in the tank gushes into the bowl. Then the flapper closes and the tank refills.

Fill tube

After a flush, most of the water passing through the fill valve refills the tank. But some water runs through the fill tube and through the overflow tub to refill the tank.

Float

As the tank refills after a flush, the float rises and closes the fill valve. Most newer fill valves are connected to a small float (see photos next page) rather than a big "ball float" like this one.

Fill valve

After a flush, the lowered float opens this valve to refill the tank. When a fill valve doesn't close completely, the toilet runs constantly.

Overflow tube

The overflow tube prevents the tank from overflowing and flooding your bathroom. If the fill valve doesn't close, for example, the incoming water will spill into the tube and down into the tank—rather than over the tank and onto your floor.

FLOAT ARM

ELJER 141-0220

1 6Gpf / 0 Lpf

D4

FLUSH HANDLE

FLUSH ROD

WATER LINE

CHAIN

Flapper

Pushing the flush handle raises the flapper; that allows water to gush into the bowl. A flapper that doesn't open completely causes a partial flush. A flapper that doesn't seal tightly when closed causes the toilet to run constantly.

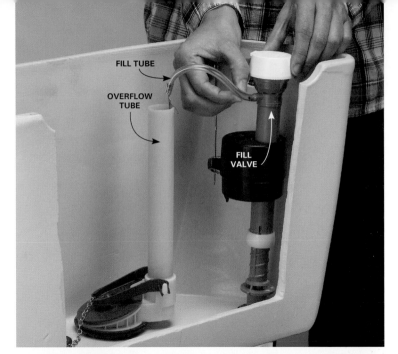

Reconnect the fill tube

If the fill tube gets disconnected or misaligned, it will squirt water into the tank rather than into the overflow tube. The bowl won't refill completely and your next flush will be wimpy. So make sure it's firmly connected to both the overflow tube and the fill valve.

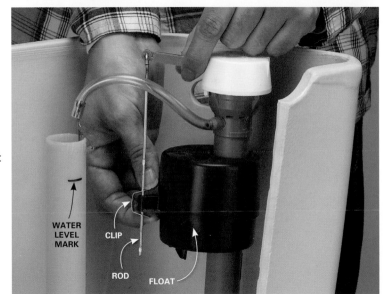

Adjust the fill height

The water level in the tank is adjusted by adjusting the float. If water level is too low, you'll get a weak flush. If it's too high, water will spill over the overflow tube, the fill valve won't close and the toilet will run constantly. To adjust a newer float, pinch the clip and slide the float up or down on the rod. With an old-style float, bend the float arm to raise or lower the float. Either way, you'll have to test-flush and refill a few times to get it right. Most overflow tubes are marked to indicate the correct water level.

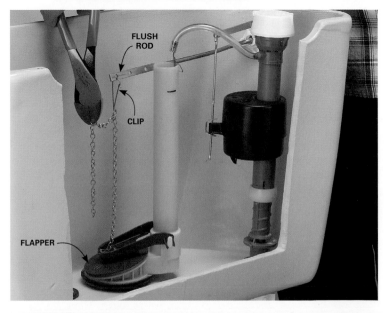

Adjust the flapper chain

The flush handle raises the flapper via a rod and a chain. The chain should have just a little slack in it when the flapper is closed. If the chain is too long, you'll have to hold the handle down to get a complete flush. If the chain is too short, the flapper won't seal when it closes and the toilet will run constantly. To adjust the chain, just move the clip to a different link. If the chain is much longer than necessary, cut off the excess to avoid tangles.

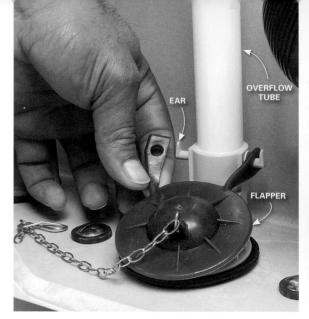

Replace the flapper

Swapping out a flapper is easy: Just unhook the chain and disconnect it from the ears on the overflow tube, then install the new one. But finding a new flapper may not be so easy. Turn off the water supply to the toilet at the shutoff valve below the tank. Then remove the flapper and search for a match. If you can't find an exact match, buy two or three close matches. Even veteran plumbers sometimes have to try a few flappers before getting it right.

Test the flapper

A worn flapper that no longer seals properly allows water to constantly seep down into the bowl. And that's the most common cause of a running toilet. To check the flapper, press lightly on it with a yardstick and listen for a minute. If the sound of running water stops, you know that the problem is related to the flapper. But before you replace the flapper, run your finger around the opening the flapper rests on. Mineral deposits on the rim of this opening will prevent the flapper from sealing. In that case, scrubbing the deposits away with an abrasive sponge or pad may solve the problem (don't use anything that might roughen the rim). If not, replace the flapper.

Don't ignore a rocking toilet

If your toilet isn't solidly fastened to the floor, there may be trouble in your future. Any movement of the toilet damages the wax seal. That leads to leaks and major repairs. To steady a rocking toilet, cut plastic shims to fit and slip them underneath (you may have to remove caulk before adding shims). Then caulk around the toilet and snug down the nuts on the bolts. But don't crank them down super-tight; that can crack the toilet.

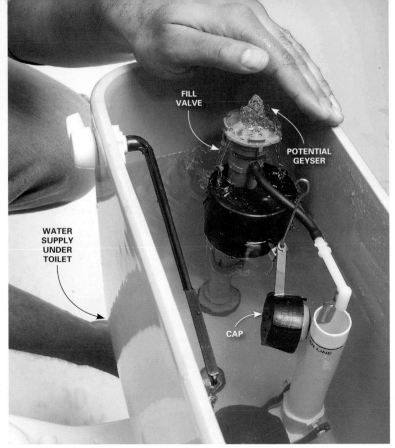

FILL VALVE

POTENTIAL GEYSER

WATER SUPPLY UNDER TOILET

CAP

Flush the fill valve

If your toilet won't stop running and none of the fixes above solve the problem, the only possible culprit is the fill valve. If you have a fill valve similar to the one shown here, turn off the water supply and remove the cap (by turning counterclockwise or removing a screw). Then turn on the water to flush debris out of the valve. Hold your hand over the valve so you don't get a cold shower. Turn off the water, put the cap back in place and test. If flushing didn't solve the problem, replace the valve.

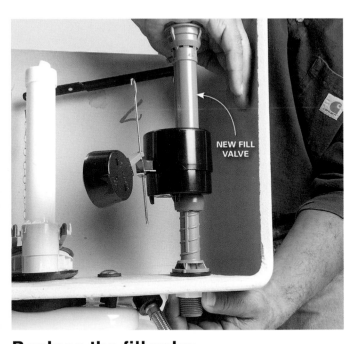

NEW FILL VALVE

NEW SUPPLY LINE

SHUTOFF VALVE

Replace the fill valve

Installing a new fill valve is mostly a matter of following the enclosed directions. But there are a few things that aren't in the instruction manual:

■ Before you do anything, make sure the shutoff valve works so you can stop the water supply. If not, you'll have to shut off the water at the main valve.

■ Yes, you can (and should!) replace an old ball-float valve with a new-style valve. The new style is easier to install and adjust.

■ When shopping, also pick up a new flexible supply line. Choose one that has a braided stainless steel sheath. Never, ever reuse an old flexible line. Flexible lines degrade over time and may eventually burst. If the existing line is solid metal tubing, you can reuse it but it will be more difficult to work with.

■ The most common fill-valve mistake is to overtighten the connection between the supply line and the fill valve. Finger-tight, plus one quarter turn with pliers is usually enough. If it leaks, just tighten it a little more.

Unplug a toilet

Simple tools and simple techniques for fast results

A plugged toilet can require professional intervention. But in the vast majority of cases, you can do exactly what a plumber would do. That means starting with a plunger and then, maybe, using a "snake." Until you've tried those methods, don't schedule an expensive house call.

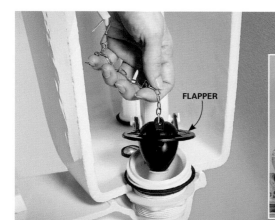

Don't flush!

When a flush seems weak, you'll wonder whether the toilet is plugged. Don't find out by flushing again. If the toilet is badly plugged, you could end up with an overflow. Instead, lift the lid off the tank and raise the flapper by hand for just a couple seconds. That will release a little water into the bowl so you can see whether it flows down the drain.

Plunger pointers

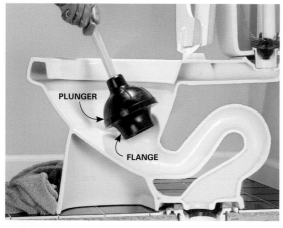

■ If the bowl is nearly overflowing, wait. In most cases, the water level will slowly fall. That may take 15 minutes or more, but better to delay than to slop sewage all over the floor.

■ Use a plunger with a fold-out flange. It will seal better around the toilet drain for a more powerful plunge.

■ Start gently. Before your first push, the plunger is full of air, so a hard push will blast out a messy sewage explosion. Slowly increase the force of your thrusts until you know how hard you can push without making a mess.

■ You need water in the bowl. Driving air down the drain won't work. So if the water level drops too low, add some by lifting the flapper (as shown above).

■ Don't give up. Clearing a stubborn clog can take 20 pushes or more.

Send in the snake

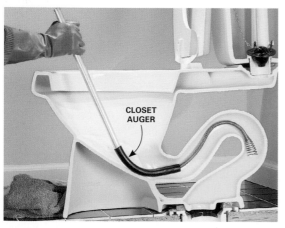

You can use a standard drain snake to unplug a toilet. Better yet, use a special snake designed just for toilets: A "closet auger" (around $20) has a rubber sleeve to protect the toilet bowl from scrape marks and a long handle that gives you some extra distance from the splashy action. It's easy to use: Just insert the snake and turn the handle that spins the snake. As it twists deeper into the drain, the corkscrew tip will either break up the clog or snag the clog so you can yank it out. When snaking fails, the next step is to remove the toilet. That allows easier access to the clog, whether it's in the toilet or in the drain lines.

DRAIN SNAKE

Stop leaks under the sink

Get rid of the drip-catching bucket—without paying a plumber

Under-sink drainpipes are the most common source of plumbing leaks. And a permanent drip bucket is the most common solution. But you don't have to live with a drip. You can end it yourself, even if you have no plumbing know-how. The solutions for a leak under a bathroom sink are similar to the kitchen-sink fixes shown here.

Be a drip detective

Before you can stop a leak, you have to find the source. And that can be tricky. Water that escapes a pipe might run horizontally for inches (or even feet) before it drops onto the cabinet floor. So do this: Get under the sink with a flashlight and look for stains or mineral deposits that reveal the trail of leaking water. Pay special attention to the joints where sections of pipe meet; that's where most leaks occur.

If you don't see any "water tracks," wipe down the pipes with a rag. Fill both bowls of the sink with warm water (cold water can cause condensation droplets to form on the pipes, making it impossible to find leaks). Let the sink drain while you examine the pipes below. Be patient. The telltale leak droplets may take a few minutes to show up.

Fixes for leaky joints

When you've found the leak location, try the simplest fix first: Just tighten the nut. You can usually turn plastic nuts by hand, but metal nuts require pliers. Either way, hold on to nearby pipes so you don't misalign other joints while you work (with metal pipes, that means having two pliers). Here are two more fixes to try:

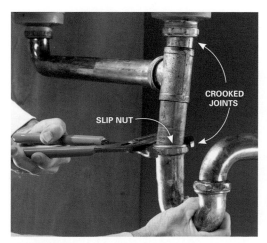

Straighten crooked joints
Joints often leak because they were knocked out of alignment by the trash can. To straighten a crooked joint, just loosen the nut, realign the pipe and retighten.

Disassemble and replace parts
Most joints contain rubber or plastic washers that can be replaced (see next page). Take the old parts to the store to find a match. You may have to disassemble two or more joints to get at a bad washer.

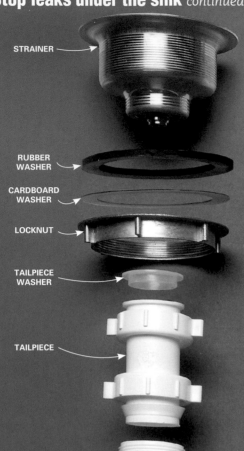

STRAINER

RUBBER
WASHER

CARDBOARD
WASHER

LOCKNUT

TAILPIECE
WASHER

TAILPIECE

WASTE ARM

Replace the whole works (no plumbing experience required!)

The fixes shown on the previous page often work. But sometimes they don't. And sometimes—especially with old metal pipes—they're just a temporary cure. So plumbers often skip the little fixes and replace the whole drain assembly. That's not as difficult as it sounds, and for $25 or less you can have a whole new drain line. Kits sold at home centers contain most of the essential parts. But snap a photo of your system and take it to the store to make sure you get everything you need. Here are some possible extra parts you may need:

■ Long tailpieces (Photo 1).The tailpieces that come with kits are often only a couple of inches long.

■ A trap arm extender (Photo 2).The arm that comes with the kit may not reach the drainpipe that protrudes from the wall.

■ A dishwasher wye that has a connection for your dishwasher hose.

■ A disposer kit that allows the waste arm to connect to a garbage disposer.

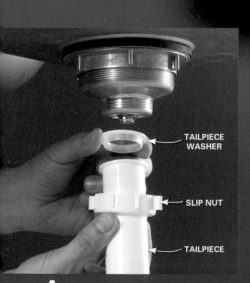

TAILPIECE
WASHER

SLIP NUT

TAILPIECE

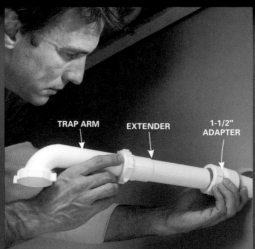

TRAP ARM   EXTENDER   1-1/2"
ADAPTER

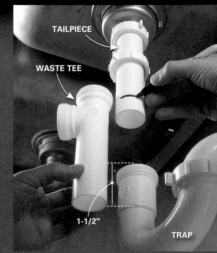

TAILPIECE

WASTE TEE

1-1/2"

TRAP

1 Start with the tailpiece
Attach the tailpiece to the basket strainer, but don't fully tighten it yet; you'll have to remove and cut it later.

2 Connect to the drain system
Slide the trap arm into the adapter where the sink drain connects to the drain pipe inside the wall. Then attach the trap and slide the arm in or out to position the trap directly under the tailpiece. You may need to cut the arm or add an extender.

3 Install the tee
Hold the waste tee alongside the tailpiece about 1-1/2 in. below the top of the trap. Mark the tailpiece 1/2 in. below the top of the tee. Cut both tailpieces to the same length and install them.

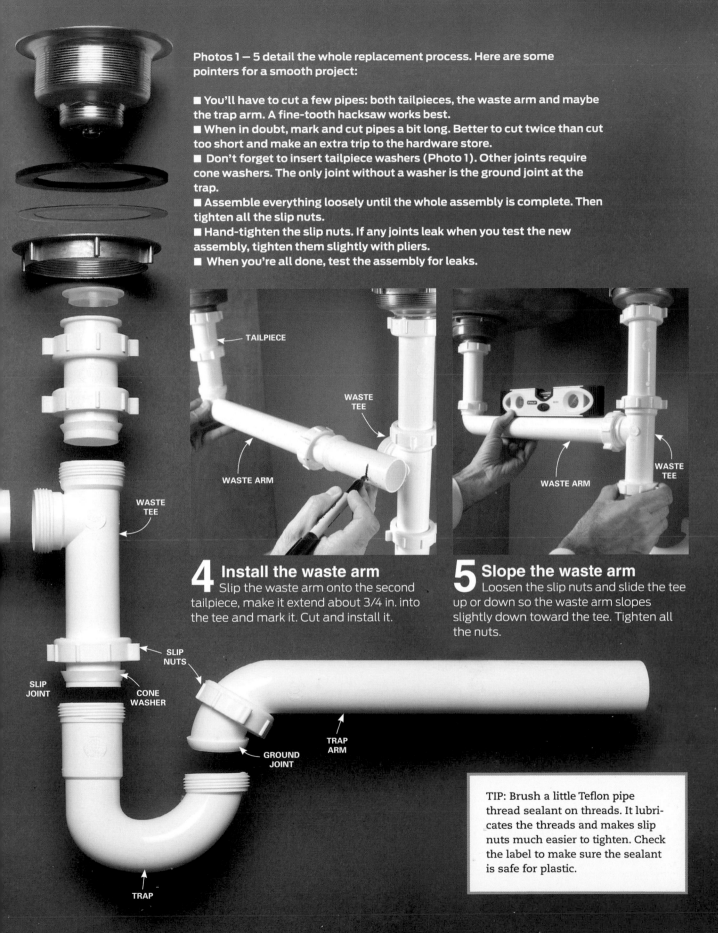

Photos 1 – 5 detail the whole replacement process. Here are some pointers for a smooth project:

■ You'll have to cut a few pipes: both tailpieces, the waste arm and maybe the trap arm. A fine-tooth hacksaw works best.
■ When in doubt, mark and cut pipes a bit long. Better to cut twice than cut too short and make an extra trip to the hardware store.
■ Don't forget to insert tailpiece washers (Photo 1). Other joints require cone washers. The only joint without a washer is the ground joint at the trap.
■ Assemble everything loosely until the whole assembly is complete. Then tighten all the slip nuts.
■ Hand-tighten the slip nuts. If any joints leak when you test the new assembly, tighten them slightly with pliers.
■ When you're all done, test the assembly for leaks.

TAILPIECE

WASTE TEE

WASTE ARM

WASTE ARM

WASTE TEE

4 Install the waste arm
Slip the waste arm onto the second tailpiece, make it extend about 3/4 in. into the tee and mark it. Cut and install it.

5 Slope the waste arm
Loosen the slip nuts and slide the tee up or down so the waste arm slopes slightly down toward the tee. Tighten all the nuts.

WASTE TEE

SLIP NUTS

SLIP JOINT

CONE WASHER

GROUND JOINT

TRAP ARM

TIP: Brush a little Teflon pipe thread sealant on threads. It lubricates the threads and makes slip nuts much easier to tighten. Check the label to make sure the sealant is safe for plastic.

TRAP

Unclog a sink

In most cases, you can do exactly what a pro would do

If you have a sink that drains slowly—or not at all—don't call a plumber just yet. There's a good chance that he will take the very same approaches shown here. So at least try the first two methods. Then, if you're willing to disassemble the drain lines, try the third. These strategies also apply to bathroom sinks, tubs and showers. If the clog is especially tough or deep in the lines, you'll have to call in a pro with more know-how and equipment.

First, try a coat hanger

If you have a two-bowl sink, look underneath to determine which bowl is above the trap. There's a baffle just above the trap that's meant to direct water down the drain. But that baffle is also a notorious clog-causer, especially along with a heavily used garbage disposer. Bend a coat hanger or other stiff wire and slip it down the drain. When you feel the wire hook onto the baffle, wiggle and jiggle to dislodge the clog.

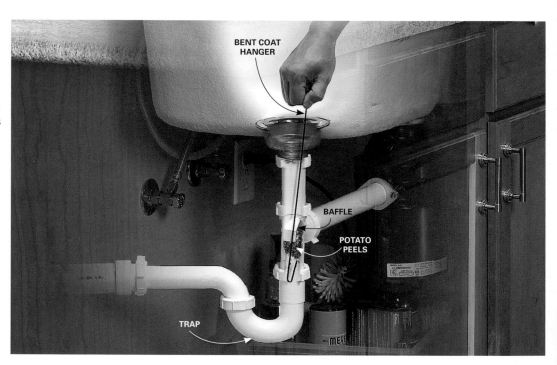

BENT COAT HANGER

BAFFLE

POTATO PEELS

TRAP

Eliminate clogs

Follow two rules to avoid kitchen clogs: First, don't use your garbage disposer as a trash can. Instead, use your disposer to handle just the tidbits rinsed off plates or a few peels dropped in the sink. Sending plate loads of food or heaps of potato peels down the drain is asking for trouble. Second, never pour grease down the drain. And running hot water doesn't help. The grease will just congeal farther down the drain where it will be even harder to clear.

Customize a drain snake

Inexpensive, effective and easy to use, a drain snake is the primary clog-buster used by most plumbers. And you can own one for less than $20. The drum contains a coil of springy cable with a spiral hook at the end. Just turn the crank and the cable spins as you feed it through pipes. Usually, the hook is too large to fit through small openings like kitchen sink baskets. But you can clip off the hook and bend the cable's end to make a smaller hook. Sometimes it also helps to bend the end.

OLD HOOK

NEW HOOK

'Snake' the drain

If the coat hanger didn't do the trick, send a snake down the drain. Loosen the setscrew to unlock the cable and feed the cable into the drain until it won't go any deeper. With about 8 in. of cable sticking out of the drain, tighten the setscrew, withdraw the cable about 1 in. and start spinning the drum. As you spin and push, the cable should wind its way through the trap. If it gets stuck, back off a few inches and try again. Don't keep spinning while the cable is stuck; that will cause the cable to twist and bend inside the pipe. Spinning fast while applying light pressure is often the best way to get past tough spots. It may take several tries to work the cable through the trap. The cable will either break up the clog or hook it so you can pull it out.

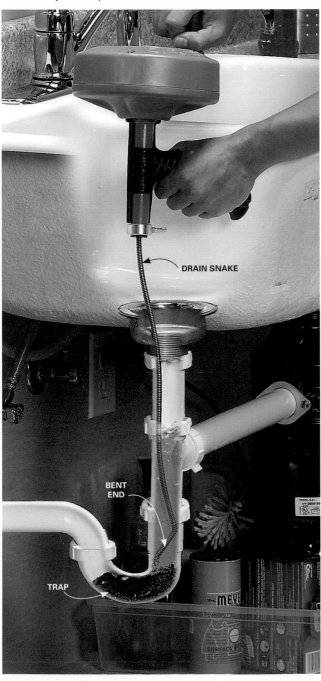

DRAIN SNAKE

BENT END

TRAP

Disassemble the drain

If the clog is far past the trap, you probably won't be able to feed the cable through all of the turns in the pipes, so the next step is to remove the drain lines under the sink. If you have plastic lines, they'll likely come apart and slip back together without too much trouble. Metal lines, especially old ones, are more stubborn; plumbers often replace them to avoid reassembly hassles. In either case, you disconnect the joints by loosening the nuts with large pliers. Be sure to have a bucket and rags handy to deal with the trapped water. With the lines disassembled, look into the trap and up into the sink drain. If they're clear, you know the clog is farther down the line. Send the snake as far as you can into the drainpipe, then reassemble the lines. Until you run water down the drain, you won't know if you cleared the clog.

GREASE AND GOO

Fix an outdoor faucet

So simple even a first-time plumber can do it

That dripping faucet isn't just a water-wasting annoyance. The constant drip contributes to basement or crawl-space dampness, while moist soil attracts ant and termites. But stopping the drip is quick and easy. If you live in a warm climate, your faucet may not be a freeze-proof model like the one shown here, but the steps will be similar.

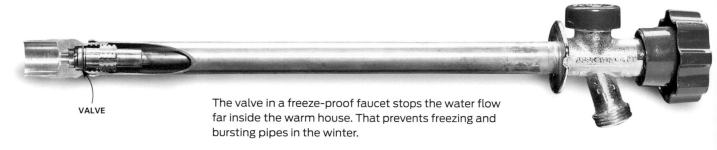

VALVE

The valve in a freeze-proof faucet stops the water flow far inside the warm house. That prevents freezing and bursting pipes in the winter.

PACKING NUTS

STEM

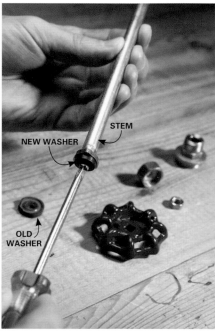

NEW WASHER

STEM

OLD WASHER

1 Dismantle the faucet

Remove the screw or nut in the center of the handle and pull the handle off (it may require a hard tug). Then unscrew the packing nut. Some models have two packing nuts. While you loosen the packing nut, hold the faucet steady; you don't want to twist the whole faucet and loosen connections inside. Wrap pliers with tape to avoid marring the faucet.

2 Remove the stem

Put the handle back on and turn it counterclockwise to remove the stem. Some stems don't need to be turned but come straight out with a firm pull.

3 Replace the washer

Unscrew the rubber washer at the end of the stem. Take it to a home center to find a match. Then screw on the new washer and reassemble the faucet by reversing the previous steps.

Why outdoor faucets leak

Sometimes, the rubber washer that seals the valve simply wears out. But often, the washer is damaged by overtightening the handle. Here's how: Even after the valve is completely closed, water continues to trickle out for a couple seconds while the long pipe inside the wall empties. That trickle makes you think that the valve is still open. So you crank the handle harder—and damage the washer. Get in the habit of closing the valve gently, and your washer will last much longer.

How to freeze a freeze-proof faucet

When you leave a garden hose connected to a faucet, it can keep the faucet filled with water, whether the valve is open or closed. Then, when the temperature drops, the faucet will freeze and burst. Don't ask how I know this.

Gary Wentz, *The Family Handyman* **Senior Editor**

Instant leak fix

Aside from outdoor faucets, lots of other valves also have packing nuts: small shutoff valves under sinks (shown here), larger shutoff valves, even some old-style kitchen or bath faucets. All of these valves are prone to slow leaks around the valve stem. In most cases, you stop these leaks simply by tightening the packing nut slightly.

VALVE STEM • PACKING NUT • VALVE BODY

Voice of experience

Shut off the water!

When my new (and very attractive) neighbor complained that her outdoor faucet was leaking, I saw an opportunity to impress her and promised to have it fixed in 10 minutes. Trouble is, I forgot to turn off the water. A cold blast knocked me flat on my back in a mud puddle. My neighbor was less impressed than I had hoped.

Dave Welk, *The Family Handyman* **Field Editor**

Clean a clogged faucet

Restore the flow in five minutes

If the flow from your kitchen or bathroom faucet isn't what it used to be, the aerator is probably plugged. That's perfectly normal. An aerator can clog slowly due to mineral buildup or instantly after plumbing work loosens debris inside pipes. Either way, the solution is to clean it out. If scrubbing with a toothbrush and rinsing won't remove tough mineral buildup, soak the aerator parts in vinegar.

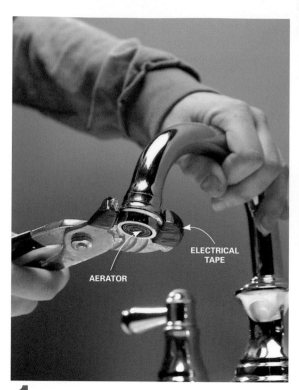

1 Unscrew the aerator
Wrap duct or electrical tape around pliers to avoid scratching the aerator. You may need a small screwdriver or knife to pry apart the components inside the aerator. Close the drain stopper so small parts can't fall down the drain.

Showerheads plug up, too

Mineral buildup can gradually turn a powerful shower into a weak trickle. The buildup may be visible around the jet holes or invisible inside the head. Either way, the solution is simple, and you don't even have to remove the head. Just fill a freezer bag with a half-and-half mix of vinegar and water. Secure the bag with a rubber band or duct tape. Vinegar dissolves minerals, but it can also damage finishes with prolonged contact, so remove the bag every 15 minutes and check the flow.

2 This is critical!
If you forget how the parts fit together, reassembly will drive you crazy. So lay out the parts in exactly the order they came apart. As you clean each part, don't forget which side faces up.

Fix a loose towel bar—forever!

Strong, simple wall anchors are the permanent solution

The little plastic drywall anchors that come with most towel bars are wimpy and guaranteed to fail sooner or later. But replacing them with strong anchors is easy. The process for towel rings, hooks and toilet paper holders is identical to the steps shown here.

1 Remove the bar and posts
Loosen the setscrew to remove the post. Some setscrews require an Allen wrench, others a tiny screwdriver. With the post off, try tightening the screws in the mounting plate. If that doesn't secure the plate solidly, remove the screws and plate. If one of the posts is solid, just leave it alone. Chances are it's screwed to a stud.

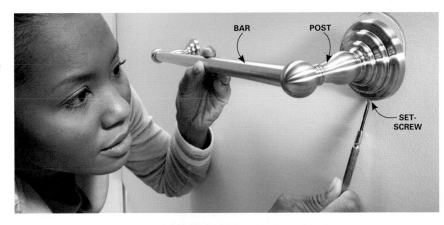

BAR POST

SET-SCREW

WEAK ANCHOR

STRONG ANCHOR

2 Install new anchors
Chances are, you'll find two plastic tube-type anchors under the mounting plate. Simply poke them with a screwdriver and let them fall inside the wall. There are several more reliable types of anchors for drywall. The screw-in toggle anchors shown here are strong, easy to install and available at home centers. Just drive them into the old anchor holes with a drill or screwdriver.

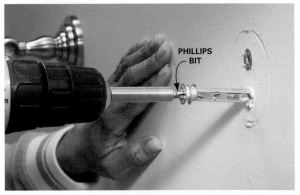

PHILLIPS BIT

3 Refasten the mounting plate
Hold the mounting plate in place and drive in the screws that came with the anchors. Reattach the posts and bar and you're done.

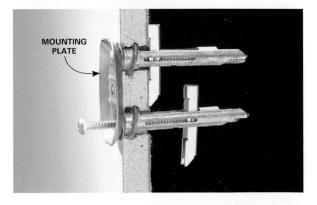

MOUNTING PLATE

Tune up your cabinets

Most problems are easier to fix than to live with

As your cabinets age, you can just give up and learn to live with all their little glitches. But there's really no reason to tolerate cabinet problems. The most common frustrations are amazingly easy to eliminate, even if you have no fix-it experience.

Adjust misaligned doors

If your doors are out of whack and you have "Euro" hinges, you can align them perfectly in minutes—just by turning a few screws. Your hinges may not adjust exactly like the ones shown here, but it will be just as easy and you can't do any harm by turning the wrong screw. To start, make sure the door screws are tight. Then follow this simple process:

1 If the door isn't flush with neighboring doors, use this screw to move it in or out. With some hinges, the door moves as you turn the screw. With others, you have to loosen the screw, nudge the door in or out, then retighten.

2 If the door is crooked—not parallel to other doors or the cabinet—turn this screw to move the door left or right.

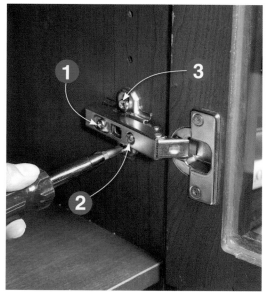

3 If the door is flush and parallel, but standing too high or low, loosen this screw and the identical one below it. Raise or lower the door, then retighten the screws. Some hinges allow the same up-down movement just by turning a single screw.

THREAD ADHESIVE

SCREW

Tighten loose knobs—forever

If you have a knob or handle that keeps coming loose, give it a tiny dose of thread adhesive (available at home centers). Some thread adhesives make future screw removal almost impossible, so choose one that allows for disassembly.

Beef up drawer bottoms

When drawer bottoms start to sag like a hammock, add a layer of 1/4-in.-thick plywood to the underside. Cut the plywood about 1/2 in. smaller than the cavity under the drawer. (Some home centers will cut plywood to size for you.) If the drawer bottom is unfinished, mount the new plywood with wood glue. If the bottom is coated, use construction adhesive. Weigh down the plywood with paint cans or a stack of books.

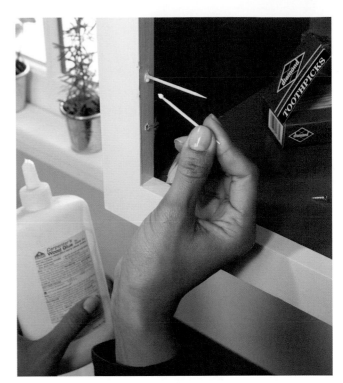

Fix stripped screw holes

Cabinet hardware screws often strip. You turn and turn, but the screw doesn't tighten. But the solution is already on your cabinet shelf: Grab a few toothpicks, dip them in wood glue and pack them into the hole. When the glue dries, break off the toothpicks and drive in the screw.

Lube stubborn drawers

To make a sticking drawer glide, coat the slides and rollers with "dry" lubricant. It goes on wet, but dries without leaving oily residue, so dust and debris won't gum up the slides later. Dust off the slides in the cabinet and on the drawer first. To avoid a mess inside the cabinet, spray the lubricant on a rag and wipe it onto the slides. You can treat the drawer parts the same or spray them.

Voice of experience

My solution for sagging shelves

I replaced my flimsy cabinet shelves with wire shelving—the stuff typically used in closets. It's strong, inexpensive and see-through, so I can locate items at the back of the cabinet without unloading the shelves. Cut wire shelving to length with a hacksaw, jigsaw or big bolt cutters. Then just set them in place on the shelf supports.

Maureen Riegger,
The Family
Handyman
Field Editor

Tune up your cabinets *continued*

Hide damage with back plates

New cabinet hardware that includes back plates can hide the wear that occurs around cabinet knobs and pulls. You'll find a small hardware selection at home centers and an endless selection online.

BACK PLATE

BACK PLATE

Ingenious (and easy) kitchen improvements

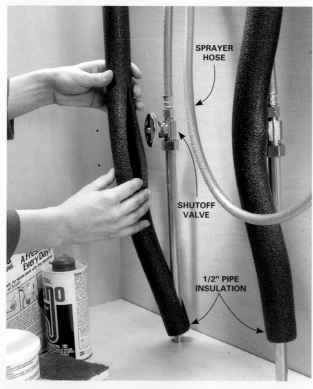

SPRAYER HOSE

SHUTOFF VALVE

1/2" PIPE INSULATION

Stop sprayer snags

If the hose connected to your sink sprayer gets caught on the shutoff handles, cover them with 1/2-in. pipe insulation. If the insulation won't stay put, add some duct tape.

Wine glass molding

T-molding designed for wood floor transitions makes a perfect rack for stemware. Just cut it to length and screw it to the underside of shelves. For a neater look, use finish washers along with the screws.

T-MOLDING

FINISH WASHER

CABINET DOOR DAMPER

Replace missing bumpers

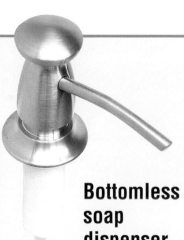

BUMPER

Your cabinets came with felt or rubber bumpers, but a few of them have disappeared and you're accustomed to the smack of closing doors. Give your ears a break for about $3. Peel off a bumper and take it to the home center. Your new bumpers don't have to match the old ones, but they should be about the same thickness.

Better than bumpers

Cabinet door dampers are the ultimate slam solution. They install with a just a screw or two and provide soft closings. They work only with self-closing hinges that hold the door shut, but that covers the majority of cabinet hinges. Find dampers at home centers or online.

Bottomless soap dispenser

Constantly refilling your sink-mounted soap squirter? Yank out the dispenser and take it to a home center to find tubing that fits over the suction tube. Run the tubing into a large jug of soap and you'll have a long-lasting reservoir.

TUBING

PEEL-AND-STICK TILE

DAMAGED CABINET BOTTOM

Under-sink makeover

The cabinet under the sink gets pretty grungy. So cover the stains with cheap peel-and-stick vinyl tiles. They're easy to cut with a utility knife, easy to install and easy to keep clean.

Renew grungy grout

When regular cleaning fails, here are your options

If a stiff brush and grout cleaner just won't do the job, don't give up. There are other steps you can take to clean, renew or replace ugly grout.

Bleach away mildew

Bleach is an effective way to clean off and kill mildew, even mildew that's growing deep in the grout's pores. Sponging on a bleach-and-water mix is fast. But if you have only small areas to treat, use a bleach pen and avoid the nasty fumes. Either way, you may also have to scour with a brush. Don't expect bleach to prevent future trouble—mildew always returns eventually.

Coat it with color

Grout coloring products are available at most home centers. They're basically paint-like coatings that can be applied by brush or pen to mask stains. If you don't find the color you want at a home center, you'll find many more color options online. You can change the color of your grout, but remember that the coating will eventually wear. And as that happens, a color that's similar to the underlying grout will look better than a drastically different color.

Steam clean

Professionals often use steam to clean grout, and so can you. A household steam cleaner doesn't have the power or speed of a pro model, but with a little extra patience, it will deep-clean grout effectively. In most cases, steam cleaning is faster and easier than scrubbing—though working with steam in a small space is a hot, sweaty job. Switch on the bath fan!

Seal out future stains

Grout is hard to keep clean because it's porous. So when you finally get grout clean, your next step should be to seal it. Grout sealer plugs tiny pores, repels future stains and make regular cleaning easier. The life span of sealer depends on its location and the quality of sealer itself. On a kitchen backsplash, a good sealer will continue to repel stains for a few years. In a shower that gets daily use, you may need to reseal every year.

Beware of acidic cleaners

The toughest grout cleaning products don't just remove stains; they actually eat away at grout, removing a thin layer of its surface. If you use them regularly, you'll eventually destroy the grout. So check the label. If it includes a caution against regular use, don't ignore it.

Replacing grout

Some grout is just plain hopeless: It's so deeply stained that cleaning won't help, it's a unique color that can't be coated over, or it's so badly eroded that it's falling out. In cases like these, regrouting is the solution. It's a common DIY project, but requires patience, know-how and a few special tools. The good news is that newer grout formulations resist staining much better than your old grout—so you can look forward to easier cleaning. Whether you do it yourself or hire a pro, here's the basic process:

1 Grind out the old grout

There are several ways to remove grout. In most cases, an oscillating tool fitted with a grout blade is the fastest, easiest approach.

2 Pack in the new grout

Grout is a cement-based powder that you mix with water. As you spread it over tile, grout fills the spaces between tiles.

Fix a door

The most common problems are also the easiest to solve

Fix a latch that won't catch

If a door won't latch—even with a hard push—it's probably because the latch is hitting the strike plate too high or too low, so it can't enter the strike plate's opening. First, tighten all the hinge screws in both the door and the jamb. If that doesn't solve the problem, take the steps below.

1 Do the lipstick test
Cover the strike plate with tape, smear some lipstick on the latch and close the door. The smudge on the tape will reveal the problem. If the latch doesn't reach as far as the strike plate opening, the door is probably warped. But if the latch is contacting the strike plate a bit too high or low, you can fix it.

2 Enlarge the strike plate opening
Remove the plate and extend the opening with a metal file. A half-round "bastard" file is perfect for this job.

Silence a squeaky hinge

1 Remove the hinge pin
With the door closed, gently hammer a nail up into the hinge knuckles. When you've driven the pin as far up as you can, grab it with pliers and yank it out.

2 Lubricate the pin
Petroleum jelly is a good lubricant for this job, because it stays in place without running. Reinsert the pin and you're done.

Fix a sticking door

When a door rubs against the jamb along the latch side, it's often due to loose hinge screws, so tighten them first. If that doesn't work, watch the edge of the door as you close it to determine if it's contacting the jamb near the top, bottom or middle. Then try the fixes below.

Adjust the hinge

Choose the hinge opposite where the door rubs against the latch side of the jamb. Remove one of the hinge screws and drive in a 3-in. screw. That will pull the door slightly away from the rubbing point.

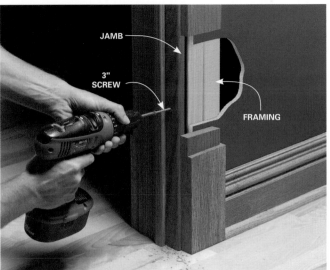

Move the jamb

At the rubbing point, drive a 3-in. screw through the jamb and into the framing behind it. This will draw the jamb slightly away from the door. It will also leave you with an ugly screw head to putty and stain, so do this only as a last resort.

Stop a door rattle

A door that rattles isn't closing firmly against the door stop molding. The simplest solution is to stick a cabinet bumper to the stop molding. Another fix is almost as easy: Remove the strike plate and bend the tab slightly. This may take some trial and error before you get it right.

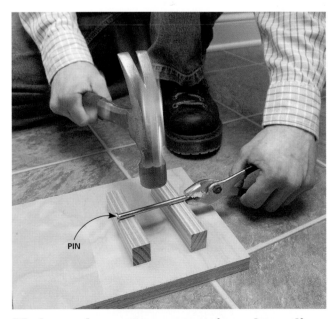

Make a door stay open (or closed)

If a door drifts open or closed, you probably have a ghost. But a little extra friction in the hinge might help. Remove the upper hinge, lay it across two blocks and bend it slightly with a hammer. If that doesn't solve the problem, do the same to the bottom hinge.

Tune up closet doors

Simple adjustments for smooth operation

"Bifold" closet doors are compact and convenient. But they have lots of moving parts that can go out of whack. That leads to an ugly, uneven fit, rubbing, binding and balky operation. You can usually solve all of those problems by adjusting the fit of the doors within the opening. Your goal is an even 1/8-in. vertical gap between the doors and even horizontal gaps above and below the doors. Here's how to reposition the doors:

BRACKET

To move the top of the door, loosen the setscrew on the top bracket and slide the bracket slightly left or right. Retighten the setscrew, close the door and check the fit. You may have to adjust and readjust a few times before you get it right.

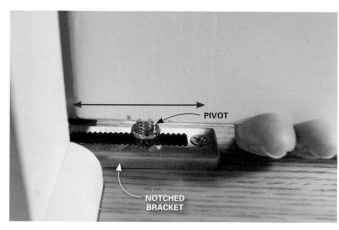

PIVOT

NOTCHED BRACKET

To move the bottom of the door, lift the door and set the pivot into a different notch. Some doors have setscrew adjustment (as shown above) rather than a notched bracket as shown here.

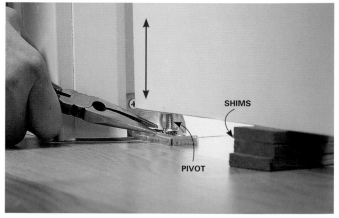

SHIMS

PIVOT

To adjust the height of the door, turn the pivot. Some pivots can be gripped with pliers; others require a wrench. For easier adjustment, lift the door and set it on a spacer such as shims or a book.

Replacement parts

Most home centers carry a good selection of replacement parts for bifold doors. You may not find an exact match, but new parts of the same type and size often work with the old door.

Top rollers are mounted near the corner of the door that glides along the track.

Top pivots lock the door into the top bracket.

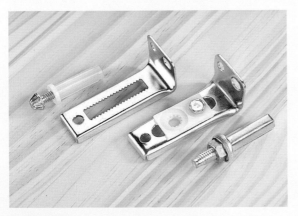

Bottom pivots connect the door to the bottom bracket and allow height adjustment.

Lube the upper track

For silky-smooth operation, spray some lubricant on a rag and wipe it onto the upper track. Use a lubricant that's labeled "dry"—it won't gather dust.

Reinforce a loose pivot

Pivots often become loose as they slowly enlarge the holes they rest in. To restore a tight fit, remove the pivot, screw on a pivot reinforcement plate and reinsert the pivot.

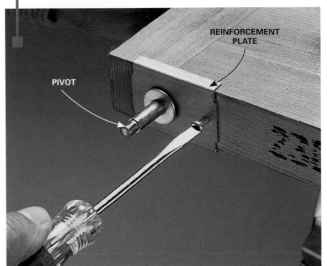

REINFORCEMENT PLATE

PIVOT

Adjust bypass doors

If you have a sliding "bypass" door that doesn't fit evenly against the opening or drags on the floor, the fix is easy. You can raise or lower one end of the door or the entire door just by turning a few screws. From inside the closet, loosen the adjusting screw (the one in an elongated slot), raise or lower the door, and tighten the screw. You may also have to reposition a locking screw. If any of the screws are stripped and won't tighten, just move the roller bracket to a new spot. With some bypass doors, you can adjust the position by turning a nut above the door.

ADJUSTING SCREW

PIVOT SCREW

LOCKING SCREW

Patch walls perfectly

With a little patience, you can get pro results

Fill small holes

For holes smaller than 1/8 in., use spackling compound. If you have a mix of hole sizes, some larger than 1/8 in., some smaller, you can use joint compound for all of them. Whatever you use, expect shrinkage as the compound dries (no matter what the label promises). Don't be surprised if you have to coat the hole two or even three times to compensate for shrinkage.

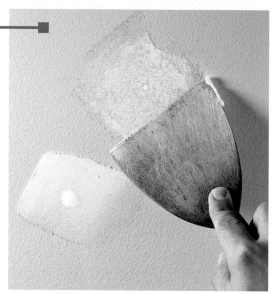

Choose lightweight compound

At the home center, you'll find premixed joint compound in plastic containers and powder in bags. Unless you want to take on a messy mixing job, buy the premixed stuff. And choose one that's labeled "lightweight." Lightweight compound shrinks less and sands easier than the standard version.

Fix nail pops—and keep them from coming back

Nail pops happen when drywall nails or screws break through the surface, usually due to shrinking and swelling of the wall studs. If you just pound them in and patch them, they'll be back. Here's how to fix them permanently:

SMASHED DRYWALL

1 Prepare for patching

Drive drywall screws into the stud above and below the pop. Don't use nails. If the drywall has puckered around the pop, slice it out. If the area is flat, leave it alone. Remove the popped nail or screw.

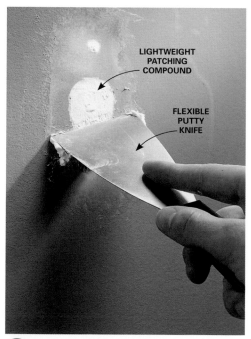

LIGHTWEIGHT PATCHING COMPOUND

FLEXIBLE PUTTY KNIFE

2 Patch the holes

Fill the depressions with joint compound. Let the compound dry and coat it again (and probably again!) until the patch is flat. Smooth the patch with 100-grit sandpaper, then prime and paint.

Patch a big hole

The usual way to cover a large hole (such as a doorknob disaster) is to cut out the damage, insert new drywall and reinforcing tape, then smooth it over with joint compound. But here's a shortcut: Home centers carry adhesive-backed metal patches in various sizes. They're cheap and save a few steps. Here's how to use one:

FIBERGLASS MESH

PERFORATED ALUMINUM

DOOR HANDLE HOLE

STICKY SIDE

1 Stick on the patch
Scrape off any protruding paint or drywall around the hole. Then apply the patch—just like a bandage.

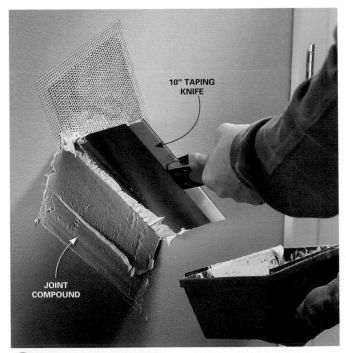

10" TAPING KNIFE

JOINT COMPOUND

2 Coat the patch
Spread joint compound over the patch with a wide knife. Smooth out the compound, let it dry and add another coat. Keep the coats thin and smooth; it's better to apply three or four coats than to create a thick buildup. Extend each coat a few inches beyond the previous coat to form edges that gradually taper.

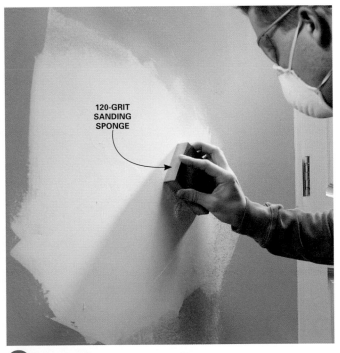

120-GRIT SANDING SPONGE

3 Sand the compound
Smooth the dried compound with a sanding sponge. If you did a good job of smoothing and tapering the compound, this will take just a few minutes and the slight hump on the wall will be invisible after priming and painting.

Fix furniture fast

Expert tricks for instant restoration

Some furniture requires professional attention (or a trip to the landfill). But furniture that shows the scars of normal use can usually be restored to excellent condition. In fact, there are people who make a good living doing just that. Here are some of their tricks:

Before anything, clean it up

Furniture restoration expert Kevin Southwick starts every project with a thorough cleaning. His secret formula is plain old soap and water, even on priceless antiques. Kevin adds a few drops of Ivory dish soap to water and gently scrubs with a damp sponge. On crevices and carvings, he uses a paintbrush. After cleaning, he wipes the surface with a sponge dampened in water only. Finally, he dries the piece with a clean towel and admires his work. Sometimes, a good cleaning is all a dull, old piece of furniture really needs.

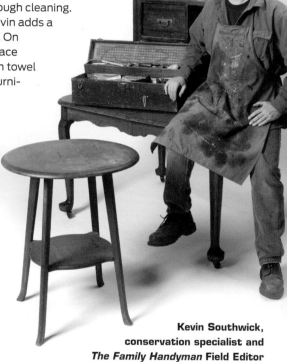

Kevin Southwick, conservation specialist and *The Family Handyman* Field Editor

Erase white rings

There are special products formulated for hazy, white blemishes (search online for "ring remover"). But try this first: Slather petroleum jelly on the ring and let it sit overnight. Often, the oil in the jelly will penetrate the finish and render the ring invisible.

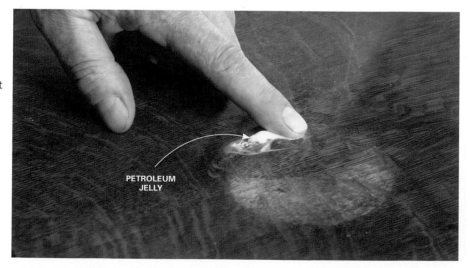

PETROLEUM JELLY

Restore the shine in minutes

A coat or two of wipe-on polyurethane is the easiest way to revive a dull finish. Just clean the old finish thoroughly and wipe on the poly with a lint-free cloth. That's it. It comes in gloss, semigloss and satin versions; satin is the best choice for hiding fine scratches. Years down the road, you can recoat it again if the luster fades. But be sure to test in an inconspicuous spot first: Wipe-on poly doesn't stick well to some finishes and might flake off.

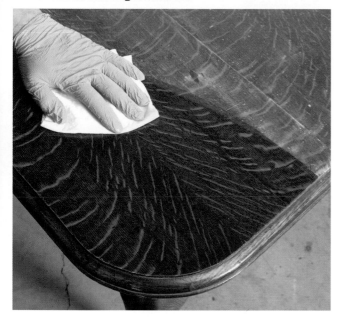

What about wax?

Finishing wax can restore the shine to a dull finish. It's easy to use and almost goof-proof: Wrap a lint-free rag around a ball of wax, rub it on, wait a few minutes and wipe off the excess. Unlike wipe-on poly, it's available in several colors so you can change the tone of the wood. But wax isn't nearly as tough or long-lasting as wipe-on poly.

DARK WAX

LIGHT WAX

MINWAX Paste Finishing Wax Protects · Polishes

WAX BALL

Better scratch removers

FINE-TIP MARKER

Home centers carry touch-up pens for scratched finishes. But stop by an art supply store instead. You'll find permanent markers in a huge range of wood-tone colors, some of them with fine tips—perfect for skinny scratches.

Spray paint upholstery

Yes, you can. Most auto parts stores and some home centers carry paint formulated just for fabric (for a huge range of colors, search online). Fabric paint has some drawbacks, though: Fuzzy fabrics like velour might feel like sandpaper when you're done, and light paint colors may not hide patterns in the fabric. So test on the back of a chair or the underside of a seat cushion first.

Make dents disappear

Moisture makes wood swell and—sometimes—heals dents. First, cut tiny slits in the finish parallel to the wood grain so that water can penetrate. Then drip a little water on the dent and wait until it dries. You can repeat this process a couple times, but after that you risk damaging the finish.

Voice of experience

Stripping furniture: Patience is the key

Refinishing furniture has been one of my hobbies for more than 30 years—and I've made every mistake in the book. One of my first projects was a set of chairs. I applied stripper and waited. And waited. Then I got a brilliant idea: heat! I fired up my propane torch, which worked nicely until the fire that turned my four-chair set into three. Since then I've used every type of stripper available. Some work faster than others, but they all work. The key to success is patience. My favorite trick is to apply the stripper, drape painters' plastic over it to prevent evaporation and leave it alone for hours or even overnight.

Gene Schmidt, *The Family Handyman* **Field Editor**

Make sticking drawers glide

Candle wax is a magical lubricant for old drawers or any furniture that has wood sliding against wood. Just rub a candle hard against the runners under drawers. Rub the tracks inside the chest, too.

Repair concrete

Options for cracks and craters

Damaged concrete isn't just ugly. Holes and cracks let in water and—unless you live in a warm climate—that water does more damage when it freezes, expanding cracks and enlarging holes. Here are your options for fixing it.

Caulk cracks

The best caulks for concrete are usually labeled "urethane" or "polyurethane," and most can fill cracks 1/2 in. wide or more (check the label). For any crack wider than 1/4 in., stuff in some foam backer rod first. Using backer rod saves expensive caulk and results in a stronger joint. And since it seals off the crack, it allows you to use runny "self-leveling" caulk, which usually provides a much neater look on flat surfaces.

BACKER ROD

Patch craters

Chip out any loose concrete and then fill the hole with concrete repair mix. "Screed" off the excess by running a board across the repair in a sawing motion. When the mix becomes hard enough so that you can't easily indent it with your thumb, finish the surface. To create a smooth surface, use a steel trowel. For a rough surface, drag a broom across it.

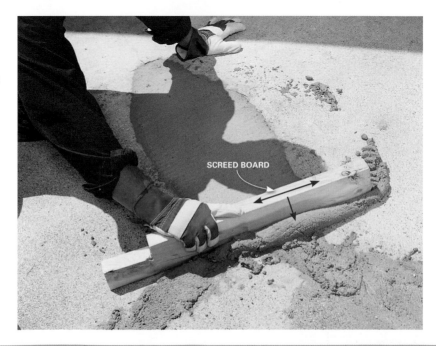

SCREED BOARD

Rebuild a corner

Assemble an L-shaped wooden form, lock it in place with bricks and fill the void with concrete repair mix. A repair mix will stick to the old concrete better than standard concrete mix. If you don't want to buy a special edging tool to round the edges of the patch, carefully shape the edges with a putty knife.

EDGING TOOL

FORM

Resurface concrete

Resurfacer is a dry powder that's mixed with water. It fills smaller holes and cracks and forms a durable new coating over the entire slab. The result is a surface that looks almost as good as new. In most cases, however, old cracks will eventually "telegraph" through the new surface.

Hide a hopeless garage floor

Sometimes the best solution for a cracked, pockmarked garage floor is to simply cover it up. Online, you'll find a huge selection of snap-together plastic tiles or mats designed to withstand vehicle traffic.

Raise sunken concrete

Sinking concrete that's in otherwise good condition can be lifted back to its original level by a "mudjacker." The contractor first drills holes in the concrete, then injects a slurry with tremendous pressure. That pressure can lift sidewalks, driveways, floors, even sinking steps.

LIMESTONE
SLURRY

Camouflage repairs

No concrete repair—caulk or patch—blends in perfectly with the old concrete. In fact, they sometimes look worse than damaged concrete. But there are a couple ways to hide the repair.

DRY CONCRETE
MIX

Coat with resurfacer

Resurfacer makes concrete look like new, hiding patches and filling small holes. The catch is that you have to coat all the concrete—resurfacing one area looks bad.

Disguise the caulk

Sprinkle a little dry concrete mix onto the wet caulk. When the caulk dries, sweep it off and the repair will be much less noticeable.

Fix appliances yourself—and save

It's crazy to pay for repairs when they're this simple

When an appliance goes on the blink, there's often a simple way to fix it without an expensive service call. Here are some common appliance problems and easy repairs to try before picking up the phone.

Jammed disposer?
Turn the blades

If your garbage disposer hums but doesn't spin, it may have something stuck in it. Switch the disposer off, then turn the blades with a special disposer wrench (sold at home centers) or by turning a bottom bolt. Many disposers have an Allen wrench for that purpose, inset on the bottom of the machine.

ALLEN WRENCH

WAY TOO HAPPY

Refrigerator shut down?
Clean the coils

If your refrigerator conks out on a hot day, suspect the coils. Service pros find this problem on half of their refrigerator calls. On many fridges, you get to the coils by removing the front grille. Then push a coil cleaning brush (sold at home centers) into the coils, pull it back and vacuum it clean. If the coils are located on the back, pull out your fridge to clean them. Bonus: The clean coils will cool more efficiently and save you money on your utility bill!

COIL CLEANING BRUSH

Gas range won't light?
Clean the igniter

If your stove burner won't come on, the likely culprit is the spaghetti sauce that boiled over a few days ago. Use a toothbrush to clean off food spills from the igniter. On an electronic ignition stove, it's a little ceramic nub located either on the stovetop or under the ceramic seal strike plate. Also make sure that the round ceramic seal strike plate is properly seated on the burner.

IGNITER

Electric stove won't heat?
Tweak the burner prongs

Turn the burner off and pull it out of its socket. Then plug it in again and wiggle it around. If it feels loose, remove the burner again and gently bend the burner prongs slightly outward for a tighter connection.

BURNER PRONG

Oven won't heat?
Check the clock and timer

Blame it on the technology. It so happens that if you set the "time cook" function, the oven, much like a programmed VCR, won't turn on until the appointed time. You may have done this inadvertently, but if your digital display reads "hold," "delay" or "time cook," then the timer is engaged. You'll have to clear it first by pushing the "off" button. On ovens with dials, be sure the knob is turned to "manual."

Oven temperature not right?
Recalibrate it

If the temperature in your oven seems off, or if your new oven just doesn't cook like your old one, you can recalibrate the temperature setting. Use the instructions in your manual or go online and search for a downloadable version using your oven's model number. Place a good-quality oven thermometer on the center shelf and wait for the oven to maintain a constant temperature. Then follow the procedure outlined in your manual to match the temperature setting to the thermometer reading.

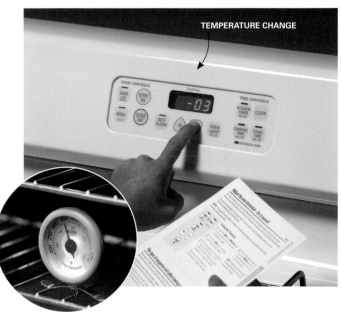

TEMPERATURE CHANGE

Noisy washing machine?
Level it

When a washing machine rocks, it makes a horrible racket during the spin cycle. The solution is to simply readjust the legs. Screw the front legs up or down until the cabinet is level. When both legs are solid on the floor, tighten each leg's locking nut. In most washers, to adjust the rear legs, gently tilt the machine forward and gently lower it down. The movement will self-adjust the rear legs.

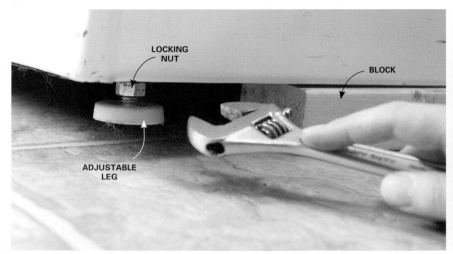

LOCKING NUT

BLOCK

ADJUSTABLE LEG

Clothes not coming out clean?
Check the water temperature

If the water in your washing machine is colder than 65 degrees F, the additives in laundry detergent won't work as well and powder detergents won't fully dissolve. Cold water for washing should be in the 65- to 85-degree range. Check the water temperature with a cooking thermometer (one that registers low temperatures). If the water temperature is below 65 degrees for cold-water washes, boost it by selecting warm water for part of the initial fill cycle. But always leave rinse settings on cold, no matter what washing temperature you choose. Cold-water rinses are just as effective as warm-water rinses, and you'll save a lot of energy.

Dishwasher not washing?
Clean the filter

When your dishwasher no longer gets your dishes clean, a food-filled filter is most often to blame. If it's clogged, water can't make it to the spray arms to clean the dishes in the top rack. The fix takes two minutes. Simply pull out the lower rack and remove the filter cover inside the dishwasher. (Check your owner's manual if you can't spot the filter.) Then use a wet/dry vacuum to clean off the screen. While you're there, slide the nearby float switch up and down. If the cover sticks, jiggle it up and down and clean it with water.

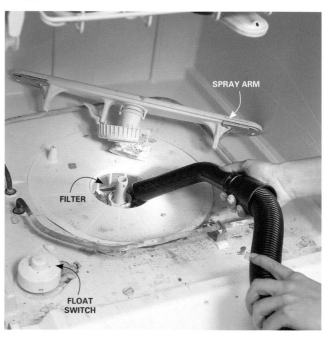

SPRAY ARM

FILTER

FLOAT SWITCH

DRYER FILTER

KIRKLAND

Dryer not heating?
Wash the lint filter

First make sure the machine isn't set to "fluff air"—a non-heat setting. If that's not it, the lint filter may be clogged. Even if the filter looks clean, it may be covered by a nearly invisible film caused by dryer sheets. Test your filter by pouring water into it. If the filter holds water, it's past time to clean it. This film reduces airflow and forces the thermostat to shut off the heat before your clothes are dry. Pull out the filter and scrub it in hot water with a little laundry detergent and a stiff kitchen brush. Also check the outside dryer vent for any lint that may have built up there.

AC won't come on?
Check the fuse

If you turn your central air conditioner on, off and then on again in rapid order, chances are you'll blow a fuse or shut off a circuit breaker or the air conditioner simply won't respond. Be patient and give the air conditioner thermostat about five minutes to reset. If it still won't come on, you may have blown a fuse. Locate the special fuse block near the outside unit. Pull out the block and take the whole thing to the hardware store. A salesperson can test the cartridge fuses and tell you if you need to replace them.

Slow-filling washer?
Clean the inlet screens

If your washing machine fills at a slow trickle, chances are you have plugged inlet screens. These screens catch debris in the water supply and protect a washer's internal parts. To get at them, turn off the water supply valves behind the washer, pull it out and disconnect the hoses. Remove the screens with needle-nose pliers. Be gentle; they're easy to damage. Clean the screens or buy new ones at a home center or appliance parts store. Carefully press them into place with a screwdriver. Before you reconnect the hoses, check them, too. Some contain screens that can be removed and cleaned just like inlet screens.

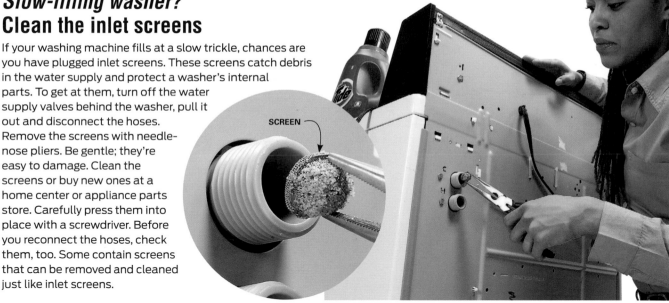

Flashing error code?
Check the manual or go online

If your appliance flashes a cryptic message on its digital display, it's a fault code telling you what's wrong. Look the code up in the owner's manual or on the manufacturer's Web site, or check an online appliance repair site. You can also usually find a list of codes somewhere in or on the appliance. Armed with a diagnosis and a make and model number, you can purchase the right part from a supplier and make the fix yourself. Or at least save some time on the service call by letting the repair service know what they'll need to bring along to make the fix.

Mike Krivit

Fix your furnace

Check the basics before you call a pro—and save $100

When heating and cooling systems misbehave, pros always check the simplest things first. Most of these checks are things you can do yourself, even if you know zilch about your system. So do it! In a few minutes, you just might save yourself a hundred bucks or more.

Make sure the thermostat is on

Thermostats, especially programmable ones, can be complicated. The more options a thermostat has, the more that can go wrong.
■ Make sure the switch is on the right setting ("heat" or "cool").
■ Check the temperature setting.
■ Compare the temperature setting to the room temperature. Set the temperature five degrees higher than the room temperature and see if the furnace kicks on.
■ Make sure the program is displaying the right day and time, as well as a.m. and p.m. settings.
■ Replace the battery. If you have a power outage with a dead battery, you'll lose your settings and the thermostat will revert to the default program.
■ Open the thermostat and gently blow out any dust or debris. Make sure it's level and firmly attached to the wall, and that none of the wires coming into it are loose.

Voice of experience

Over the phone, I always ask: Is the power on? The gas? Did you check the thermostat? And still—when I go to the home—I often find that one of these simple things was the problem.

Bob Schmahl, HVAC technician and *The Family Handyman* **Field Editor**

The best thing you can do: Change filters regularly

Dirty filters are the most common cause of furnace problems. If the blower is running but no warm air (or cool in the summer) is coming out, replace the filter. A dirty filter also reduces the efficiency of the furnace and shortens its life. Check your owner's manual to find out where the filter is located and how to remove it. Change inexpensive flat filters at least once a month. Make sure that the arrow points toward the furnace. Inspect pleated filters once a month. Hold them up to the light and if you can't see the light clearly through them, replace them. Manufacturers say pleated filters are good for three months, but change them more frequently if you have pets, kids or generate lots of dust.

Lost your owner's manual?

Most major-brand manuals are on the Web—just go to the manufacturer's Web site.

HVAC message board

It's hard to keep track of the furnace maintenance schedule. To make it easier, stick a small white magnetic board on your furnace duct. Write down the furnace filter size, brand, date the filter was last changed and when the furnace was last serviced. Update the information when you change the filter or have the furnace cleaned or checked.

1. Check the heat pump

If you have a heat pump, clear away grass and leaves. If the fins on the outside of the unit are caked with dirt and debris, rinse them off.

2. Look for blocked registers

If your furnace comes on but one or two rooms are cold, make sure all the room registers are open and clear.

3. Make sure the gas is on

Just as with switches, someone may have turned off a gas valve and then forgotten to turn it back on. Trace the gas line back from the furnace to the meter, and if you see a handle that's perpendicular to the gas pipe, turn it so it's parallel. If you have an old furnace or boiler, you may have a pilot light. Remove the front panel and the burner cover and check to make sure it's lit.

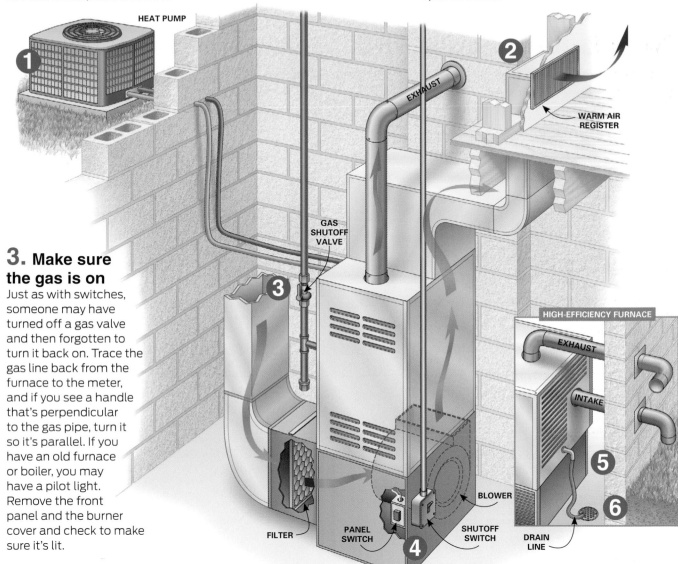

4. Check the shutoff switch and breaker

Furnace technicians often find that the only "repair" a furnace needs is to be turned on. Look for a standard wall switch on or near the furnace. Check the circuit breaker or fuse for the furnace as well. Make sure the front panel covering the blower motor is securely fastened—there's a push-in switch under it that must be fully depressed for the furnace to operate.

> **CAUTION!** Always turn off the shutoff switch and turn the thermostat off or all the way down before changing the filter or working on the thermostat or furnace.

5. Clear the intake and exhaust

Some furnaces exhaust through a pipe in the wall of the house rather than through a chimney. These furnaces also draw in air through a pipe. Make sure both pipes are clear, especially after heavy snow.

6. Flush the drain line

A drain tube plugged with sediment or mold will cause the furnace to shut down. To clean the line, remove it and fill it with a mix of bleach and water (25 percent bleach).

Lube it right

Solutions for squeaking, sticking, stubborn stuff

Every home has some moving parts that stick or squeak. So lubricants are an essential tool for every home-owner. Here's how to choose them and use them.

Two lubricants you must have

General-purpose lubricant

This stuff is amazingly versatile. Aside from lubricating just about anything, it penetrates rust, inhibits rust and even works as a cleaner on gummy stuff like adhesives. For most jobs, there are better products; but no other product can do as many jobs.

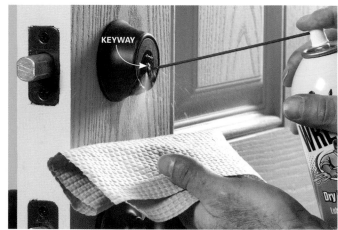

Dry lubricant

It goes on as a thin liquid but dries fast to form a slippery film that won't gather dust. That's a huge advantage. In some situations—on drawer slides, for example—a grimy mix of oil and dust looks bad. In other cases—like locks—grime will cause parts to stick.

And two more you might need

Lithium grease

Available as a paste or spray, this is the best lubricant for high-load parts like axles and bearings. It also lasts longer and inhibits rust better than most other products, so it's great for outdoor tools and hardware.

Penetrating oil

To free up stuck screws or rusty bolts, this is the best choice by far. But it's not a good permanent lubricant; after using it, clean off the parts and then lube with a different product.

Avoid the off-brands

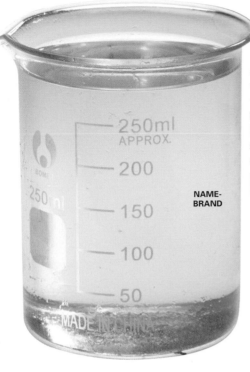

Cheap lubricants often contain more solvent and less of what matters. These two beakers show how much lubricant was left after the solvent and propellant evaporated from a brand-name product and a no-name brand.

NAME-BRAND

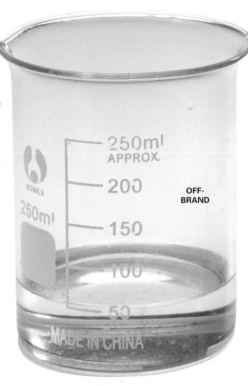

OFF-BRAND

Lube weather stripping

If you have sticky weather stripping on doors or windows, or on your home or car, spray some dry lubricant on a rag and wipe it onto the weather stripping. Allow the lubricant to dry before closing the door or window.

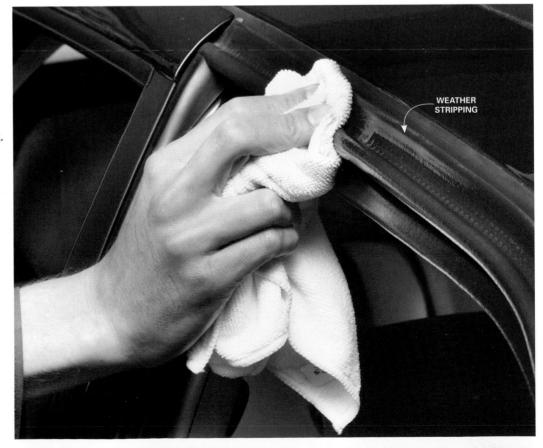

WEATHER STRIPPING

Beware of overspray

Spray lubricants are easy to apply where you want them—and where you don't. Aside from just making a mess, some types will damage paint or plastics, and some (especially dry lubricants) prevent adhesion during a future painting project. Often, the best way to prevent overspray is to spray lubricant on a rag then wipe it on. When that won't work, protect surfaces with plastic or cardboard.

Lube stubborn windows

Often, a little lubricant can make sticking old windows glide like new. If you have double-hung windows, spray some dry lubricant on a rag and wipe the tracks on both sides of the window opening. If you have tilt-in double-hung windows, you can also lubricate the sides of the sashes. On casement windows, lubricate all the moving parts on the crank-out mechanism and the sliding bracket at the top.

Warm up a cold room

Restore cozy comfort—without paying a pro

Some rooms are always cold in winter, some get cold occasionally and some that have never been cold in the past develop a sudden chill. Whatever the situation, here are some simple solutions to try before consulting a pro. If you have forced-air heat and central air-conditioning, some of these tips will apply to summertime hot rooms too.

Troubleshooting: Check the simple things first

If the room was comfortable in the past but is cool now, here are some quick things to check:

■ **ARE THE REGISTERS OPEN?**
Every furnace technician has a story about a cold room that was cured by opening a register or two. Don't make yourself the star of one of those stories.

■ **ARE THE REGISTERS BLOCKED?**
Rearranging the furniture or shoving a rug aside can block airflow.

■ **ARE THE DAMPERS OPEN?**
Some ductwork contains dampers to adjust airflow. Look for handles and markings on the ductwork such as "summer" and "winter." Set the damper handle parallel to the duct line for maximum airflow.

■ **IS THE FURNACE FILTER FILTHY?**
This is the most common cause of heating (and cooling) troubles. Change the filter and the problem usually disappears.

■ **ARE THE RADIATORS CLEAR?**
Whether you have electric or hydronic baseboard units or old-fashioned radiators, they won't throw maximum heat unless air can flow through them. If you move the bed against a baseboard unit or toss a blanket across a radiator, the room might get chilly.

■ **IS THE RADIATOR AIR-LOCKED?**
If you have a hot-water radiator that's not heating, the cause is usually trapped air, and getting rid of it is simple. Use a radiator key, 1/4-in. 12-point socket or a flat screwdriver (depending on your valve type) and slowly turn the valve counterclockwise until water drips out. This will release trapped air and let hot water flow. While you're at it, repeat the process on your other radiators. Bleeding the radiators will lower the pressure in your system, so you might have to slowly add water to increase the pressure. Do this by opening, then

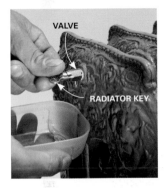

VALVE

RADIATOR KEY

closing, the valve on the water pipe above the boiler. If you're unfamiliar with your system, call a pro. How much pressure you need depends on how high the water has to rise. The basic rule is 1 lb. of pressure for every 2 ft. of rise. Your gauge may read in pounds, feet or both. A basic two-story house, with the boiler and expansion tank in the basement, needs 12 to 15 lbs., or 25 to 30 ft., of pressure.

Give your furnace a boost

If you have forced-air heat, one of the easiest ways to warm a chronically cold room is to set a duct booster fan (available at home centers) on a register. It works simply by drawing more warm air into the room. There are also in-line fans that can be installed in the ductwork.

REGISTER DUCT BOOSTER

IN-LINE DUCT BOOSTER

Heat the floor

There are two types of in-floor heat: Hydronic, which pumps hot water through tubing, and electric, which heats with cables, much like an electric blanket.

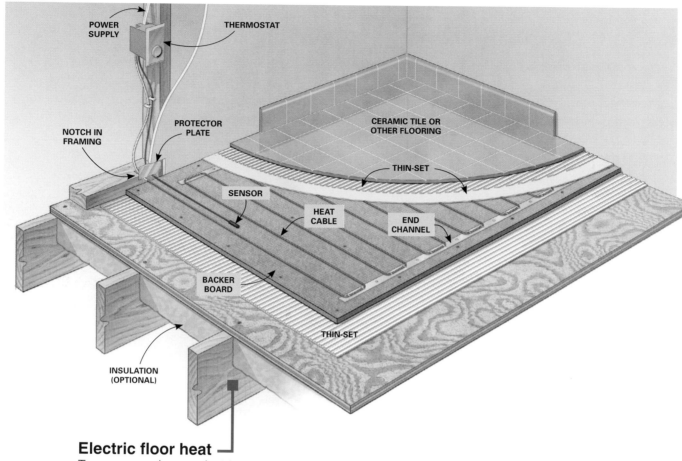

POWER SUPPLY

THERMOSTAT

NOTCH IN FRAMING

PROTECTOR PLATE

SENSOR

HEAT CABLE

END CHANNEL

BACKER BOARD

CERAMIC TILE OR OTHER FLOORING

THIN-SET

THIN-SET

INSULATION (OPTIONAL)

Electric floor heat

To warm a cool room, electric systems are usually more practical than hydronic systems. Some electric systems consist of mats or mesh that contains cables. Others rely on channels to hold cables in place. Electric cables are most often installed with tile flooring.

Not just for tile

Some electric mats can heat floating floors such as laminate or engineered wood flooring. Because floating floors aren't fastened to the subfloor, you can simply lay the flooring over the mat. Some electric mats also work with carpet, though the carpet acts as an insulator and reduces heat gain in the room.

THERMOSTAT BOX

LAMINATE FLOORING

DUCT TAPE

MAT

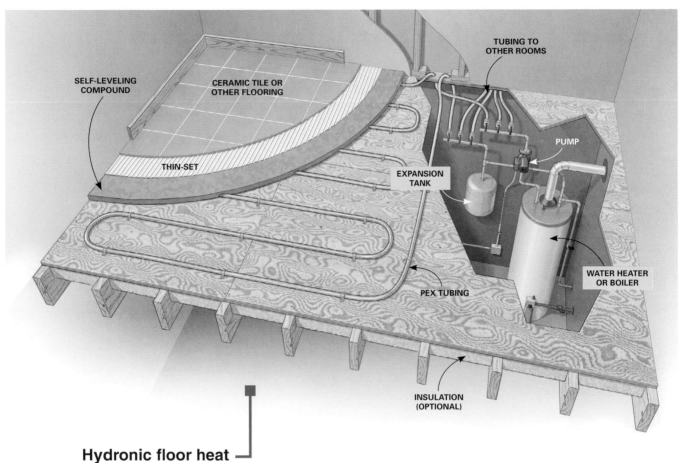

SELF-LEVELING
COMPOUND

CERAMIC TILE OR
OTHER FLOORING

TUBING TO
OTHER ROOMS

THIN-SET

EXPANSION
TANK

PUMP

WATER HEATER
OR BOILER

PEX TUBING

INSULATION
(OPTIONAL)

Hydronic floor heat

Hydronic systems require a hot water source, tubing and a built-up floor to embed the tubing. It's a major project that can heat an addition or an entire home. But in most situations, there are much more economical ways to add a little heat to a cool room.

Under-floor heat

If you already have a hot-water heating system and unfinished space below the floor, hydronic tubing installed under the floor may be a cost-effective way to warm up a room. Otherwise, electric systems are far more economical. There are also electric mats that can be installed from below.

PEX TUBING

HEAT
TRANSFER
PLATE

Cool a hot room

Alternatives to central AC and window units

Whether you're building an addition or just tired of wrestling with your window unit twice each year, here are three ways to cool spaces without the expense of adding or extending a central AC system.

Portable air conditioner

Friedrich

Portable air conditioners are similar to window units in operation. They sit on the floor (on casters) and use an adapter kit to vent the hot air through a hose running through a window, a wall or a sliding glass door.

MAIN ADVANTAGES
- They are easy to install and use.
- You can move them from room to room.

MAIN DISADVANTAGES
- They're almost twice as expensive and use more energy than a window unit with the same cooling capacity.
- The vent hose can be a nuisance.
- They take up valuable floor space.

Spring cleaning is mandatory

A window air conditioner can hold some nasty surprises after winter storage. Aside from harmless stuff like dust and dead bugs, it might contain health threats like mold or mouse droppings. So before you lug it to a window, vacuum all the surfaces, especially the fins on the exterior face of the unit (that's good for efficiency and performance). Also pull off the cover panel, and vacuum and clean the foam filter. Finally, plug it in and fire it up. Better to blow dust around the garage than your bedroom.

Harry Kashuck,
The Family Handyman **Field Editor**

Mini-split system

Long popular in Europe and Japan, a mini-split system air conditioner (sometimes called ductless AC), is a hybrid of central air and a window unit. A small condenser sits outside and connects through a conduit to an inside evaporator mounted high on the wall or ceiling.

MAIN ADVANTAGES

■ Quiet operation. The condenser sits outside, it doesn't let in street noise and the indoor fan is whisper-quiet.

■ The system can be mounted anywhere thanks to the small size of the indoor and outdoor components. The conduit, which houses the power cable, refrigerant tubing, suction tubing and a condensate drain, runs through a 3-in. hole hidden behind the indoor evaporator.

■ Zoning flexibility lets you cool rooms individually.

MAIN DISADVANTAGE

■ Cost. The two units, plus professional installation, typically total $1,500 to $3,000.

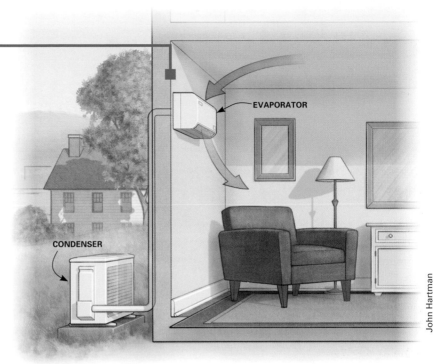

EVAPORATOR

CONDENSER

John Hartman

Split AC system
It doesn't require ductwork and can be run to one or more rooms. The small size, quiet operation and individual zoning let you cool only the room you're using, which can save energy and money.

In-wall AC unit

An in-wall air conditioner is basically a window unit reengineered for in-wall operation. The primary difference is that it stays put year round.

MAIN ADVANTAGES

■ Permanent installation means you don't have to lug it in and out twice a year, and it's not an easy entry point for burglars.

■ It doesn't block a window.

■ The size of the unit isn't limited to a standard window opening, so it can be bigger and more powerful than a window unit.

MAIN DISADVANTAGES

■ Installation is a substantial construction project, involving siding, framing and interior walls.

■ You may need to install a new electrical circuit. Some larger units require 240 volts (although most smaller units can be plugged into a standard 120-volt outlet).

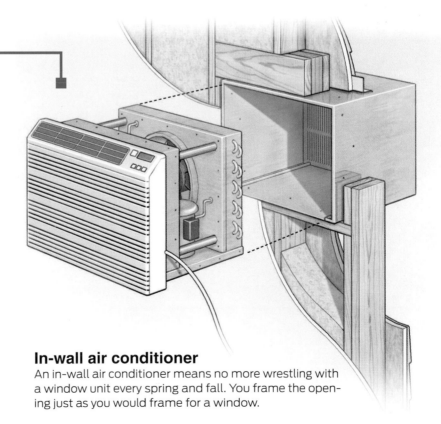

In-wall air conditioner
An in-wall air conditioner means no more wrestling with a window unit every spring and fall. You frame the opening just as you would frame for a window.

John Hartman

Cure condensation

Water pulled out of thin air can do serious damage

Every home has some condensation somewhere, sometime. And most of it is harmless. But in heavy doses, those little droplets of water can add up to real damage. Here are the main trouble spots:

What is condensation?

When warm, humid air contacts a cold surface, water vapor in the air becomes liquid, forming droplets on the surface.

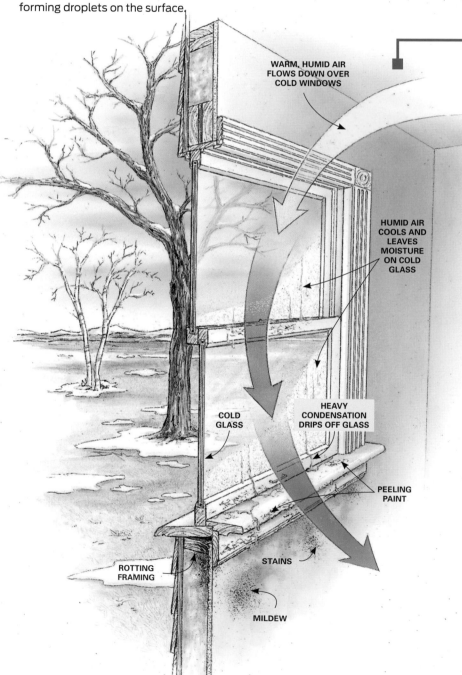

WARM, HUMID AIR FLOWS DOWN OVER COLD WINDOWS

HUMID AIR COOLS AND LEAVES MOISTURE ON COLD GLASS

COLD GLASS

HEAVY CONDENSATION DRIPS OFF GLASS

PEELING PAINT

ROTTING FRAMING

STAINS

MILDEW

Windows

In winter, windows are the coldest surface in your home, so that's where condensation is usually worst. Light, occasional condensation isn't a big problem, but heavy, continuous condensation damages windows and trim, leading to peeling paint or varnish, stains and rot. Worse, water can seep into walls, causing rot and mold. Aside from lowering indoor humidity, the only real cure is new windows that insulate better and stay warmer.

Basements

Warm, humid summer air reaching cold basement walls and floors is the perfect recipe for condensation. The result is mold, mildew and musty odors. You might be tempted to air out a dank basement by opening windows, but that often makes the problem worse by boosting the supply of humid air. Finishing a basement with well-insulated walls and floors greatly reduces condensation. A quicker, easier solution is to run a dehumidifier.

Toilets

After a flush, the tank refills with cold water and the tank can "sweat" and drip, causing flooring damage and wood rot. This condensation sometimes tricks homeowners (and even plumbers) into searching for a toilet leak. One cure for tank condensation is an insulated tank; some new toilets offer that option, and insulating kits for existing toilets are also available. Another solution is to install a tempering valve, which feeds a mix of hot and cold water into the tank.

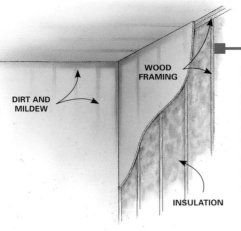

WOOD FRAMING

DIRT AND MILDEW

INSULATION

Walls

Like any other cold surface, walls can gather moisture. Condensation on walls is usually light, more like fog on a mirror than large droplets on a window. But that light moisture can gather dirt and support mildew growth. Since wood is a poor insulator, you may see stripes of dirt and mildew that show the framing behind the drywall, an effect called "ghosting." Condensation on walls may also reveal poorly insulated areas. Aside from upgrading insulation, air movement can reduce condensation on walls. Running a ceiling fan or leaving closet doors open, for example, can reduce condensation by circulating warm air and raising the temperature of walls. Moving air also quickly dries any condensation that does occur.

Voice of experience

Wet wallpaper

One cold autumn day, I put 15 gallons of maple sap on the stove, boiling it down to make syrup. After raking the yard, I returned to a steamy kitchen and serious condensation on the walls—so much that the wallpaper was falling off. I was able to rehang the wallpaper, but could have avoided that mess just by switching on the exhaust fan.

Neal Cook, *The Family Handyman* **Field Editor**

Lower the humidity

Condensation requires cold surfaces and humid air. So there are two ways to prevent it: Raise the temperature of surfaces or lower the humidity. Raising temperatures is sometimes expensive, difficult or both. But there are simple ways to cut humidity:

■ **Exhaust fans**
Cooking and bathing pump a lot of water into the air. But the solution is as easy as flipping a switch. Run kitchen and bath exhaust fans for 15 to 30 minutes after a shower or pot of spaghetti.

■ **Dehumidifier**
It will raise your electric bill by a few bucks, but a dehumidifier is one of the easiest and best ways to fight condensation.

■ **Air conditioner**
Air conditioning doesn't just cool the air—it also dries it. So you might solve summertime condensation problems by using your AC more often.

■ **Dryer vents**
The vent pipe carries all the moisture removed from your laundry outdoors. Make sure it's sealed tight at joints and blows air outdoors.

■ **Furnace settings**
Some furnaces have a built-in humidifier that adds a little moisture to dry winter air. But if the setting is too high, it can cause condensation troubles. Check the manual or call in a pro.

Defeat odors

Proven solutions for stinky situations

Don't be ashamed—bad smells develop in even the cleanest homes. But with a little knowledge, you can overcome odors. Here are solutions for some of the most common stinky situations.

Moldy washing machine

Eliminating the moldy smell in your front-loading clothes washer is easy. Just run the empty washer through a cycle once a month with a mold cleaner designed for front loaders. Affresh is one brand. If you don't want to use the tablets, you can substitute a cup of bleach. To prevent mold in the future, keep the door open between washings so the interior can dry out. The ultra-tight seal on front-loader doors doesn't let the interior dry, and mold can grow inside between washings.

ANTI-MOLD TABLET

Smelly floor drains

Under every drain in your house, there's a trap that holds water and prevents sewer gas from flowing out. But if you have a rarely used shower or floor drain, the water in the trap can eventually evaporate. That lets in stinky sewer gases. The solution is a few ounces of cooking or mineral oil. Dump a bucket of water down the drain to refill the trap. Then add the oil. The floating oil forms a seal over the water and prevents evaporation.

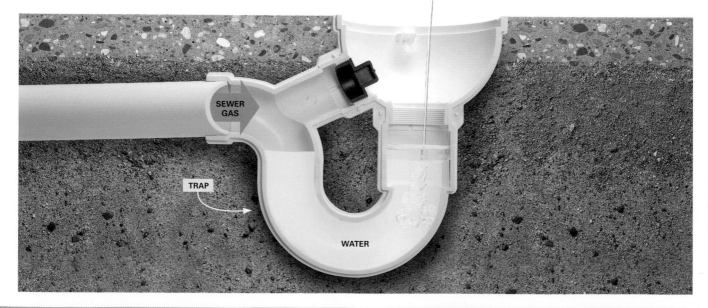

SEWER GAS

TRAP

WATER

Disposer odor

Run cold water and drop in a few slices of orange or lemon peels. Run the disposer for five seconds, then turn off the water and the disposer. Give the acidic peels about 15 minutes to work. Turn on the water and the disposer and drop in a few ice cubes to "sandblast" the disposer clean. Plug the drain and fill the sink half-full. Then pull the plug and let the accumulated water flush the disposer and pipes clean. Gunk buildup around the disposer's splash guard can stink too. A careful cleaning will remove that stink source.

Deep-clean the disposer
Citric acid from orange or lemon peels will soften the gunk inside so you can rinse it out by running the water.

Clean the splash guard
Lift the flaps and scrub them with a toothbrush and grease-cutting cleaner.

Refrigerator stench

When your power goes out and the food in your fridge and freezer goes bad, you've got a really stinky mess on your hands. Here's what to do:

■ Remove the food and wipe everything down with a disinfecting cleaning spray.

■ Clean all the nooks and crannies inside the freezer, especially the shelf supports.

■ Smash about 12 charcoal briquettes and spread the chunks on two trays. One goes in the fridge, the other in the freezer.

■ Crunch up newspaper and fill the shelves with it.

■ Close the doors and walk away, giving the charcoal and newspaper time to absorb odors.

■ Replace the old newspaper and charcoal with fresh stuff every day for about a week or until the smell is gone.

Stinky dishwasher

If your dishwasher stinks, don't reach for the bleach. Bleach is corrosive to metal parts and doesn't solve the root problem. The smell comes from bacteria that feed on trapped food and grease in the screen at the bottom of the machine, in the jets in the sprayer arms and along the bottom edge of the door. Clean these areas, then pour in some dishwasher cleaner (Dishwasher Magic is one brand).

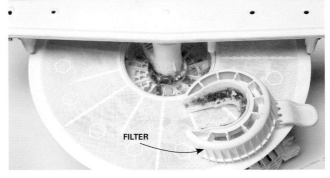

Clean the filter
Remove the bottom rack and sprayer arm. Clean and rinse out the filter screen at the bottom of the tub.

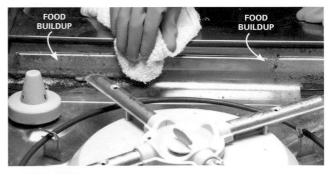

Clean the whole compartment
Wash out any food lodged in the jets of the sprayer arm and scrub the area below the door.

Quiet your home

Silence annoying noises

Houses make sounds. Some of them are tough to diagnose or cure. But others are surprisingly easy to silence. Here are some simple solutions.

Appliance hum

Washers and dryers transfer vibrations to floors and telegraph noise throughout the house. The solution is to set their feet on rubber anti-vibration pads (available at some home centers and online).

ANTI-VIBRATION PADS

Exhaust vent chatter

When the wind blows just right, the damper on a dryer or exhaust fan vent can slam open and closed. Add some weight to the damper to resist the wind. On a steel damper, stick on a magnet or two. Then run the fan or dryer to make sure the damper still opens. Add or remove magnets as needed. On a plastic or aluminum damper, use glue and steel washers. Note: Don't try this fix on gas dryer vents; too much weight could keep the damper closed and prevent dangerous exhaust gases from exiting the house.

MAGNET

Voice of experience

Soffit clatter

The metal soffit panels under overhangs fit loosely into channels. And when the wind blows, they can make a racket. After installing metal soffit on dozens of homes, I finally found a solution to soffit clatter: Pick up some screen spline (used with window screens) at a home center. Stuff the spline into the channels and the clatter will stop.

Mark Peterson, contractor and *The Family Handyman* Contributing Editor

PLASTIC PUTTY KNIFE

SCREEN SPLINE

SILENT CHECK VALVE

CLAMP

Sump-pump thump

The check valve above a sump pump prevents water from flowing back into the house. It also makes a huge thump when it slams shut. The solution is a check valve that's designed to close quietly (available at some home centers and online). Installation is usually easy; just loosen and retighten a couple clamps.

Creaking pipes

Pipes expand and contract as they heat up and cool down. That can mean ticks, creaks or groans as they slide against wood and the straps that secure them. One solution is to remove straps and wrap the pipe with felt before reinstalling the strap.

VINYL BUMPER

Slamming toilet lid

A soft-close toilet seat (available at home centers) solves the slam-down problem. To prevent the seat from slamming up against the tank, stick a clear cabinet door bumper to the tank lid.

NYLON ROLLER

WORN STEEL ROLLER

Garage door rumble

Nylon rollers are a whole lot quieter than metal rollers. You can buy them online or at garage door suppliers. Install them one at a time, removing each hinge, slipping the new roller into the hinge and then refastening the hinge before moving on to the next hinge. Be sure to unplug the garage door opener while you work.

INCREDIBLY EASY FIXES

Pro solutions—but easy enough for beginners

Every professional handyman occasionally gets called in to a job that's so easy that an honest pro feels a little guilty about charging. Here are a few of those fixes from our crew of professional (and honest!) handymen.

Clean a vent hood grease filter

The standard way to clean the filter from a kitchen exhaust fan is to stick it in the dishwasher. If that doesn't get your filter clean, try an auto mechanic's approach: Buy some water-based degreaser at an auto parts store, fill your laundry tub with hot water and degreaser, and let the filter soak for a few minutes. After that, all it takes is a rinse.

Remove a broken lightbulb

How many homeowners does it take to change a broken lightbulb? Just one—if he or she knows a couple tricks. The most reliable method is to find a stick that fits inside the bulb's metal base and slather the stick with a big blob of glue from a hot-melt glue gun. Shove the stick into the base and let the glue cool for few minutes. Then just turn the stick counter-clockwise. Another trick is to carve the end of a potato to fit into the base, push it in hard and turn while pushing. With either method, *turn off the power before you do anything*. You may also have to break out any glass remaining in the base with pliers.

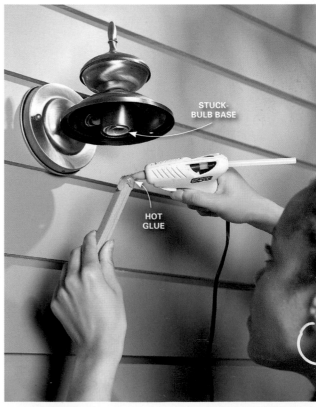

STUCK-BULB BASE

HOT GLUE

Dead doorbell?

A wireless doorbell is an easy, inexpensive solution: Just mount the button by the front door and the chime anywhere indoors. But before you do that, check your existing doorbell button. The button is the most likely culprit and it's connected to low-voltage wiring, so you don't have to worry about getting shocked. Here's how to do it:

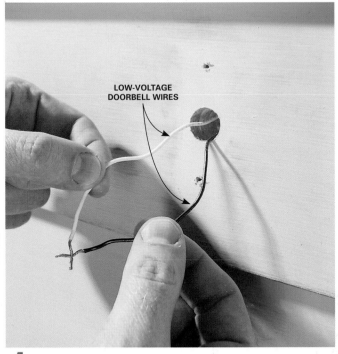

LOW-VOLTAGE
DOORBELL WIRES

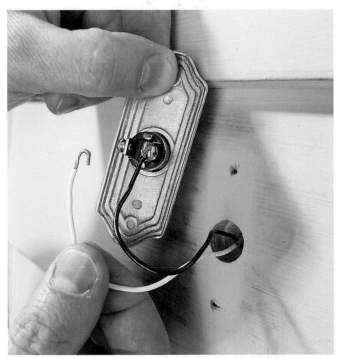

1 Test the doorbell

Unscrew the doorbell button to remove it from the wall. Loosen the screws on the back of the button and disconnect the wires. Then touch the two wires together. If the chime rings, the button is bad. If not, the chime, transformer or wiring is bad.

2 Replace the button

Connect the wires to the new button just as they were connected to the old one. Screw the button to the wall and you're done.

Patch a laminate floor

A dropped knife can leave an instant chip in a laminate floor. Luckily, home centers carry fillers formulated to patch laminate damage. If you have a leftover scrap of the flooring, take it to the store to help you find a good match. You may have to buy two colors and mix them to get the right color. Also pick up some solvent of the same brand as the filler. Apply the filler with a putty knife. Don't worry about perfection on the first coat; results are often better when a chip is filled twice. Use the solvent to clean any filler off the surrounding laminate. A smooth, flat patch will look pretty good, but you can make it even better: After the filler dries, scratch some fake "wood grain" lines in it with a utility knife. Then rub a brown marker over the scratches and wipe off the excess ink. The ink left in scratches will help blend your patch with the surrounding laminate.

PLASTIC
PUTTY KNIFE

Surgery for snagged carpet

If you have a running snag in carpet with woven loops, don't worry. You can make a repair so perfect that it will be invisible to everyone but you. All it takes is scissors, a small screwdriver, tape and some carpet adhesive, which is available at home centers.

SNAGGED YARN

CARPET ADHESIVE

SEALER

1 Cut the yarn
Gently tug the loose yarn to find the point where it's still firmly attached to the backing. Snip it off as close to the backing as possible.

2 Glue down the yarn
Protect nearby carpet with tape and apply a bead of carpet adhesive into the run. Use a screwdriver to press each "scab"—spots where bits of backing cling to the yarn—into the adhesive.

Tighten a wobbly table leg

Whether it's a dining table, coffee table or end table, it probably has a leg-fastening system similar to the one shown here. To tighten this type of leg, flip the table upside down or crawl under it. Then simply tighten the one or two nuts that secure the leg. While you're at it, you can make sure that the nut won't loosen up again by applying a little thread adhesive. Just remove the nut, apply a little adhesive and screw on the nut. But be sure to choose a version of thread adhesive that allows for easy removal later. Some types will make it almost impossible to disassemble your table.

Adjust a dragging shower door

If the sliding doors on your tub or shower don't slide smoothly, repair them soon. The dragging will eventually cause permanent damage to the doors, tracks or rollers.

First, make sure the rollers on both doors are riding on the tracks inside the upper rail. Sometimes a roller falls out of the track. In that case, all you have to do is lift the door and guide the roller back into the track. If an off-track roller isn't the

problem, you'll have to remove the dragging door so you can adjust its height. Many doors have a plastic guide at the middle of the bottom rail. To remove it, just remove a single screw. Other doors have a guide rail screwed to the door (Photo 1). Remove the door (Photo 2) and adjust the rollers so the door no longer drags (Photo 3).

1 Remove the guide rail

Unscrew the guide rail at the lower edge of the door so you can remove the door.

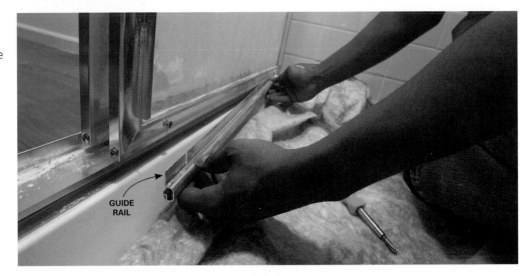

GUIDE RAIL

UPPER RAIL

2 Remove the door

Tilt the door in or out and lift it carefully out of its track. Make sure the rollers turn smoothly.

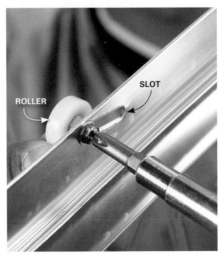

ROLLER

SLOT

3 Adjust the rollers

Loosen the roller's screw, then raise or lower the door by repositioning the roller in its slot. Tighten the screw and hang the door in place to check the fit.

Replacement rollers

If you find a broken roller or any of them don't turn, remove one and take it to a home center to find a match. Often, a roller of slightly different size will work, but rollers with flat or rounded edges aren't interchangeable.

ROUND EDGE

FLAT EDGE

Adjust a sticking patio screen door

Badly aligned rollers inside the bottom of a patio screen door will cause the door to bind or stick when opening or closing. This stresses the corners of the door, and if the corner joints become loose, the door will eventually fall apart. But you can adjust the door to glide smoothly with just a screwdriver. You'll find two adjustment screws at the bottom of the door, one at each end, that raise or lower separate rollers. Adjust them as shown here.

ADJUSTMENT SCREW

ADJUSTMENT SCREW

DOOR FRAME

ROLLER   TRACK

1 Lower the door
Turn the adjustment screw counterclockwise and lower the door until it rests on the track. Do the same at the other end of the door.

2 Raise the door
Raise one roller until it lifts the door about 1/4 in. off the track. Slowly raise the other roller until there's an even gap between the door and the track.

Reglue countertop edging

End caps and other laminate edges sometimes come loose and can break off if left loose. But as long as the particleboard backer is in good shape, the fix is simple.

Gently scrape off any chunks of debris or dried glue on the laminate. Then grab your clothes iron, switch it to a medium-hot setting and try to iron the laminate back in place. Sometimes heat reactivates the glue, sometimes not. If not, you'll need to reglue it with contact cement as shown here. Chances are, you'll end up with little blobs of cement squeezed out along the edges of the laminate. Let them become gummy overnight and then simply rub them away with your finger.

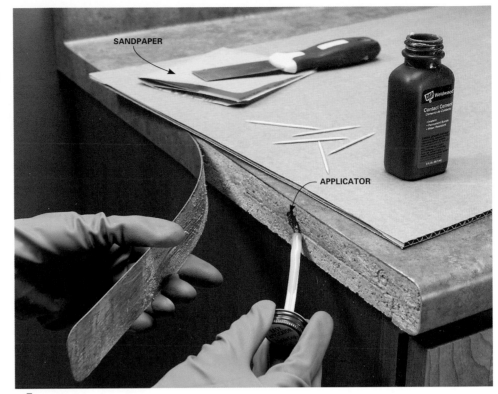

SANDPAPER

APPLICATOR

1 Apply contact cement
Coat both the laminate and the backer with contact cement. Open a window for ventilation.

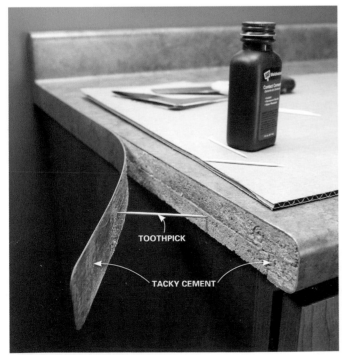

TOOTHPICK

TACKY CEMENT

2 Let the cement dry
Keep the two sides apart until the cement is dry, but still tacky. Usually, that takes about 20 minutes.

3 Rub the laminate into place
Force the laminate against the countertop with a smooth block of wood. Make a light pass first, then rub hard to embed the laminate.

Reattach a storm door closer— for good

A gust of wind or a high-velocity kid can swing a storm door open so hard that it rips the closer off the door or jamb. But you can reconnect the closer to the door or jamb as shown here. If the mishap also bent the closer's arm, remove it and take it to a home center to find a similar model. When installing a new closer, throw away the short screws that came in the package and use long screws as shown in Photo 1.

1 Reattach the closer bracket
Drill screw holes and drive screws at least 3 in. long into the jamb. Those long screws will pass through the jamb and bite into the framing behind the jamb for a rock-solid connection.

2 Reattach the closer to the door
If the closer's screws were yanked out of the door, simply toss out the old screws and replace them with thicker (but not longer) screws.

Straighten a crooked fridge door

A sagging fridge or freezer door doesn't just look bad. It can cause the door gaskets to seal poorly and means the fridge will burn more energy to keep the milk cold. It can also lead to frost buildup in the freezer. To realign the door, just loosen and retighten hinges. If only the upper door needs adjustment, move the top hinge only. If the bottom door is crooked, you'll have to move the hinge that's between the two doors. Moving that hinge also affects the fit of the upper door, so you'll have to adjust the upper door after adjusting the lower door.

1 Loosen the hinge
Pry off the plastic hinge cap and loosen the screws. Keep loosening until you can lift the door by hand.

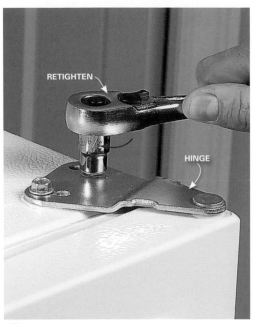

2 Tighten the hinge
Hold the door even with the side and top of the fridge while you tighten the screws.

Stiffen a wobbly deck

Some otherwise solid decks tend to sway or wobble as you walk across them, especially decks that stand on posts a few feet off the ground. If you have this problem, you'll be amazed at how a simple 2x4 brace stops the sway. Run the brace diagonally across the undersides of the deck joists, fastening it to each joist with nails or screws. You can use a single long 2x4 or a couple shorter 2x4s. If you use more than one, lap over at least two joists, running them side by side.

2x4 BRACE

Fix a dead light fixture

Lots of things can go wrong with a lamp or light fixture, causing bulbs to burn out quickly and lights to flicker or not work at all. Here's the first thing to check: Unscrew the bulb and peer into the socket. The little contact tab in the center of the socket should be tilting slightly outward, away from the bottom of the socket. But sometimes the tab gets bent flat against the socket so it can't make contact with the base of the lightbulb. The fix is easy. But before you do anything, unplug the lamp or turn off power to the fixture. Make sure the power is off using a noncontact voltage tester. Then simply bend the tab outward with a small screwdriver.

TAB

Cover a loose flooring seam

If you have an open seam in a vinyl floor, don't procrastinate. Foot traffic will eventually wreck the exposed edges and make repairs difficult or impossible. The usual cure for a loose seam is to reglue and reseal it. But here's an easier fix: Buy a section of metal transition strip at a home center and cut it to length with a hacksaw. Then nail or screw the strip over the seam and you're done!

TRANSITION STRIP

DAMAGED SEAM

Prevent floor damage

Furniture manufacturers often put small metal buttons on chair and table legs. That's fine for carpet, but those buttons can damage wood, laminate, vinyl or even ceramic floors. So it's a good idea to replace the factory buttons with softer feet.

Pads
Felt or cloth pads are gentle on floors, but they don't slide as easily as plastic feet.

Glides
Plastic glides slide smoothly, but don't use them on wood flooring—chemicals in plastics can stain wood finishes.

1 Remove the metal buttons
Usually, you pry them off with a screwdriver or grab them with pliers. If that doesn't work, drill a 1/4-in. hole in the button and lever it out with a screwdriver.

2 Nail on soft feet
You can stick adhesive-backed pads on furniture legs, but nail-on feet stay put better. With hardwood legs, first drill a hole slightly smaller than the nail shank.

Index

Index

Are you a smart homeowner?

A little knowledge can save you money, help you avoid frustration and make you happier with your home. Once you've read *100 Things Every Homeowner Must Know*, you'll know the answers to the questions below—and a whole lot more.

Which type of faucet valve is least likely to develop drips?
See page 128

When an appliance isn't working, what should you do before you call a repair pro?
See page 14

What's the easiest way to avoid furnace trouble?
See page 258

■ **What's the best way to prevent catastrophic water damage while you're on vacation?**
See page 99

■ **Who should you call before digging in your yard?**
See page 103

■ **For better home security, which two areas should you focus on first?**
See page 84

■ **How can you protect appliances and electronics from power surges —and instant destruction?**
See page 38

Which method of killing ants actually makes them harder to eradicate?
See page 43

How can you reduce soap scum buildup effortlessly?
See page 198

■ **If you fertilize your lawn just once a year, when should you do it?**
See page 205

■ **When your smoke alarms are about 10 years old, what should you do?**
See page 80

What type of paint is best for most interior and exterior projects?
See page 142

What causes most problems with lawn mowers and other small engines?
See page 56